SOUTHERN AFRICA: TOWARD ECONOMIC LIBERATION

*Papers presented at the Arusha and Lusaka
meetings of the Southern Africa Development
Co-ordination Conference*

SOUTHERN AFRICA
TOWARD ECONOMIC LIBERATION

Edited by AMON J. NSEKELA

REX COLLINGS   LONDON   1981

First published in Great Britain by Rex Collings Ltd.
6 Paddington Street, London W1

© Southern Africa Development Co-ordination Conference 1981

ISBN 086036 154 3

Typesetting by Malvern Printers
Printed in Great Britain by Photobooks, Bristol

Zimbabwe appears throughout this volume except in the case of some pre-independence statistical tables where Southern Rhodesia has been left

CONTENTS

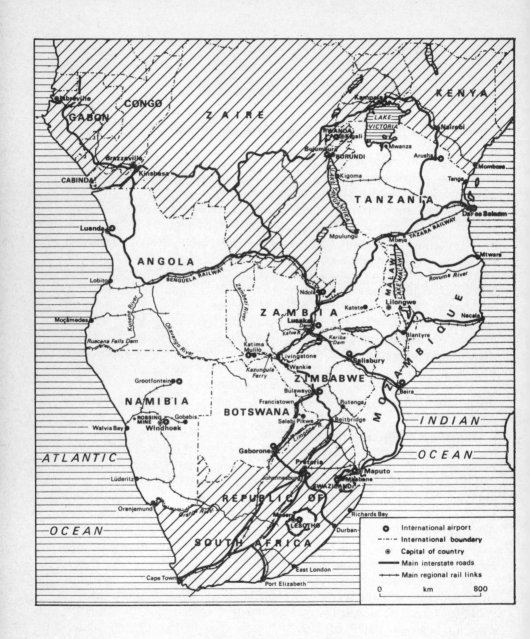

Southern Africa
(specially prepared for SADCC)

vi

Introduction*

Sir Seretse Khama

I am happy to be able to introduce this volume on development co-ordination in southern Africa. I do so as the spokesman for all my colleagues in the Southern African Development Co-ordination Conference and, whenever appropriate in this Introduction, I shall use their own words.

I have long believed that political and economic liberation are phases in the same struggle. At the independence of Mozambique, President Machel said, 'the first day of our political independence is the first day of the longer and harder struggle for economic independence'. Our experience in Botswana certainly has borne this out. The greatest single constraint upon our being able to realize the potential opened to us by our political independence has been the total dependence for transport and communications on neighbouring white-ruled territories.

I have also long recognized that achieving economic liberation must be a regional as well as a national struggle. In the political realm, the struggle for the liberation of Angola, Mozambique and Zimbabwe and the continuing struggle for the liberation of Namibia have taught all of us in southern Africa that lesson.

Geography enforces it in the economic sphere, for six of the nine independent states of southern Africa are landlocked. Economic factors point in the same direction, for all of us are relatively small. So too do power realities. President Nyerere's warning applies as much to economics as to politics—'Small nations are like indecently clad women, they tempt the evil minded.' Only in co-ordinated action can the small independent states of southern Africa achieve the economic strength and power necessary to resist those who are tempted to continue to exploit us and to perpetuate our economic fragmentation and dependence.

Although individually small and economically weak, collectively our nine states, together with the yet-to-be-freed Namibia, are not insignificant. We speak for 60 million people living in an area of 5 million square kilometres, with an aggregate GDP of US$20 billion even in our present under-developed condition. We have within our borders the raw materials for

*This introduction was written and the final text agreed shortly before Sir Seretse's tragic death.

industrialization—energy and base metals. We have energy in the form of oil, coal, uranium, hydroelectric power, and of course limitless solar energy when it can be harnessed; and we have base metals such as iron, copper, nickel, cobalt, chrome, lead, zinc. Add to these our diamonds and gold and the wide variety of our agricultural products including cotton, sisal, tea, coffee, tobacco, sugar, wool, maize, wheat, leather, beef, wood pulp and mohair. Given the political will established at Lusaka and the co-operation of investment-exporting countries, greater economic self-sufficiency for each of our countries and for the region as a whole is a realizable objective.

This publication may persuade concerned readers that economic co-ordination in southern Africa is no longer a dream. Nor is it just an ideal for the future. It is in the process of becoming a reality. At the Lusaka Economic Summit held on 1 April 1980, the nine independent states of southern Africa took the historic decision to act in concert for co-ordinated development of our region in order to reduce the excessive economic dependence from which we all suffer.

It is a source of great satisfaction to me that at the request of the other Front Line States, Botswana convened and chaired the Lusaka Summit and the 1979 Arusha meeting of the economic ministers of the Front Line States which preceded it. This volume is a record of what has been initiated at Arusha and Lusaka and of the next steps we hope to take.

First and foremost, it includes the Lusaka Declaration and Programme of Action, as well as eight sectoral papers on aspects of Southern African Development Co-ordination. These were prepared by the Conference Secretariat for the Arusha Meeting and have been a valuable source of insights, ideas and information to both the Arusha and Lusaka meetings. They will help the reader understand the problems and potential of the independent states of southern Africa, see the need for and possibilities of regional co-ordination, and grasp the aspiration and realities which underlie the Lusaka Declaration and Programme of Action.

Co-ordination for Political Liberation
Our drive for economic co-ordination originates in our experience of political co-ordination in the struggle for independence which first gained momentum in southern Africa in the 1950s. In the 1960s six of our number achieved independence: Tanzania, Malawi, Zambia, Botswana, Lesotho and Swaziland. Their independence was not won without effort and sacrifice, but by and large it did not require sustained armed struggle.

It was otherwise with Mozambique, Angola and Zimbabwe and it remains otherwise with Namibia. The peoples of the Portuguese colonies and of Zimbabwe faced entrenched racist and imperialist power which until the eleventh hour refused to negotiate genuine majority rule. In these colonies nationalist movements found themselves faced with no alternative but to respond to the violence of repression with the violence of liberation. The armed struggle in Mozambique, Angola and Zimbabwe required and received solidarity and support from the independent states of the region that was intensive, co-ordinated and sustained.

In Namibia, SWAPO's struggle continues to command the same support. Early in 1969 in the Lusaka Manifesto the States of East and Central Africa called for negotiated change but warned that the alternative was armed struggle. This regional solidarity in support of political liberation was endorsed by the OAU later that year.

In due course after Mozambique won its independence the struggle in Zimbabwe intensified and the Front Line States developed a co-ordinating mechanism which gave the struggle for political liberation a new regional dimension. The strength and effectiveness of co-ordinated action in the political liberation struggle encourages us to believe that a similar dynamic of co-ordination is attainable on the economic front. This is not to ignore or to gloss over national economic interests or differences of opinion. These are real but no less real have been national political differences of opinion which the Front Line States have overcome in the political liberation struggle. The nine independent states of the region can do as much in the interest of Southern African Development Co-ordination.

The need for economic co-ordination was posed squarely by President Kenneth Kaunda in his welcoming address to the Lusaka Summit: 'Let us now face the economic challenge. Let us form a powerful front against poverty and all of its offshoots of hunger, ignorance, disease, crime and exploitation of man by man. Let us form an African Movement to wage a militant struggle against poverty. Let this Summit be our workshop for sharpening our tools, forging new weapons, working out strategy and tactics for fighting poverty and improving the quality of life of our peoples.'

The first necessity in such a programme is to enlarge our freedom of choice. When there are no options the process of decision taking is an empty one.

There is need for choice of transportation routes and communications channels, for choice of sources of energy, for choice of markets and of suppliers, for choice of investment sources and enterprise partners. We need to develop programmes to reduce one-sided dependence and to increase the options open to our national economies and governments. This need is probably greater and more urgent in southern Africa than anywhere else in the world. The fragmentation of our economies and their enforced integration into that of the Republic of South Africa have created an excessive national and regional dependence on that country which we seek to reduce.

President Samora Machel in his address at Lusaka highlighted the need both to reduce dependence and to build programmes and institutions related to what we perceive as our real regional needs. 'Therefore the economic plans have to be conceived and prepared by ourselves. There is no one better than ourselves, no one who knows better our needs and priorities. We must not accept the habit of plans made outside of our region.'

ix

Basis for Co-ordination

Economic co-ordination among the independent states of southern Africa requires that the Programme of Action must offer and be seen to offer real benefits to each state. There must be a perception of common regional interests but the pursuits of these common interests must provide for the real and immediate needs of each co-operating state.

Effective co-ordination means the regional utilization of the specific characteristics, strengths and experiences of each economy and of its natural resources and geographic location for the benefit of all the countries of the region and their peoples. Among equals there is a very real role for specialization and division of labour. None need be exploited by it. All may benefit from it. No independent southern African state is large enough to pursue economic autarchy. Among genuine partners acting in agreed co-ordination there is nothing wrong with mutual interdependence. It is the one-sided dependence of the weak on the strong which destroys self-reliance, corrodes initiative, and distorts development. Southern African development co-ordination will be achieved by southern Africans for southern Africans. How could it properly be otherwise? But that is not to say we reject outside help. Indeed at Arusha and at Lusaka it was made plain that the independent states of southern Africa seek external co-operation. These outside co-operators have a variety of reasons for seeking to help us to co-ordinate our development. Some are concerned for southern African liberation. Some are moved by a humanitarian commitment to support national and regional efforts to overcome poverty. Some hope to secure access to the region's mineral resources and markets. All of these are valid interests over-lapping with each other and with our own to create a solid foundation of mutuality on which we can build a sustained programme of practical co-operation and imaginative assistance.

Initial Proposals and Actions

Southern African development co-ordination did not arise as a new concept at Arusha. As early as 1974 when Mozambique's independence was in sight President Kaunda spoke of the day when the independent states of southern Africa 'could meet to discuss liberation—not liberation from political oppression but liberation from poverty'. In his speech in Dar es Salaam on 7 July 1974 he called for the creation of a 'Transcontinental Belt of independent and economically powerful nations, from Dar es Salaam and Maputo on the Indian Ocean to Luanda on the Atlantic'. Arusha and Lusaka are the latest steps on the journey to the realization of that vision.

For there are already practical examples of economic co-ordination and much of that experience has centred on transport. Following the illegal declaration of independence in Rhodesia in 1965, Zambia faced a transport crisis. As a result of the joint actions of Zambia and Tanzania, aided by a wide range of external co-operators including China, the World Bank, Italy and the USA, the region now has the Great North Road from Lusaka to

Dar es Salaam, the Zambia-Tanzania Road Services Company, the Tanzania Pipeline, the Tazara Railway, and Zambian support for expanding harbour facilities at Dar es Salaam and Mtwara as well as the airport at Mtwara. Similarly Mozambique and Zambia have co-ordinated highway development programmes while Angola and Zambia have worked together on plans to rehabilitate the Benguela Railway.

Zambia and Botswana have co-operated to secure a land route between the two countries that did not cross Rhodesia. Mozambique has co-ordinated national transport development and route use with Malawi, Swaziland, Tanzania and Zambia.

Preparation for the Arusha Conference

Given this history of economic co-ordination at bilateral level since 1965, why did Heads of Government wait until 1980 to launch the Lusaka Declaration and Programme of Action? I regret that it has taken us so long to consolidate our efforts but that is the wisdom of hindsight. In the early days we were caught up in quite specific day to day crises caused by the struggle against minority rule in Rhodesia and the Portuguese colonies. Supporting the Liberation Movements, keeping our own economies functioning, and succouring our hard hit neighbours occupied us full time. In addition, our approach to regional co-operation has changed since the 1960s. There was then a hope which seemed realistic that the East African Community could form the core of a broader eastern and southern African grouping. Zambia was actively negotiating for membership and other states in the region held more tentative discussions. In the end this hope proved a vain one. Moreover, global economic problems which reached a critical level in 1973/4 forced all the independent states of southern Africa to concentrate attention and resources on keeping their heads above water in the very rough seas of the world economy.

Nevertheless, discussions continued among the Front Line States on how we might extend our common effort in support of political liberation to the pursuit of economic liberation. Background papers, technical data and notes for possible agendas and programmes were assembled in 1977/8. In May 1979, Foreign Ministers of the Front Line States met in Gaborone at Botswana's invitation, and decided that a Conference of Economic Ministers should be convened at Arusha, to which representatives of bilateral and multilateral external co-operating agencies and institutions should be invited to express their views on our proposed programme of action.

The Arusha Conference

At the Arusha Conference in July 1979 we made very considerable progress. In fact there were two meetings at Arusha. At the first, Economic Ministers of the Front Line States agreed on the broad lines of the declaration and programme of action which required final ratification by Heads of

xi

Government. It was also recognized that southern African development co-ordination affected all the independent states of the region.

The second meeting took place between the Ministers of the Front Line States and representatives of development agencies, whose views and support we wished to secure from the start. I believe this may be the first time a group of Third World countries has taken the initiative in setting out its priorities and programmes and inviting selected potential partners from the developed world to attend a forum to discuss them.

The level of interest and indications of potential support were generally gratifying and the discussions were of considerable value to us in refining our priorities for the Programme of Action.

Trade, Production and Co-ordination

Our states believe that it is vitally important that we trade more among ourselves within the southern African region. We must diversify domestic production as well as outside import sources. Reducing import dependence on the Republic of South Africa cannot mean of course that each state should produce everything for itself: in each individual country the natural resource base, the national market, the supply of skilled personnel at all levels are too small. But we should not be satisfied by substituting European or North American or Japanese or any other goods for South African products. We must also trade among ourselves.

Intra-regional trade can increase without the creation of a free trade area or a common market. Each of our states in SADCC has experience with those models of trade creation. The Federation of Rhodesia and Nyasaland, the Portuguese colonial 'economic union', the East African Common Market, the Southern African Customs Union—all were, or are, free trade areas or common markets. All have served to limit our development, to enrich externally based firms and interests and to hamper national planning. The words of Mozambique's Finance Minister, Rui Baltazar Santos, at Arusha are very relevant: 'We must look squarely at our mistakes lest we fall into repeating them.'

We collectively reject models which would lead to growing gaps between stronger and weaker states and to conflicts of interest which would seriously undermine mutual trust and contain the seeds of dissolution.

None of this means that there should not be preferential trade arrangements among our countries. But they should be planned ones so as to flow from and serve the needs of co-ordinated national and regional development. Our trade arrangements should not be at the mercy of free market forces or foreign companies. The Tanzania-Mozambique annual trade plan is one example of such a preferential trade arrangement.

Nor can trade be considered in isolation. Production is the first goal. And reliable transport links must precede lower tariffs.

Botswana's agricultural development is a case in point. We wish to reduce food dependence on the Republic of South Africa and to build up food security against drought. First this requires that we build up our own crop production. There are three ways in which southern African co-operation can assist this goal. The most obvious is in research. All of us face the problems of semi-arid areas; we need to co-ordinate and share research. External co-operation needs to be regionally oriented—hence the Lusaka Programme of Action includes an approach to the International Crops Research Institute on Agriculture in Semi-arid Tropics to establish a regional unit for southern Africa in Botswana.

Next comes water, although this does not as yet form part of the agreed Programme of Action. A major water source in Botswana is the inland delta of the Okavango River. The Okavango is a regional river rising in Angola and passing through Namibia into Botswana. Its effective use in each of these countries would require that we agree on who can draw how much water at what times of the year. Finally in much of northern and western Botswana agriculture is deterred by the absence or high cost of transport. A Trans-Kgalagadi Railway would not only give us access to the Atlantic through an independent Namibia for our coal and for other minerals, but could also assist agricultural production. So even domestic agricultural output growth is closely linked to regional co-ordination.

For Botswana, self-sufficiency in food is at best a long-term goal. But we can shift our import sources to SADCC partners; Zimbabwe can supply maize and sugar; vegetable oil could come from Swaziland; and in time fish from Namibia, if production can be co-ordinated and transport improved. Botswana can export meat and meat products. It is because trade development in southern Africa is important that we must begin by co-ordinating transport and production.

SADCC and African Economic Co-operation
Southern African development co-ordination does not preclude SADCC states from participating in other economic co-operative groupings within Africa. Nor is it in any way inconsistent with the Lagos OAU Summit's endorsement of a phased, long term strategy toward African continental economic integration.

On the contrary, most SADCC member states participate in the Eastern and Central African Management Institute based in Arusha, in the Eastern and Central African Multilateral Planning and Operational Co-ordination Centre (MULPOC) in Lusaka, and in the ECA's new Eastern and Central African Mining Institute in Tabora. But these useful ventures among a broader group of states are not enough by themselves to form a coherent programme of co-ordination for liberation and development. The southern African transport and communications challenges are very real, very appropriate for regional action, and very different from the equally real problems of the Sudan, Seychelles or Burundi. There is no contradiction between the SADCC and other eastern and central African co-operation agencies.

Equally, several SADCC states are members, or may become members, of other co-ordination groupings. The most prominent present case is the Kagera Basin Authority which brings together Tanzania, Burundi and Rwanda and which Uganda is likely to join. These States have real common interests in energy, transport and communications, production and trade. They are largely separate from the particular common concerns of the SADCC states but in no way inconsistent with them. Similarly the need for co-ordinated sectoral or regional development may involve Zambia and Angola in co-operating with Zaire in a variety of specific projects. And once SADCC is firmly established and producing concrete results other states may wish to join, for example the Indian Ocean island states of Mauritius, Seychelles, Madagascar or the Kagera Basin states of Rwanda, Burundi and Uganda. But we must first achieve real successes among ourselves.

I fully endorse the judgement of President Shehu Shagari of Nigeria on the OAU's first economic summit held, like the Lusaka Summit, in April 1980. The Lagos meeting was indeed 'the signal for the commencement of Africa's struggle for economic independence'. In President Shagari's words: 'It will be a long battle but a battle which we are determined to win, for we know that without political independence it is impossible to achieve economic independence and without economic power, political independence is meaningless, incomplete and insecure. African economic co-operation is not simply a lofty ideal. It is a fact of life, a necessity. We are determined that our role in shaping the economy of this great continent can no longer be determined for us. This role can only be determined by ourselves.'

Nothing could be more consistent with the Lusaka Declaration 'Southern Africa: towards Economic Liberation'. Nor is there any conflict between the Lusaka Programme of Action and the Lagos call for continental preferential trade arrangements by 1984 and an African Economic Community by 2000, which is a phased, long term strategy.

SADCC is fully consistent with that strategy and can contribute to its success. Action is needed now that will achieve quick, concrete results. There can be no sounder foundation for pan-African economic co-ordination than the success of African regional economic groupings such as SADCC and ECOWAS.

We must first develop, at the regional level, the habit of inter-state co-ordination of major economic decisions, in order to create a basis of trust and solidarity and to demonstrate the very real concrete gains which can be made to flow. This will also help us develop our transport and expand our production so that by the end of this century our economies will be strong enough nationally, regionally and continentally for the visions of the Lusaka and Lagos Economic Summits to be realized.

From Arusha to Lusaka
I know that the interval between the Arusha Conference in July 1979 and

the Lusaka Summit in April 1980 raised questions in the minds of some as to our seriousness of purpose. That delay was unavoidable if the Lusaka Summit was to be a success.

At Arusha only the five Front Line States—Angola, Botswana, Mozambique, Tanzania and Zambia—were present. It was natural that we should take the initiative because our perception of the need for co-ordinated economic action had arisen out of the realities of co-ordination and co-operation among us in the political struggle.

However, at Arusha our ministers agreed that it was imperative that SADCC should be open to all independent southern African states and should also co-operate where feasible with the Liberation Movements in preparing for their struggle for economic independence after political liberation.

Accordingly the Front Line Heads of State agreed that the meeting of Heads of Government to adopt the Declaration on Southern Africa Development Co-ordination and determine its initial Programme of Action should include all independent southern African states. Moreover we felt that the newcomers should not simply be presented with a draft declaration and agenda from the Arusha meeting in whose preparation they had not participated. They had to be actively involved in the preparations for the Summit. And to accomplish the necessary process of consultation took time. During this period progress was being made toward the political liberation of Zimbabwe. From the Commonwealth Heads of Government Meeting in Lusaka, through the Lancaster House Conference, to the February election, Zimbabwe was of central concern to all of us. A genuinely independent Zimbabwe was clearly going to be a crucial member of SADCC. It would not have been sensible to hold the regional Summit before the Prime Minister of independent Zimbabwe could attend.

The nine months which elapsed between Arusha and Lusaka were thus put to good use. The presence at the summit of all nine independent states and the agreement on the Declaration and the Programme of Action involving each SADCC member is evidence of this.

The Lusaka Declaration
The Lusaka Declaration 'Southern Africa: towards Economic Liberation' is a commitment by the nine independent states of southern Africa 'to pursue policies aimed at economic liberation and integrated development of our national economies'. It was adopted because the nine governments were agreed that the time had come to build on the experience of unity and cohesion which the Front Line States had gained in the struggle for political liberation, to extend it to the struggle for economic liberation and development, and to broaden it to include all independent southern African States.

Unity of action is fundamental in this endeavour. To free the peoples of southern Africa from misery, hunger and chronic dependency we must

xv

mobilize collectively the creative capacities, resources, personnel and potential wealth of the region. Our unity cannot be an abstraction. It must be based on perceived mutual interests, embodied in concrete projects, and cemented through the experience of successfully working together.

This requires that we identify priorities and that we create the means to achieve them. One overriding priority is the reduction of our dependence on the Republic of South Africa. A necessary means to that end is to free all our minds—politicians, public servants, technocrats and consumers alike—from the belief that there are no viable alternatives. Mental liberation is not enough by itself but it is an essential first step to understanding what choices exist and what actions can be taken to broaden our options.

Therefore the Lusaka Declaration makes it very clear that it is we ourselves who must co-ordinate southern African development. Co-ordination must be decided upon, planned, directed and in large part paid for by southern Africans. None of the states gathered at Lusaka were in any doubt on that score.

Towards Broader Co-operation
Regional self-reliance is not inconsistent with our desire and need to seek the co-operation of 'the peoples and government of the many countries who are interested in promoting welfare, justice and peace in southern Africa and the international agencies who share this interest'. The Declaration is specifically addressed to them as well as to the peoples of southern Arica. Economic liberation, designed and implemented by southern Africans, can proceed more rapidly and be more effective within a framework of co-operation.

There were no illusions at Lusaka that the advances of the recent past are now secure. Still less was there any failure to recognize that there would be opposition. The drive for national and regional development through co-ordinated action may be seen by some as a threat to their self-interests. The struggle for economic liberation may therefore be bitterly contested.

The tactics of opposition will vary. Perhaps the most dangerous will be that of the false friends who will whisper in southern African ears that the road chosen is too difficult, that fellow southern African states are not trustworthy, that the struggle is not worth the effort. Their purpose is clear—to destroy our solidarity and to divide the southern African states.

To free ourselves from economic dependency will therefore require vigilance. We must resist the temptation of short-term national advantage at the expense of other southern African states and of regional integration. We must hold fast to the faith that southern African economic and political salvation rests on southern African unity.

The First Steps Forward
We also require a sense of realism and of perspective. It is necessary to be

modest in our immediate objectives and to be ambitious in our long-term goals. To claim too much too soon would destroy credibility and undermine our realization of the value of what has already been achieved. To set long-term goals too low would prevent us from achieving all that we are capable of achieving.

Firm first steps are possible in several fields. Development of co-operation in each of them depends on an adequate regional system of transport and communications, without which co-operation in production, security, energy and trade would simply not be feasible.

The initial projects must yield direct benefits for national development and enhance the scope for regional economic co-operation. We must begin with concrete actions which help us to gain experience and to define further fruitful ways of co-operation. We should not begin by building elaborate institutions and interstate bureaucracies. Any institutions should be instrumental to co-operation or result from it.

The Programme of Action

The Programme of Action adopted at Lusaka is multifaceted. The first priority is transport and communications. The co-ordination of our use of existing facilities is a priority. So is the reconstruction of systems damaged by enemy raids and by lack of adequate maintenance during the economic crises of the past five years.

The rail systems of Angola, Botswana, Mozambique, Swaziland, Tanzania, Zambia and Zimbabwe all need attention. In addition new regional road and rail links are needed, especially after the independence of Namibia. To begin implementing the initial projects as well as planning and designing the long-term ones a Regional Transport and Communications Commission is to be created in Maputo.

Agriculture is our common denominator. We are all nations of farmers. Yet time after time famine sweeps our lands, finds us unprepared and once again forces our people to rely on the charity of foreign governments. This is an absurdity in a region where there is no scarcity of land.

Our programme of co-ordinated action seeks firstly to control foot and mouth disease which, crossing political boundaries, all too frequently decimates our livestock. Secondly, internationally linked research can help us find ways of overcoming the constraints on crop production in the semi-arid conditions which characterize much of our land. Thirdly, we must devise a regional food security plan which would ensure prompt remedial action against anticipated shortages and provide for times of emergency.

People are both the instruments and the beneficiaries of development. We recognize that as a region we are deficient in the skills necessary for our economic liberation. This will be an area of priority concentration beginning with a survey of existing training institutions and leading to regional policies and programmes to accelerate the pace and lower the cost

xvii

of training through the intensive development and utilization of regional facilities.

If we are to reduce our dependence on imported manufactured goods, if we are to expand trade among ourselves, we must build up our industrial and manufacturing output. This cannot be done on the basis of separate industries for each of our small national markets.

Nor is it acceptable, as President Nyerere has said, 'for any country— however small—to be merely a purchaser of industrial goods from others. We have to plan development which is balanced between nations, so that each contributes and each benefits. Otherwise attempts at co-operation will collapse.'

We will therefore carry out a pragmatic search for strategies for the harmonization of our industrial development.

All of the southern African economies have faced energy problems—of cost, of availability and of dependence on South Africa. However, the region is potentially more than self-sufficient in energy and some countries have surpluses of certain energy sources. A Regional Energy Conservation and Security Plan should be able to contribute to reducing the energy import drains on foreign exchange, providing markets for national surpluses and increasing regional and national security of supply.

The programmes and projects now envisaged will not be cheap. In the field of transport and communications a very rough first estimate of financial requirements for regional projects during the 1980s is $1,500 million. We are therefore examining suitable financial mechanisms for the mobilization, management and deployment of funds of this magnitude for co-ordinated regional projects.

Finally co-operation with external governments and institutions requires a forum for discussion and pledging. We have therefore decided to hold the Southern African Development Co-ordination Conference annually. The first in Arusha in 1979 did not go much beyond the discussion of general issues. But the second which is to be held in Maputo in November 1980 is to include specific project and programme proposals.

It is our hope that internnational and bilateral aid agencies will at that time be able to pledge their support for the various components of our Programme of Action.

Decision to go Forward

The Lusaka Declaration and Programme of Action do not represent a final achievement. Rather, they constitute a beginning. The independent states of southern Africa have chosen to go forward to solidarity and to co-ordinate their efforts towards economic liberation. This is a momentous decision with consequences which stretch far into our future. A movement has begun which, if sustained, could in time fundamentally change the economic direction of our continent.

To those who seek a deeper understanding of the motivations and modalities, the aspirations and personalities of this movement towards economic integration, I recommend a study of the documents in this volume.

SERETSE KHAMA

Communiqué issued at the Lusaka Summit

Today, in an historic summit meeting, leaders and representatives of the nine independent countries of southern Africa made a joint declaration of their strategy for a closer integration of their economies. This marks a new commitment to co-ordinate their economies so as to accelerate their development and reduce their dependence on the Republic of South Africa.

The Leaders approved a programme of action which included:

— The creation of a Southern African Transport and Communications Commission based in Maputo.

— Measures to control hoof and mouth disease in cattle throughout the region.

— The preparation of a food security plan for the region.

— The establishment of a Regional Agricultural Research Centre specializing in drought-prone areas.

— Plans for harmonization of industrialization and energy policies.

— Sharing of national training facilities within the region.

— Studies leading to proposals for the establishment of a Southern African Development Fund.

The Summit agreed that a meeting of Ministers should be held in Zimbabwe in September, 1980.

The Summit agreed that an International Donors Conference should be held in Maputo at the end of November, 1980.

The Summit requested the Government of Botswana to examine the need for institutional mechanisms for overall co-ordination of the programmes. Meanwhile, the Government of Botswana was given responsibility for taking immediate follow-up action until appropriate institutions have been established and are operational.

The Declaration by the Governments of Independent States of Southern Africa made at Lusaka on 1 April 1980

We, the undersigned, as the Heads of Government of majority-ruled States in Southern Africa, offer this declaration to our own peoples, to the peoples and Governments of the many countries who are interested in promoting popular welfare, justice and peace in Southern Africa and to the international agencies who share this interest. In it we state our commitment to pursue policies aimed at the economic liberation and integrated development of our national economies and we call on all concerned to assist us in this high endeavour.

Dependence in Context
Southern Africa is dependent on the Republic of South Africa as a focus of transport and communications, an exporter of goods and services and as an importer of goods and cheap labour. This dependence is not a natural phenomenon nor is it simply the result of a free market economy. The nine States and one occupied territory of Southern Africa (Angola, Botswana, Lesotho, Malawi, Mozambique, Namibia, Swaziland, Tanzania, Zambia and Zimbabwe) were, in varying degrees, deliberately incorporated—by metropolitan powers, colonial rulers and large corporations—into the colonial and sub-colonial structures centring in general on the Republic of South Africa. The development of national economies as balanced units, let alone the welfare of the people of Southern Africa, played no part in the economic integration strategy. Not surprisingly, therefore, Southern Africa is fragmented, grossly exploited and subject to economic manipulation by outsiders. Future development must aim at the reduction of economic dependence not only on the Republic of South Africa, but also on any single external State or group of States.

Liberation: Political and Economic
While the struggle for genuine political independence has advanced and continues to advance, it is not yet complete. We, the majority-ruled States of Southern Africa, recognize our responsibilities, both as separate nation

2

States and as a group of neighbouring majority-ruled African countries, to assist in achieving a successful culmination of our struggle.

Our urgent task now is to include economic liberation in our programmes and priorities.
In the interest of the people of our countries, it is necessary to liberate our economies from their dependence on the Republic of South Africa, to overcome the imposed economic fragmentation and to co-ordinate our efforts toward regional and national economic development. This will be as great for Namibia as it is for all the independent States of the region.

Southern Africa is a focal point of conflict. How can it be otherwise when a racist regime holds Namibia under military occupation, grossly exploits the people and the economies of the independent states and is a major barrier to our national development? It is not the quest for liberation, but the entrenched racism, exploitation and oppression which is the cause of conflict in Southern Africa. The power behind this is in large measure economic. Economic liberation is, therefore, as vital as political freedom.

We, the majority-ruled States of Southern Africa, do not envisage this regional economic co-ordination as exclusive. The initiative toward economic liberation has flowed from our experience of joint action for political liberation. We envisage regional co-ordination as open to all genuinely independent Southern African States.

In this spirit we call on Governments, international institutions and voluntary agencies to give priority to increasing financial resources to support Southern African efforts toward economic liberation and independent economic development.
This we believe is the route to genuine interdependence and represents the best hope for a just and co-operative future for the region as a whole.

Development Objectives

The development objectives which we will pursue through co-ordinated action are:
1. the reduction of economic dependence, particularly, but not only, on the Republic of South Africa;
2. the forging of links to create a genuine and equitable regional integration;
3. the mobilization of resources to promote the implementation of national, interstate and regional policies;
4. concerted action to secure international co-operation within the framework of our strategy for economic liberation.

Strategies and Priorities.

We will identify areas in which, working in harmony, we can gear national development to provide goods and services presently coming from the

3

Republic of South Africa and weave a fabric of regional co-operation and development.

Key to this strategy is transport and communications.
The dominance of the Republic of South Africa has been reinforced and strengthened by its transport system. Without the establishment of an adequate regional transport and communications system, other areas of co-operation become impractical. The economic liberation of Namibia, following its attainment of genuine political independence, will require the creation and operation of adequate transport and communication links with its natural partners to replace the artificial ones which currently bind it to the Republic of South Africa.

We will therefore create a Southern African Transport and Communications Commission to co-ordinate the use of existing systems and the planning and financing of additional regional facilities.

The ports of Mozambique serve four States in the region and with the genuine independence of Zimbabwe can be developed to serve two more. Zambia uses transport facilities in five regional States. The development of Mozambican, Tanzanian and Angolan ports and the co-ordination of facilities more effectively to meet requirements of the land-locked States are necessarily of regional concern. Transport and Communications will be a major focus of regional action. The co-ordination of transport facilities to meet the needs of land-locked States is crucial. With the attainment of genuine independence in Zimbabwe it is urgent to restore transport routes linking it to the Indian Ocean through Mozambique. Additional areas in which co-ordinated action will be needed include major new projects such as a possible railway from Botswana through Namibia to the Atlantic Ocean, thereby creating an alternative route to the sea for Botswana, Zambia and Zimbabwe; the co-ordination of airline schedules so that movement within the region is practicable; the study of existing and proposed micro-wave and ground satellite facilities to identify how they can be interlinked, possibly through the Rift Valley Station. The Commission will be located in Maputo and serviced by a small technical unit. It will co-ordinate transport and communication links among participating States. The Commission will seek participation of all genuinely independent States in the Southern African region. In addition, in many fields, notably in transport, observer status will be open to Liberation Movements wishing to participate in anticipation of genuine independence. Similarly, in manpower development and research, the involvement of Liberation Movements is essential to amass the knowledge and train the personnel necessary once political liberation is achieved.

Regional co-ordination must be operational—it must result in concrete programmes and projects. This will require both domestic and external finance. Present estimates, for example, show that in excess of US$1.5

billion will be needed to finance urgent transport and communications projects over the next decade.

We emphasize the importance of additional resources being made available to assist efforts to co-ordinate regional economic development projects. In the first instance, we intend to use the Regional Transport & Communications Commission to mobilize finance for urgent projects in priority sectors by holding ad hoc pledging sessions with existing bilateral and multilateral funding agencies. As economic co-operation develops, a Southern African Development Fund will be created and research to this end is being initiated. Its scope would be subsequently broadened and it might prove desirable to create a separate regional development bank. We therefore urge the friends of Southern Africa to pledge financial support to this Fund.

Concerted Actions

Regional co-operation in the field of transport and communications is seen as crucial to economic liberation and has therefore been given the greatest attention. In other sectors, similar programmes of concerted action are envisaged.

For trade development we recognize that many of us have existing bilateral and multilateral trade and customs arrangements. But even within these constraints we believe that there is room for substantial increases in trade among ourselves. To this end existing payment systems and customs instruments will be studied in order to build up a regional trade system based on bilaterally negotiated annual trade targets and product lists.

A majority of the people of Southern Africa are dependent on farming and animal husbandry. Their future livelihood is threatened by environmental degradation and in particular by desert encroachment as well as recurrent drought cycles. Even today few of the States of the region are self-sufficient in staple foods. Both environmental protection and food security are major challenges both nationally and regionally. We, therefore, urge that the International Centre for Research on Agriculture in the Semi-Arid Tropics (ICRASAT) should set up a Southern Africa Regional Centre in Botswana.

We further urge the development of the existing facilities in Botswana for production of foot and mouth disease vaccine to provide for the needs of all of the majority-ruled countries in Southern Africa. The spread of this disease currently threatens Angola, Botswana, Namibia, Zimbabwe, Swaziland and Mozambique. A co-ordinated approach to its control and elimination is urgently needed.

Likewise, we will undertake concerted projects in order to exploit natural resources, in particular those of common hydrological basins.

It is a matter of urgency to identify ways in which the co-ordination of research and training as well as the exchange of information can strengthen programmes to protect our environment and increase food production. In

5

the field of food security the possibility of the co-ordination of national reserve policies and the facilitation of interstate exchanges will receive priority attention.

We have decided to give special attention to the sharing of training and research facilities.

We have further decided to stimulate the exchange of information aimed at achieving a concerted policy in the fields of mining, industry, energy and agriculture. In particular, consultations among those States requiring petroleum products and electricity on the one hand and those with petroleum refining capacity and electricity surpluses on the other must be undertaken to achieve regional solutions.

The effort for economic development is an essential condition to free the Southern African States from the exploitative migrant labour system.

External Co-operation

We are committed to a strategy of economic liberation. It is a strategy which we believe both needs and deserves international support. Southern African regional development must be designed and implemented by Southern Africans. It will, however, be achieved more rapidly and will be more effective if development takes place within the context of global co-operation.

International bodies and States outside Southern Africa are therefore invited to co-operate in implementing programmes towards economic liberation and development in the region.

This preliminary identification of aims, strategies and sectors illustrates both the magnitude of the task facing us and some of the broad areas within which outside assistance will be welcomed.

It is envisaged that Southern African Development Co-ordination meetings of member Southern African States and other invited participants should be held annually. This will provide a mechanism for surveying results, evaluating performance, identifying strengths and weaknesses and agreeing on future plans. Economic liberation and development in Southern Africa cannot be attained either easily or speedily. What is therefore needed is sustained co-operation.

We view this declaration as a statement of commitment and strategy. Under-development, exploitation, crisis and conflict in Southern Africa will be overcome through economic liberation. The welfare of the peoples of Southern Africa and the development of its economies requires co-ordinated regional action. It is our belief that in the interest of popular welfare, justice and peace, we in Southern Africa have the right to ask and to receive practical international co-operation in our struggle for reconstruction, development and genuine interdependence. However, as with the struggle for political liberation, the fight for economic liberation is neither a mere slogan to prompt external assistance nor a course of action from

6

which we can be deflected by external indifference. The dignity and welfare of the peoples of Southern Africa demand economic liberation and we will struggle toward that goal.

JOSE EDUARDO DOS SANTOS
PRESIDENT OF THE PEOPLE'S
REPUBLIC OF ANGOLA

SERETSE KHAMA
PRESIDENT OF THE
REPUBLIC OF BOTSWANA

SAMORA MOISES MACHEL
PRESIDENT OF THE PEOPLE'S
REPUBLIC OF MOZAMBIQUE

JULIUS K. NYERERE
PRESIDENT OF THE UNITED
REPUBLIC OF TANZANIA

KENNETH D. KAUNDA
PRESIDENT OF THE
REPUBLIC OF ZAMBIA

MABANDLA F. N. DLAMINI
PRIME MINISTER OF THE
KINGDOM OF SWAZILAND

ROBERT GABRIEL MUGABE
PRIME MINISTER
ZIMBABWE

MOOKI V. MOLAPO
MINISTER OF COMMERCE, INDUSTRY,
TOURISM AND LABOUR,
THE KINGDOM OF LESOTHO

DICK TENNYSON MATENJE
MINISTER OF EDUCATION
REPUBLIC OF MALAWI

This Declaration is produced in ten original copies, eight in the English language and two in the Portuguese language. All are equally valid.

SECTORAL PAPERS

Introductory Note

Prior to the Southern Africa Development Co-ordination Conference (SADCC) in Arusha, in July 1979, a series of studies was commissioned on the prospects for regional integration in each of the major sectors of the economy in southern Africa. These studies were undertaken by C. Colclough, D. Clarke, J. Faaland, R. H. Green, J. Isaksen, Y. Kyesimira, J. Loxley, P. F. M. McLoughlin and J. K. Moyana.

The SADCC Steering Committee, which was set up at the preparatory meeting in Gaborone in June 1979, hereby wishes to place on record its indebtedness to these consultants for their willingness, under considerable pressure of time, to make this important contribution to the success of the Arusha Conference. The papers were edited for presentation to the Arusha Conference by an editorial sub-committee consisting of Reginald Green, Iddi Simba, Tim Sheehy and Margaret Feeny, to all of whom the Steering Committee is also much indebted.

At the request of the Conference, the Steering Committee then undertook the further revision and editing of these studies for publication. Under the Committee's direction this revision and final editing has been carried out by Reginald Green and Cranford Pratt, who were, once again, ably assisted by Margaret Feeny. The SADCC Steering Committee owes the editorial team an indescribable debt for the care and attention they have given to this work.

These papers do not represent official positions of the SADCC, its participating governments, the Steering Committee or the editors. The Steering Committee, rather than the authors, is responsible for the final editing and presents the papers as a contribution to the discussion on greater regional co-ordination of the development policies and projects of the independent states of southern Africa.

Amon J. Nsekela
Chairman of the SADCC Steering Committee

First Steps Toward Economic Integration

Instruments, Institutions, Instrumentalities

Even the longest journey begins with the first step.

—Chinese Proverb

INTRODUCTION

The case for economic co-operation, co-ordination and integration among peripheral poor Third World economies is compelling. Within the Third World it would make collective selfreliance more effective and it would help assure a more secure and more rapid rate of development. Globally it would be a means of forming an effective 'Trade Union of the Poor'.

The experience of Third World economies to date, while mixed, can hardly be described as massively successful. Indeed it cannot be claimed even to show a general forward trend. The East African Community, for example, collapsed because of unequal division of gains, interstate ideological differences and external influences. This was hardly an exceptional event, disappointing though it was. Unequal gains, inadequate political, economic and ideological homogeneity and very real external influences both economic and political are likely to characterize any grouping of African states and to plague any effort at closer co-operation.

In respect of southern Africa the approaching independence—however won—of Namibia, the attainment of independence by Zimbabwe, the growing concern of independent southern African states to reduce their dependence on RSA and the increasing internal struggle and international tensions associated with the liberation struggle in the Republic of South Africa itself, have given rise to special concern over the potential for regional economic co-operation. This interest exists in the states and liberation movements of the region, in neighbouring African states, in the Economic Commission for Africa and among outside bodies such as the EEC and USAID. Whether the goals and approaches of all those interested are compatible may be open to doubt. To date agendas and questions have not become clear enough to resolve what is practicable and whose interests overlap to what extent on which issues. Yet the breadth of the interest in greater economic co-operation amongst the independent peoples of southern Africa is undeniable.

11

This paper seeks to present a sketch of the problems with which economic integration in southern Africa would seek to grapple; the characteristics which will constrain integration; the various ways which the constraints and past experience suggest are ill-conceived or are premature leaps; and a sketch of approaches which are both compatible with constraints and potentially able to loosen them over time and of areas in which action is practicable. It is in no sense definitive and is much more oriented to posing issues than to answering questions. Indeed until more questions are asked in a systematic fashion, especially by the decision takers of the states concerned, it will remain impossible for anyone (most of all an academic analyst) to offer operationally practicable answers.

By its nature much of this survey is critical or sceptical, and its positive conclusions as to what may be practicable today are disappointing when set in contrast either to the nature of the problems confronting the people and states of the region or to the broader aspirations of long term integration. However, the intention of the criticisms is not to discourage first steps but rather to indicate directions in which any step is likely to be a misstep. Equally, the value of limited but significant initial joint action is likely to be greater both in the short term and in building a base for broader and deeper future integration if the burden of expectations laid upon it is realistic and relatively modest. The failure of grand aspirations in the field of economic integration among peripheral economies has been all too frequent and has usually led, at least for a time, to a cold reaction against co-operation, making new starts ever harder to achieve. Southern and eastern Africa have been no exception to that pattern of experience.

TOWARD WHAT GOALS?

Many of the reasons for interest in economic integration in southern Africa are common to other regions, but those which relate to disentanglement (partial or total, selective or across the board) from the region's dominant power, the Republic of South Africa, are distinctive. The key considerations can be stated either as negative—present conditions which must be overcome, or as positive goals to be furthered. In either case they appear to form five clusters:

1. *Reduction of concentrated unilateral dependence on RSA*

Except for Angola and Tanzania, every economy in the region is dependent to a significant extent on RSA for sources of supply, key personnel, markets, finance, transportation, enterprises and/or employment opportunities. For Lesotho, Swaziland and Namibia the degree of subordinated economic integration is in some respects more like that of the outland provinces of a single state than that of even an extreme dependence of weaker independent states. Clearly the principal ways to reduce this dependence must be national. Even in respect of international co-operation it is clear that regional co-operation is not the only form though it may be the dominant one. Its possible achievements and limitations have to date been clouded by a greater degree of generalized moderate verbal enthusiasm than of serious posing of questions, articulation of projects or acceptance of costs.

2. *Reduction of external economic dependence.*

In a global sense this is a possible parallel goal to reduction of dependence on RSA. It is not an identical one. Diversification away from RSA, e.g. to EEC, may serve the first goal by shifting dependence. It may also reduce dependence on any one external economy, thus giving some gains in bargaining potential and degrees of freedom. Those routes, however, have limited and uneven direct relevance to regional co-operation—limited and uneven, not negligible, because in certain cases diversification of dependence requires a greater integration of transport with neighbouring states if trade with, for example, Europe is to increase. Thus the Tanzanian-Zambian road, rail, pipeline and oil projects, the proposed and partially operational Mozambique-Zambia and Mozambique-Malawi links are important aids to the diversification of southern Africa's dependence. The relevance of regional integration is greater still in broadening the scope of regional production—of goods and services including education/technical assistance—trade and selfreliance. Here significant questions of costs, gains, intraregional dominance and the 'logic' of the region (however defined) as an economic unit have been posed incompletely and fitfully rather than systematically and intensively.

3. *Increased co-ordination of external economic relations.*

This has rather special meanings in the southern African context. One strand of this which has been secondary to date, turns on the joint management of economic interests of two or more states vis-à-vis foreign firms or states as happens, for example, in respect of diamonds between Angola, Botswana and Namibia and—only partly within the region—in the operation of the Kenya-Uganda-Tanzania-Zambia Interstate Standing Committee on Shipping to negotiate on rates with international shipping conferences or cartels. The major strand has been that of co-ordinating initiatives; negotiation and use of extraregional assistance in respect of the costs imposed on the independent southern African states by the liberation struggle in general and the transition to lessened dependence on RSA in particular. The interest of EEC and USAID seems to focus in particular upon this category.

4. *Joint development of particular common assets.*

This is a goal which has substantial attraction for several states in the region. For example use of Botswana's Okavango Swamp waters, potentially its largest single source of agriculture, is dependent on water

13

agreements and possible joint river development with Namibia and Angola. Development of its western mineral deposits as well as reduction of dependence on RSA transport, appear to depend on integrated action with Namibia in respect of rail and harbour facilities. Equally, if Cabora Bassa's dependence on RSA is to be reduced and/or the scheme brought to full utilization, then Mozambican/Zimbabwean joint action in respect of power use and transmission is critical. To date the short term stresses of the post 1965 regional struggle (including breaking the links of an imposed economic integration) and the continued occupation of Zimbabwe and Namibia, have limited thinking on issues of this kind to generalities rather than detailed programme or project proposals. With the successful conclusion of Zimbabwe's struggle for independence, the time has come for these matters to be further pursued.

5. *Broader, mutually beneficial economic integration.*

This is an obvious final goal. Nevertheless though obvious, it has tended to be seen in terms of trade expansion with flows posited on the basis of present difficulties in resource endowment and industrial capacity. This seems risky for three distinct reasons. First, it raises the spectre of Zimbabwe establishing an industrial hegemony like that which it held in the Central African Federation long before independence or that which some feared Kenya sought to consolidate in the EAC. Second, it risks overlooking the possibility that the major gains will lie in production not now carried on in the region and especially in those lines of production not economically practicable except in the context of integration. Third, by placing trade first it accepts, however unintentionally, the liberal, neo-laizzez-faire political economic ideology which most if not all of the governments reject both domestically and in their criticisms of the existing international economic order (or disorder). Selective integration of production, with trade as an implementing consequence, has been seen as the medium term goal in the Tanzania-Mozambique economic co-ordination approach (again an initiative crossing regional lines) but even in that case articulated proposals have been limited to short term, gap-filling or capacity-utilizing trade both because of the short run Mozambican need to reactivate the existing economic units following the Portuguese exodus and the limited capacity which each government has for detailed forward planning.

These five clusters represent areas in which regional economic integration is already seen as a means of meeting challenges. In respect of each there is a belief within the regional states that common interests do exist. These are necessary conditions for identifying institutional approaches and concrete areas for joint action. They are, however, by themselves, by no means sufficient conditions for launching a strategy to promote greater integration.

Five imperatives must be obeyed if efforts and greater integration are in fact to succeed:-

14

1. Have a genuine commitment to and involvement in the working through of proposals by national decision takers, civil servants, managers;

2. Avoid hasty adoption of approaches which recreate older, usually colonial linkages or copy models from academic analysis or other regional experiences or are drawn up by outside bodies or expatriate advisors (no matter how well intentioned);

3. Centre on areas in which regional action is critical and its gains to participants readily perceived e.g. transport;

4. Avoid precipitate action in areas (e.g. free trade) in which conflicts among states are likely, even if working out how to avoid or to resolve conflict, delays action or requires initial progress to be ad hoc;

5. Relate initiatives directly to the economic front of the southern African liberation struggle by reducing economic dependence on RSA.

DIVERSITY AND CONFLICT OF INTEREST

The potential regional gains from integration cannot be captured unless there is full recognition of the structural and political diversity of the states which are likely to participate and careful attention to how gains and costs will be shared. Only on that basis can institutional arrangements and areas of joint activity be negotiated and operated to create a framework perceived by each participating state to be in its separate as well as its regional interest.

The diversities and the potential conflicts arising from them are unfortunately numerous:

A. There are wide variations in structures and levels of productive forces. Zimbabwe's industrial sector is much stronger than Botswana's; Namibia's level of output per head and potential state revenue per head is very different from Lesotho's. These diversities do not prevent mutuality of gains: they do mean that they must be planned and bargained for, not expected to emerge from market forces, and that cost-bearing must be discussed in relation to ability to pay as well as to potential short term gains;

B. Resource patterns are equally diverse, e.g. Malawi appears to have its greatest strength in arable agriculture where for example Namibia is weakest; Zimbabwe to have the greatest short term potential and need for regionally oriented manufacturing; Mozambique and Angola to possess hydroelectric capacity and/or potential relevant to their neighbours. Again the variation suggests a need for co-ordinated planning and negotiations especially in respect of goods trade and its interaction with other joint activities, including trade in services such as transport and power;

15

C. By definition *the development of special assets* will rarely if ever involve all of the states in the region, nor will those concerned necessarily all be within the region, e.g. the Kunene is of direct concern to Angola, Namibia and perhaps Botswana, but hardly to Mozambique; Ruvuma Basin development is an area in which Mozambique and Tanzania have common concerns; Kagera Basin development links Tanzania with Rwanda, Burundi and Uganda, not with the other southern African states. Any approach to regional integration which tries to straightjacket all activities as if they were of concern to all states, or which excludes some because they involve non-regional states, will fail to meet the very real need to facilitate overlapping multistate joint actions. These can be a significant and even, in the early years, the dominant part of regional economic integration;

D. *Ideological and/or strategic diversity* within the region is high. To pretend otherwise, or to act as if this fact did not affect what types of integration were viable, would be very shortsighted. In particular the diversity rules out any normal free trade area. In certain cases it will require creating parallel (and apparently duplicative) transport and commercial flow links in more than one direction. Such diversity need not prevent co-operation, but the divergences and limits need to be understood by all parties if unpleasant and damaging surprises are to be avoided as the institutions of co-operation are being built and as they begin to operate;

E. Partly linked to the foregoing diversities are different *priority areas and approaches* for co-operation. However these differences also relate to historic (e.g. Central African Federation membership) and physical (e.g. landlocked) factors. Reduction of dependence on RSA is a fairly uniform objective. However, what this reduction requires varies. For example, for Mozambique the key sub-areas are wage employment, port revenue and power sales, whereas for Swaziland they turn more on access to transport, commercial infrastructure, water and power development and sources of goods. Some of the variations may be complementary e.g. Swaziland's need for alternative transport and for commercial infrastructure and goods might provide some domestic employment power-use and port activity for Mozambique. To make them fit together requires case by case co-ordinated study and negotiation;

F. Definitions of the region, or more to the point partners for economic integration activities, differ widely. Zambia's and Mozambique's closest links and their greatest range of joint operations are with Tanzania. Some regional definitions limit themselves to Botswana, Lesotho, Swaziland, Zimbabwe and Namibia; the standard one includes these plus Mozambique, Angola, Zambia and Malawi; the broadest add Tanzania, the Malagasy Republic and Mauritius—plus presumptively the Comoros and Sao Tomé e Principe. The problem is not primarily one of drawing lines but of deciding

16

what regional framework fits the objects and political needs of the region (however self defined), how open to geographic expansion it should be and with what provisions for joint activities involving regional and adjoining non-regional states.

G. Degree of priority or commitment to regional integration, especially in terms of ability—narrowly or politically defined—to bear costs, varies markedly. At one extreme Lesotho would find a total break with RSA either impossible or economically suicidal. On a somewhat different level, Zambia has paid a very high level of costs for delinking with pre-independence Zimbabwe over 1965–75 and has had high ongoing security expenditures related to the liberation struggle in that country and in Namibia. These interacted with a disastrous global economic situation in respect to its key export. Zambia today cannot afford a net loss or even an absence of short term gains from regional integration activities. Any acceptable package must ease its economic plight. More generally, some leaders and senior officials have not, at least in the past, shown a firm belief that regional integration was important or promising enough to make large commitments to it. These considerations may suggest the need for allowing for quite uneven degrees of participation.

Discussion of diversities should help accommodate them or might help to reduce them. Misperceptions are quite as damaging when false as when true. For example many Tanzanians perceive Zambia as relatively wealthy and able to be lavish in its use of foreign exchange; not a realistic view since 1974. Many Zambians see Tanzania as little affected, or even positively helped, by global economic crises (a startling perception of the state ranking number 3 on the UN's 'most severely affected' list). Lack of open discussion may avoid official acrimony but it also reinforces views which hamper the perception of similarities in the degree of external shocks and the cost of domestic adjustments. A lack of such discussion also blocks the emergence of a wider recognition that these are potential common interests, as for example, exist in two way trade using surplus manufacturing capacity available in each state and substituting for purchases from outside economies.

Real understanding of goals, costs and benefits is critical because costs, whatever their subsequent gains, are high. The trade and transport costs of Zambia's delinking from pre-independence Zimbabwe and, to a degree, RSA totalled about £500 million over 1965–78; the Tanzanian fixed investment in transport facilities designed primarily to support Zambian delinking was in excess of £200 million over 1965–75, i.e. over 20 per cent of Tanzania's total fixed investment. To accept costs, whether recurrent or capital, of such orders of magnitude, decision takers need to know what gains can be projected, at what dates. Only in that way can they be sure there is agreement on the division of costs and gains; only in that way can they be certain that the commitment of all parties is firm.

Because of the diversity of goals, resources, past experience and economic circumstances that pertain in eastern and southern Africa, several institutional and programmatic approaches are likely at best to be minimal and ineffective and at worst divisive and damaging. Unfortunately each has a certain appeal (not necessarily inappropriate in other times and places) and some seem to be under active promotion and consideration by certain of the organizations involved.

No form of free trade area or customs union is a desirable first step nor even a very promising medium term goal. A standard free trade zone among states as diverse as those of southern (or southern and eastern) Africa would generate cumulative inequalities registered by rising imbalances in trade. Further, given the very different attitudes to transnational corporations (TNCs) in general and to specific TNCs like Lonrho in particular, unplanned free trade areas would give rise to acrimonious charges and countercharges. These would almost certainly lead to cumulative restrictions and breakdowns.

The case against a free trade area is partly historic and ideological. The failure of the common market in the Central African Federation and in the East African Community are seen, partly if not wholly accurately, as demonstrating that a free trade area means 'to him who hath shall be given'. Moreover, if the means chosen for industrial expansion in the states with stronger existing manufacturing sectors were TNCs, then the standard historic operational definition of free trade as the right of the economically stronger to enter without let or hindrance into the territory of the economically weaker would pertain in full measure. None of the southern African states accepts the desirability of that type of free trade in respect to industrial economies. Indeed the decision takers of Botswana, Lesotho, Swaziland and Namibia are convinced that such free trade within the South African Common Market has prevented the emergence of serious industrial sectors in their economies. It is therefore unrealistic to suppose that those states with weaker industrial sectors would accept it in respect of say, Zimbabwe or, in a bi-regional grouping, Kenya.

However, the ideological and historical perceptions also relate to a serious analytical case. Inequalities, however originally generated, are likely to increase cumulatively under free trade. Domestically, various redistribution tools can be used which are not available intraregionally or are not very effective. Free trade without long term co-ordination of production is unlikely to maximize economically viable regional output or to lead to relatively less unbalanced regional trade. Indeed it may concentrate on precisely those commodities in which gains from centralized production are low and avoid those in which regional size plants with consequential trade flows are critical; certainly both tendencies were notable in East Africa. Therefore a planned, and by inference selective regional trade development approach appears more promising economically as well as politically more practicable.

A planned free trade area would need to be *based on production, with trade as a consequence*, (an inversion of the laissez-faire model) or on a selective fiscal/protective system which would help the weaker economies. The former seems unlikely to be attainable on a broad range of products in the near future for technical even more than political reasons. Experience with the transfer tax in East Africa suggests that the latter is both hard to operate effectively and unclear in results.

A preferential area, for example, establishing that customs duties will be 5 per cent lower on imports from regional states than from elsewhere, would be more practicable. The variant of the three tier system with RSA goods paying 5 per cent above the standard rate might be even more plausible, at least for states which are not now members of the South African Customs Union (SACU) or are in a position to extricate themselves from it.

However, taken by itself, the first variant would have negligible effects on imports from RSA except for former SACU members. Importers do not in fact shift sources of supply speedily in response to marginal relative price changes, especially not when commercial information, trade, commercial credit and transport channels are as weak as those now existing among the regional or bi-regional group of states. Therefore, while a general preferential area would probably be a visible symbol of commitment and might be worth adopting as such, it would be no substitute for much more detailed regional, subregional and bilateral trade preferences, contracts and development schemes for specific, selected products.

A tight multisectoral regional integration scheme seems equally un-promising either as a starting point or as medium term goal. It may well be true that the East African co-operation structures would have been dismantled in 1967–8 except for the gain which each received from the then common transport and communications corporations. It is also the case that the structures proposed for the co-ordination of sectoral planning in the Kampala Agreement (1965) between the three East African Heads of State and the implementation of these arrangements in the years 1968–70 were the EAC's most innovative and potentially productive provisions and initiatives. Nevertheless, the corporations would not have been created in 1967–8 had they not already existed. They are hardly suitable models for the much broader southern African region. Further, their operations raised controversies deeply damaging to the EAC after 1971. Similarly the planning co-ordination proceeded slowly and had achieved but little momentum so that it did little to create new links to cement the Community before the Amin coup largely halted its further development.

Even more directly relevant to the initiatives to be taken in southern Africa is the fact that negotiations on the enlargement of the EAC over 1968–72 were constantly bedevilled by the fact that it was very difficult for any new member to participate in only some Community sectors. It is clear, however that a much more selective participation plus new areas of co-operation not equally interesting or equally acceptable to the three founding members would have suited the potential new members much better. The diversity of southern (or southern and eastern) Africa suggests that similar difficulties would face any all-or-none multi-sectoral approach.

At present neither homogeneity, knowledge, experience of working together, nor trust in the stability of relations are wide enough to allow a comprehensive economic integration community. This may not be a permanent situation but it is much more likely to be overcome by the success of more limited and more loosely structured joint action than by ignoring the present lack of adequate foundations for a broader EAC or an African Andean Pact.

However, totally ad hoc arrangements, individually valuable as they can be, seem less than adequate to meet the goals underlying interest in southern African economic integration. Pure bilateralism among nine of 15 countries would require a remarkable number of agreements. It would fail to capture the benefits that would flow from broader co-operation and from the mutual support which each would receive from overlapping co-operation links. The same inadequacies would be true for a set of sectoral projects and/or joint ventures for as long as these were introduced without any interstate co-ordinating and planning framework.

In particlar, reduction of dependence on RSA does appear to require co-ordinated action including joint approaches to external states and organizations. Experience elsewhere is that very narrow projects or sets of unlinked projects while useful in themselves do not generate any real dynamic toward broader exploration and exploitation of potential areas for mutually profitable integrative action.

INSTITUTIONAL APPROACHES

In the context of southern Africa, what can be said more positively about potentially suitable institutional approaches?*

A. A broadly and flexibly defined region seems appropriate. Present links strongly suggest the inclusion of Tanzania. This could imply later extension to include Rwanda and Burundi because of the projects which link them with Tanzania and, arguably, Kenya because of its trade with shipping links with Zambia. Whatever institutions are created, they should be open to new members without major renegotiation. Over time, the southern and eastern African regions may well merge and conceivably expand to include Zaire. At present the eastern region does not exist and its rebuilding, if it takes place, is not likely to be rapid.

*See also the discussion on organizations and institutions in the following paper.

20

B. Regionalism should be inclusive rather than exclusive. If a participating state has special integration links with neighbours outside the region—for example, Tanzania with Rwanda and Burundi if, as is probable, the latter two were not initially involved in southern African regionalism—it should not be the business of regionalism to prevent or discourage these but to accommodate and, where appropriate, encourage them.

C. An umbrella organization to co-ordinate regional integration is needed with a consultative council of all participating states, probably backed by full time resident directors from each state and a limited advisory and technical secretariat. Such a body would serve as a forum for consultations and for negotiating new, or renegotiating old regional or subregional programmes, as a venue for co-ordinating the various aspects of regional integration and as a centre and service unit for sectoral and project units.

D. Committees and project boards would be appropriate to handle sectoral policy co-ordination e.g. transport, trade, research, to engage in specific joint policy operations e.g. shipping rate negotiations with conference lines; to manage or to co-ordinate management of interstate projects e.g. a Kagera Basin Development Authority; to serve as boards of directors to multistate joint ventures e.g. Eastern African National Shipping Line, or a new Zimbabwean-Zambian Kariba Power Corporation were it to be established. Membership of any particular council, committee, authority or board would not be compulsory: there is no need to presume that each would be of interest to all members. Equally the relations with the umbrella organization would vary. Councils and co-ordinating committees would presumably meet at, and be serviced by, the secretariat; operational activity committees might need their own staffs, offices and legal personalities. Neither would necessarily supersede bilateral contact and co-ordination bodies like those existing between Tanzania and Mozambique. Nationally, each participating state would need a co-ordination unit. Experience in East Africa suggests that desk officers with regional responsibilities in major ministries and parastatals meeting regularly with an independent co-ordination officer as chairman/secretary can work well, especially if the unit reports to a similar committee at ministerial level.

E. *Related institutions* and *co-ordination forums* may be critical and can be more productively related to the overall regional integration process by liaison and loose association than by seeking rigid legal and functional relations. Central bankers and treasury ministers/officials prefer their own 'club'; even in the EAC neither was formally covered by the Kampala Treaty, yet right up to the breakdown, these were two of the more critical and more smoothly working forums of integration and co-ordination. Some institutions, for structural or historic reasons e.g. the East African Institute of Management, will prove easier to handle in ways somewhat separate from the main cluster of integration bodies. While administratively untidy

21

and somewhat less than ideal for communication and co-ordination, such diversity need not be, or be seen as, an obstacle to building up coherent integration strategy and practice.

F. Pre-existing institutions, through broadening their membership, may help give southern (or southern/eastern) African economic integration a more rapid operational buildup. The Interstate Standing Committee on Shipping, as a means for co-ordinated action on freight rates and conditions, could be extended to Malawi, Rwanda, Burundi, Botswana, Mozambique, Swaziland and Zimbabwe for the east coast trades and perhaps develop a west coast branch to service Angola, Namibia, Zambia and potentially Botswana and Zimbabwe. The same lines of development could be explored for the Eastern African National Shipping Line. The East African Development Bank has the initial resources and staff and the institutional operating experience to form the base for a broader eastern and southern African investment finance and industrial co-ordination promotion body. The former EAC facilities in Arusha might form a core for the umbrella organization and the East African Institute of Management for a specialized training institution. Similarly ECA's MULPOC programme for encouraging regional integration can afford experience, data and perhaps staff toward creation of a regional umbrella institution's initial secretariat and operations.

G. Joint ventures are multistate units which either produce goods or provide services. They are particularly suitable for self-financing enterprises such as railroad, industrial unit, hydroelectric project, but may be useful for specialized service bodies e.g. management institute. In certain contexts they can be a south-south alternative to TNCs. Their vital characteristic is that the participants see that important ends can be more readily accomplished jointly than separately. Whether and in what form this requires joint ownership varies. For example, if Tanzania or Mozambique develops a natural gas-based petrochemical industry to produce fertilizer, plastics and feedstocks, a regional venture covering petrochemicals, fertilizers and plastics might be desirable. However, joint ownership of plants in the three sectors would be neither necessary, sufficient nor probably even desirable. A series of term contracts for petrochemicals, plastics and fertilizers with quantity purchase and supply guarantees, and with clear formulas for determining price, would be the most logical core of the joint venture. A jointly owned company to exchange data, oversee contract fulfilment and adjustment and to assist in regional planning for the industries, would be desirable but on the face of it the case for cross shareholdings in the plants is rather weak. However, in the case of a development bank or regional trading company—whether to handle intraregional trade or specialized extraregional purchasing—participation in the capital and management of the operating company of each state would appear the most practicable organizational approach.

22

H. Initial expenses, including meetings, institutional personnel and finance, need to be held to the minimum consistent with setting a process of integration in motion. High expenses and large institutions before significant gains are visible are likely to erode support and to create divisive debates about cost sharing, personnel appointments and venues of meetings among participating states. Assuming a modest central budget with operating units self-financed or at least on separate budgets, annual national fees proportionate to GDP and paid half-yearly in advance would initially seem more suitable than either an elaborate automatic financing scheme (like that of the EAC) or very heavy dependence on financial support from institutions or states outside the region. The case for separate budgets for operating units is strong. It is, of course, self-evident for joint ventures. However, the case for it is broader. If many of the units, such as for example a Standing Committee on Shipping, do not include all the regional states, then separate budgets for each of the operating units and co-operation would reduce arguments about contribution levels.

The successful creation, operation and expansion of economic integration is based on perceived common interests and perceived gains by each participant. The gains need not be the same: an industrial co-ordination programme may indeed be easier if one participating state's dominant concern is employment, another's is use of domestic raw materials and a third's augmenting investible surplus. Nor need the common interest be perceived in the same way by all parties. For instance a Namibian/Botswanan railway may be most valuable to Botswana for furthering access to the sea and lowering the cost of western Botswanan mineral development, and to Namibia for achieving access to Zambian and Zimbabwean markets/sources of supply and augmenting invisible export earnings with no derogation from the existence of a common interest in its creation. Nor is it necessary that each programme and project yield net benefits to each participating state. What is necessary is that each state perceives them as a group and evaluates their costs and benefits jointly as well as separately.

If common interest and net gains are to survive, it is desirable that activities be safeguarded from external shocks. Any project whose survival is dependent on extraregional support is weak on this count. Any project which builds up a community of interests that a new government will find costly to dismantle, or that an external economic dislocation will render more valuable, rates highly. For example a joint power project linked to several industrial plants with high built-in regional trade links is not readily dismantled by one party and probably becomes more valuable if oil prices rise or general world inflation escalates manufactured import costs.

However, common interests are not necessarily permanent. Gains can go down as well as up; some shocks cannot be insulated against. Certain projects by their nature have built in obsolescence, especially joint universities to judge by experience. Therefore, regional integration

23

frameworks should be designed so that it is possible to modify membership of or to dissolve specific projects or programmes with minimum damage to other projects and programmes which are not themselves the causes of contention. While the difficulty of doing this in the EAC was not a major contributory cause of its breaking, it did—especially in the case of railways—contribute to a climate of opinion which spread dissatisfaction from one programme to the next.

SOME SECTORAL PERSPECTIVES

Because most of southern Africa has been economically integrated with the Republic of South Africa and the balance of the area was integrated with one or other of two different colonial powers, the gaps in communication and even in the infrastructure are far greater than they were in the CAF or EAC: and consequently so is the need to create linkages. As a result of this there are many sectors in which integrating activities can now be instituted with fairly self-evident benefits to each participant and with the prospect that there wll be set in motion a positive development dynamic.

TRANSPORT SYSTEMS

Transport within southern Africa and between southern and East Africa is marked by gaps ranging from the 50 or so kilometres from the Namibian highway at Katima Mulilo to the Zambian system, to the several hundred kilometre gap between the Tanzanian and Mozambican main highway systems. The main road links needed are between Tanzania-Mozambique, Tanzania-Malawi, Namibia-Zambia, Namibia-Angola, Zimbabwe/ Botswana-Namibia. Links between Mozambique and Malawi, Zambia and Swaziland require improvement as does the Zambia-Botswana link. The major rail links that would be advantageous are Zimbabwe/Botswana-Namibia, to link with the Atlantic, and perhaps Angola-Namibia. Although presently canvassed, a link between Malawi and Tazara, the Tanzania-Zambia railway, appears at first sight less desirable than road connections. Regional air communications are almost equally patchy, especially in respect to air cargo. They are also hampered by inadequate airports in Botswana, Lesotho and Swaziland.

The first requirement is to identify the key missing links. Whether the actual construction of highways and railways (or the operation of the two rail links) needs to be joint is a different issue, and one to which the general answer is probably no. However, if the highway systems are to be used, long distance lorry operators will be needed. Co-ordinated national or multistate lorry fleets are likely to be the most satisfactory. While a regional airline is not likely to be practicable, co-ordination of schedules to maximize service and possibly some joint ventures between smaller states e.g. Namibia-Botswana, offer early possibilities for joint action. For railways many combinations are possible. For example, joint ownership of fixed assets and rolling stock, systemwide planning, through traffic procedures and rates could be combined with national operating and domestic traffic/rate planning companies. Problems of return of rolling stock, transfers of funds and maintenance are not solved by total joint ownership/operation and those of wage/salary structures and industrial relations may be exacerbated.

WATER AND POWER

Water, power and river basins are a triad of sectors of critical importance to several states in the region. No one project or river basin involves all or even a majority, but most states have concerns with one or more. Major areas of joint interest include: Namibia-Botswana-Zambia-Zimbabwe-Mozambique (Zambezi), Botswana-Zimbabwe (Shashi), Angola-Namibia-Botswana (Cuando-Makwegana, Okavango), Tanzania-Mozambique (Ruvuma), Angola-Namibia (Kunene).

The particular topics: water use agreements, power dams, reservoirs and pumping stations, bridges, basin development, vary from case to case. Few, if any, of the potential schemes are well enough studied to allow instant action beyond an agreement to undertake joint development beginning with joint studies. However, this sector could well involve a larger capital outlay and have a greater impact on rural incomes over the next two decades than any other.

EMPLOYMENT

Employment is not in African experience a promising area of integration. However, in the southern African context it needs at least to be explored. At least five states, Lesotho, Botswana, Swaziland, Mozambique and Malawi, receive a substantial proportion of their foreign exchange earnings as remittances from citizens working in RSA. In the case of Lesotho the number of wage employees in RSA is much larger than those working for wages at home. Phasing down this element of dependence is of considerable concern to each state. Second there are substantial numbers of workers from some southern African states working in others, e.g. Malawians and Zimbabweans in Zambia and Malawians and Zambians in Zimbabwe. Whatever the long run attitude towards employment of non-citizens, co-ordination and, if more nationalist employment policies are adopted, phasing down of non-citizen regional employment appear to be in the mutual interest of the individuals and states concerned.

In practice, employment gains, including shifts away from migrant work in RSA, are likely to be indirect:

A. Certain joint development projects such as transport, water and river basin development, will lead to significant gains in employment in each participating state;

25

B. If economic integration results in expanded production, then this will increase employment, easing reabsorption of those now working in RSA and reducing pressures to repatriate residents who are citizens of other southern African states;

C. Coordinated southern African approaches to external sources could increase funding of immediate (construction, reforestation, erosion control) and longer term (enhanced agricultural production) employment and output generation schemes. These should be designed with special reference to the problems of persons, communities and states now dependent on employment in RSA and to those of refugees, especially from Namibia, Zimbabwe and Angola, requiring transitional support for reintegration in their home countries.

FISHING

Fishing requires joint action to create uniform economic zones, uniform regulation of foreign fleets and the establishment of a valid convention or conventions covering the Indian and Atlantic ocean waters surrounding Africa from the equator south. The present regulations and conventions are anachronistic creations of Portugal and RSA. They are of dubious validity and negligible effect in protecting resources. Joint action to supersede them would involve accession to the relevant FAO South Atlantic and Indian Ocean Fisheries Conventions and the working out of adequate quota rules to safeguard stocks and revenues, plus means to enforce them. All of this appears to be both urgent and practicable now that Namibia is a full member of FAO. Further co-operation (especially if landlocked states wish to participate) in joint research institutions, quota allocation, crew training, distribution systems and perhaps catching and processing firms are potentially significant and merit case by case study.

PROMOTION OF TRADE

Trade initially is likely to be most usefully promoted in terms of gap filling. Most of the southern African states, especially Angola, Mozambique, Zimbabwe (because of colonists' exodus) and Zambia (because of depression flowing from copper prices) have some severely under-utilized industrial capacity. Some of these states have actual or potential surpluses of certain key agricultural commodities—notably maize, sugar and dairy products. Others have deficits in the same lines of production usually currently met by extraregional sources including RSA.

Experience in the promotion of trade between neighbouring African states, as for example between Tanzania and Mozambique, suggests that a useful and not insignificant volume of trade can be built up on this basis. It also suggests several other points:

A. An ongoing commercial/economic search and monitoring operation

26

is needed to identify opportunities for trade: a function which could usefully be done regionally as there is no reason all exchanges should be bilateral;

B. The lack of adequate commercial infrastructure (including extra-regional bias by state commercial bodies) and transport pose serious problems which need to be tackled in parallel with, and co-ordinated to, trade development;

C. Tariffs are the least serious barriers and can where necessary be dealt with by exemption orders. An effort at this stage to achieve a common tariff system and a reduction of tariffs on intraregional trade appears to be a misdirection of effort;

D. Longer term and broader trade development requires the co-ordination of production development to achieve a planned expansion of trade.

The work done in regard to the eastern and southern African preferential trade area which was catalyzed by ECA is useful in this context. While preferences by themselves will do little, the negotiations and draft agreement do focus attention on other obstacles to trade. By creating a concern with intra-African trade and with reduction of tariff, transport, information, procedural, clearing and other obstacles to trade development, they can create a setting in which positive trade and production oriented initiatives are more likely to succeed. It is also the case that the broad eastern and southern African framework is appropriate to such facilitating measures as the reduction of tariffs and the creation of preferences.

REGIONAL PRODUCTION CO-ORDINATION

Production co-ordination can be carried out bilaterally in the short term but evidently has greater scope regionally. There are several reasons for this. First a regional export orientation is less risky than one directed to a single market. Second for some products a single plant could well serve more than two markets. Third the range of co-ordinated production and trade is greater within the region than among any two countries.

The form of co-ordination requires both analysis and negotiation. Proposals which either threaten large existing sub-sectors or reinforce present imbalances are unlikely to be practicable. There will need to be early umbrella secretariat attention to preparatory studies leading to the ministerial negotiation of guidelines for the process of identifying products, projects and locations, of negotiating locations and joint venture or contractual relations and of moving into production requires several years, and the initial trade dynamic from gap filling is likely to prove a finite and wasting asset.

27

How to initiate studies is both simple and complex. Any competent technocrat and any production oriented political leader can rapidly run up a working list. However, experience suggests that some pre-study dialogue is needed to identify:

a) areas in which there is a real multistate interest in acting jointly if the studies warrant it, not just one technocrat's intellectual drive or one state's desire for a production unit;

b) a package of production lines which allows something for each participant without exorbitant costs of fifth best locations. This may mean several lines of production (e.g. cement in Mozambique, fertilizer in Tanzania and Swaziland, rayon in Zambia, fabricated construction steel in Zimbabwe) and/or distribution of different stages of production (e.g. fertilizer in Zambia and Swaziland, ammonia and plastic raw material in Tanzania, plastic final products in Zimbabwe and Mozambique);

c) a broad framework for agreeing on production location, trade arrangements, ownership patterns, financing, fiscal and price arrangements once data exists to identify the actual industries.

The framework should if possible be regional, even if the co-ordinated production/trade arrangements vary in participants and in specific terms. The case is strong for a committee of ministers backed by a subcommittee of officials with support from a regional secretariat and from development bank personnel.

Emphasis on regional arrangements does not necessarily exclude parallel agreements crossing regional lines. For example the potential Swaziland (iron ore, coal)/Kenya (limestone/iron and steel production) arrangements need not be seen as incompatible with regional production and trade co-ordination in iron and steel at the metal production and fabrication stages. Nor should manufacturing exclude considerations of agricultural production and trade co-ordination.

MONETARY AND FINANCIAL INTEGRATION

The responsibilities of monetary and financial integration probably cluster on two poles: trade and transport payments need to be facilitated and development finance needs to be mobilized with special attention to matching it with desired integration projects. The first, at least initially, requires not a formal clearing union but a frame agreement on regulations and procedures by participating state central and public sector commercial banks. The provision of credit beyond a two to four week clearing period is unlikely to be necessary for trade and transport promotion and will lead to major obstacles to agreement. A small co-ordinating unit to act as a clearinghouse for multistate settlements probably initially located at one of

28

the larger and more experienced central banks (say in Zambia or Tanzania), might be useful.

While joint export finance and export insurance with regional or broader coverage would be technically desirable and feasible, co-ordinated national action to encourage domestic bank credit and insurance company risk cover appears likely to be more practicable in the short term. However, a regional reinsurance corporation could both reduce extraregional outflows of premiums and operate profitably because much of the region's business, especially fire, is of above average quality.

Initially a joint meeting of regional treasury, trade ministry, central bank, commercial bank and insurance company representatives would appear useful. It could work out common national and financial institution approaches to:

a) commercial credit for regional exports;

b) exchange control authorization for—and actual remittance of payment for—regional imports;

c) normal (loss or damage in transit) insurance on regional trade and on interstate transport vehicles;

d) bilateral or multilateral reinsurance agreements among national companies;

e) central bank procedures for approving and facilitating clearing of transactions denominated in regional currencies;

f) the possibilities for building up medium term i.e. one to five year export credit facilities and/or credit/remittance risk insurance cover.

However, these arrangements would not, in fact, be so simple or so purely technical as they appear. They require parallel political decisions actually enforced on and implemented by central banks:

a) to move away from financing deficits by delaying payment on normal commercial transactions: 12 to 30 month delays weigh especially heavily on regional producers, export houses and banks;

b) in the interim, to give clear indications as to the delay to be expected in receipt of payments and to accept invoices providing for interest charges on delayed payments;

c) to give at least 'most favoured nation' treatment to regional payments. At present, because regional creditors are less able to exert international leverage, they believe, with justification in some cases, that they are put at the end of the queue;

d) to devise a preferential system so that remittance for new regional visible and service imports are made within 180 days, whatever the general lag on backlog and extraregional transactions;

e) to create a legal and payments context in which regional insurance and reinsurance transactions are not rendered unsound by risks or unpredictable delays in approval of transactions and of payments.

These are not minor points. If they cannot be achieved, regional trade cannot flourish nor can an amicable climate of dialogue toward developing it be achieved. However it is also true that the remittance lags and uncertainties arise from severe foreign exchange scarcities, not from procedural bottlenecks, much less from illwill. Frank discussion is needed on what is possible now and how soon improvements can be achieved. Mozambique/Tanzania experience suggests that, in the context of planned trade, intraregional payments problems can be overcome even by states with very major foreign exchange problems.

Since one purpose of economic regionalism is to reduce extraregional dependence and therefore foreign exchange constraints, it is ironic that external foreign exchange crises should be allowed to choke the development of intraregional trade. However, in the absence of an agreed trade framework and probably of target levels of imports and exports linked to preferential remittance provisions, such choking is only too likely, and too easy to understand, as both EAC and Zambia-Tanzania experience illustrate.

Development finance could make a head start through an enlargement of the membership of the existing East African Development Bank. Since no regional state will be eager to participate in a bank from which it does not receive at least as much in loans as it pays in as capital, and will for many purposes see a national investment bank as more suitable than a regional, a successful regional development will need to meet most of the following tests:

A. It must have the ability to raise foreign finance on easy terms and to extend it rapidly (e.g. to serve as a channel for external assistance to southern African transition programmes);

B. It must have a capacity to act as a merchant bank in identifying projects, sources of finance (including packages melding diverse sources), ownership structures and markets and helping bring these strands together as a partner in company promotion;

C. It must be able to assemble analytical expertise to provide regional studies on sectoral and project level, keyed to identifying projects (especially in directly productive sectors) which could be undertaken by two or more states or by enterprises formed or approved by them with profit to the region and to each state;

D. It must emphasize financial mobilization for multistate projects and/ or interstate joint ventures in addition to merely helping to promote them.

30

Personpower and Knowledge (education and research) development are areas in which a number of co-ordinated programmes, inter-institutional contractual arrangements and specialized joint institutions and programmes can be useful, but in which grand designs and assumptions as to the permanence of arrangements can be damaging.

In education the most generally practicable approach may be a series of contractual relations allowing national institutions to specialize, and states to be confident of places in those specialities not covered at home, without the problems posed by full scale joint institutions. The latter may be useful in some fields in which common concern is high and the practicability of effective national programmes low, e.g. a rechristened East African Institute of Management, an anti-desertification research and training unit.

Research probably requires systematic exchange of information and co-ordination of programmes on a broad front together with a more limited number of joint institutions. In the case of the latter, more attention is needed to relate their work to action, especially in states beyond their immediate host and in some cases to joint research/action bodies. The control of insect or bird pests characterized by interstate migration could be strengthened by regional or subregional bodies responsible for research, control and co-ordination of national action (a model in some respects followed by the Nairobi-based Locust Control Organization).

The umbrella secretariat could also play a useful role in co-ordination and information exchange. This would probably need to go beyond being a postbox and forwarding address in order to generate a systematic search for information backed by a programme of meetings and exchange visits among national institutions and officials of relevant national bodies responsible for personpower and knowledge development and for employing personnel and making use of research findings.

FUEL AND POWER

Fuel and Power is an area covering both research and, potentially, trade. Taking the region as a whole, there have been surpluses in hydroelectric power, petroleum and coal and a potential surplus in natural gas—whether as fuel or as chemical feedstock. However, individual states are importers of electricity, of petroleum and refined products and of coal from extra-regional sources, and the development of natural gas is hampered by the absence of an assured regional market for its (fertilizer, plastic, explosive) base and other chemical products. Further, the region faces two interlocked common problems. The first is the increasingly destructive pattern of meeting household fuel needs from charcoal. The second is the need for locally relevant research on alternative small scale power sources. These local sources are many. The feasibilities include quick growing trees for charcoal, solar energy, methane from animal or human waste (itself linked

31

to waste disposal and natural fertilizer production) and windpower—
windmills are common in RSA and the assertion that wind changes at the
Lesotho, Botswana, Swaziland and Namibia borders renders their use
elsewhere impracticable is, on the face of it, implausible. Small scale hydroelectric units, for example at village level, linked to small scale irrigation are
another possibility and so is geothermal power in areas of natural hot-
springs or subsurface hot water/steam concentrations such as occurs in
parts of the Rift Valley.

The three regional lines of action which seem practicable now are:

1. a study of regional and national fuel/power requirements and
production by source with a ten year historical record and a rough 10 to
20 year projection;

2. a study of alternative power sources, existing research, ongoing
national research, potential national uses;

3. specific studies of ways to assist reduction of the dependence of
Botswana, Lesotho and Swaziland for petroleum products and electric
power on the Republic of South Africa. The Ndola and Maputo
refineries and Cabora Bassa dam would appear relevant to such studies
with commercial and transport questions dominant (not physical
possibility constraints) at least in the Botswana and Swaziland cases.
General issues of RSA dependence reduction, the uncertain outlook for
RSA oil procurement and cost and the eventual real possibility of oil
sanctions against RSA all point to the clear desirability and potential
urgency of collaborative pre-planning in this field.

What further joint or co-ordinated action would be appropriate should
be clearer after the results of the first two studies. Electricity sales within the
region may prove desirable and practicable albeit almost all the states have
the potential for their own hydro or thermal plants. If Angola locates oil
near Luanda, a pipeline from the Atlantic to Ndola might be viable. Joint
planning and some joint ownership of refineries, plus a co-ordinated plan
for by-product (chemical feedstocks, petrochemical, creosote, asphalt)
production specialized by refinery, should increase regional production and
reduce regional imports with related cost reductions to participating states.

In the case of research, co-ordination of national programmes to provide
maximum exchange of information would seem clearly desirable. In some
cases e.g. solar energy, waste to methane/fertilizer units, in which research
and pilot project costs are likely to be high in personnel as well as money
and for which results are likely to be fairly widely applicable, some regional
or subregional research and pilot projects centres might be appropriate. The
research should be linked to pilot project work designed to identify and to
devise means to overcome implementation problems. For example the waste
to gas/fertilizer technology is simple to engineers but not to villagers who
would need to build and maintain units. Further, waste collection, gas use

(whether bottled for cooking or used to power an electric generator), fertilizer distribution, and sanitary issues pose very real problems which need to be studied from a village, not a laboratory or research institute, point of view. Finally the institutional form of such units requires consideration from a social as well as a technical perspective. If private and appended to large farms or ranches, small gas/fertilizer units could contribute to further institutionalization of the already very high degree of inequality characterizing many of the cattle raising communities of the region.

EXTERNAL REGIONAL INITIATIVES

External action is potentially another major area for co-ordination. Some aspects are of general interest to all states in the region while others will be of real concern only to one or two and need the involvement of states from outside the regions. The first is perhaps best illustrated by external regional programmes. Several external agencies are engaged in regional perspective planning intended to result in co-ordinated initiatives by them toward southern Africa. If the southern African states are to control and make use of such external regional initiatives, they must act together. Otherwise the external regional plans will at least in part be implemented without serious African consideration of their regional—as opposed to national—impact. Indeed in some cases, notably the USAID exercises, national consultation has been so sketchy and uneven as to create the appearance of a plan for the region that has been almost entirely externally designed. This is not a matter of evil intentions. It is for example perfectly reasonable and proper for DGVIII (the Development Division of EEC) to seek to plan a co-ordinated regional co-operation programme for southern Africa. However, such programmes can only meet African perceptions of regional needs and priorities if there is a clear regional perspective and bargaining stance on the African as well as on the external side.

The need for co-ordination in matters that are of concern to only one or two states but involve states outside the region as well, is exemplified by diamonds. Botswana, Angola, Namibia, Tanzania and Lesotho are the producers of a substantial proportion of the world's diamonds and especially of its gem diamonds. Because the industry is dominated by a knowledge, production, selling cartel centred on De Beers, they face a number of common problems as to taxes, ownership, personnel development, output quotas, price determination and marketing. While not essential to joint action in this or similar fields, the umbrella organization might be of value in facilitating joint consultations and in providing supporting services. This would remain true if the regional members decided to invite, say Zaire (the world's largest industrial diamond producer) Sierra Leone and Ghana into their working group, in order to add to their knowledge and bargaining weight.

Policies vis-à-vis taxation, incentives to foreign investors, relations with TNCs, technology transfer and related fields offer opportunities for integration ranging from quasi-formal discussions and agreements to much more detailed and definite regional codes—like those of the Andean Pact in respect of technology and foreign investment. Such operational co-ordination at regional level would be complementary to the programme of issue identification, negotiation strengthening and harmonization of national action being launched by the Economic Commission for Africa/United Nations Transnational Centre joint unit.

EXTERNAL FINANCE CO-ORDINATION

Aid/external finance is an area in which co-ordination is especially urgent. As noted earlier, external agencies are already developing southern African regional strategies. If these are met by, placed in a dialogue with, become complementary to, a southern African regional strategy on aid/external finance by and for southern Africans, the results can be positive. If not, they could possibly serve to increase the external dependence and internal fragmentation of the region and of the states which comprise it.

Advocating that all aid/external finance be regionally negotiated and allocated is neither acceptable to southern African states, plausible from the point of view of donors/lenders, nor technically practicable. Equally, however, a situation in which three external agencies are carrying out studies on a project and dangling hints of implementation finance to two states and to a regional group of three states (including those two) may be practicable—indeed has happened—but is deeply corrosive of both regionalism and national decision taking. It leads to a grab-now-on-whatever-terms-before-somebody-else-grabs attitude. That syndrome is useful to project salesmen and perhaps to the prestige of the external agency, but it is inimical to self-reliance, to proper negotiation, to meaningful national planning and to the reduction of external dependence through regional co-ordination.

What is likely to be practicable regionally? The following five points are open for serious discussion:

1. A regional position could be prepared on desired types and patterns of external finance and its terms and channels both to strengthen national aid negotiating teams and to make it more likely that external finance, whether to individual states or via regional channels, will assist rather than erode regional selfreliance and solidarity;

2. Regional meetings could be held with those states and institutions (e.g. USAID, EEC UNDP/UN) which have their own southern African regional strategies including the use of aid/external finance;

3. Regional channels could be created including ultimately a development bank for external finance which is directed to projects of regional and multistate interest; the objective being to negotiate finance for these

34

projects jointly whenever practicable and to encourage the use of regional channels for its disbursement;

4. Regional institutions could be developed, with a capacity for identifying and assembling packages of external finance for national, multistate and regional projects;

5. Broad guidelines could be established for co-ordinated national policies on acceptable terms and conditions of foreign loans and for foreign investment. The aim would not be to impose a straightjacket on the states but to improve their bargaining position by exchanges regarding their negotiating experience and by avoiding mutually damaging competitive bidding for loans or investments.

The last two points go well beyond aid. This is only realistic. Aid is only one source of external finance and is frequently inextricably linked with bank borrowing, export credits, IMF drawings and private foreign investment. In the case of each of these sources, each state in the region would be in a stronger position if national experiences of negotiation and implementation (successes and failures) were pooled and joint guidelines adopted. Otherwise there will be cumulative pressure by donors, lenders and investors to impose 'least favoured nation' (from a southern African perspective) treatment by generalizing the worst terms and the widest concessions, a process materially damaging to each state and psychologically even more damaging because it places the individual states in a hostile relationship with each other in courting the favours of the outside source of finance or investment.

While major decisions to act on external finance/aid co-ordination need to be taken by ministerial meetings, these need to be backed up and serviced by exchange of information and official level meetings. Negotiating experience and achieved terms/conditions could readily be exchanged via the regional secretariat, perhaps supplemented by occasional seminars of negotiators and/or intraregional technical assistance in respect of specialized negotiating personnel. The working of the guidelines, the possibilities of their further development or the need for their alteration, and the general lines and impact on the region and its member states of external aid/finance programmes, procedures, terms could be reviewed by semi-annual meetings of senior officials.

The sketch of areas is not, nor is it intended to be, exhaustive. Its purpose is to indicate some probable priority, high mutual benefit areas and to give examples of other areas in which regional or subregional integration appears potentially desirable and practicable.

A CONCLUDING SUMMARY

Building regional co-ordination in southern Africa will not be easy. This does not relate to lack of potential gains nor to lack of political concern for increasing regional selfreliance. Region building, like nationbuilding, is a long, slow, tedious process. It requires overcoming compelling interests and balancing divergent ones. In situations of multiple domestic demands on resources, and on the ability which exists to resolve or transcend conflicts, there is always the temptation to solve short term national problems at the expense of longer term regional development and to postpone consideration of regional issues in order to concentrate on national ones. The southern African region historically has been integrated with RSA and two metropolitan powers while fragmented within itself. The heritage of this process is a set of physical and institutional structures which hamper attainment of regional co-ordination and a resulting lack of any extensive experience in co-operation or even an extensive range of contacts to provide a shared basis from which to begin to construct regional selfreliance.

The struggle for southern African liberation since the early 1960s has partially filled this last gap. Most of the experience in co-operation—whether economic or political, in transport or in diplomacy, arises out of that struggle. At the same time, it has increased the perception of southern African states that southern Africa is potentially an area for common action as well as being merely a geographical entity. Building on those common experiences and perceptions is possible—indeed they form a much better basis than any intellectualized theories of regionalism and they provide a more self-evident core of mutual interest than the ASEAN (Southeast Asian) or Andean Pact (northern South American) states had when they initiated their now important structures of regional integration. To argue that the present basis of regional solidarity is primarily against RSA and its South West African occupation regime is true. However, almost any solidarity is to a degree against a common enemy. For example the 13 North American colonies were notoriously separatist and squabbling until their determination to end British overlordship forced them to begin a process of acting in common. The common struggle in fact provides for southern Africa opportunities for integration which parallel the opportunities which these erstwhile colonies in North America faced in the 1780s.

APPROACHES

Diversity of interests is a fact. Only a clear recognition of that diversity and respect for it can provide a basis for a negotiated programme transcending it. For example to insist either that all regional states form a single joint airline or that there are no regional initiatives in aviation is a recipe for inaction. Co-ordination of international schedules, cross leasing of equipment, some joint international services, one or more two-country carriers, a joint training facility, might transcend differences by recognizing them and going beyond them to perceive common concerns. Equally a free trade area would, even if negotiated, either become riddled with safeguards and exceptions or collapse in rising intraregional deficits, blocked balances

36

and acrimony. Even the apparent short term export gainers, notably Zimbabwe, have no real interest in such a result. A planned expansion of trade linked to filling gaps, reducing dependence on RSA and identifying production for national use or regional export possibilities in each state, may seem slower, more complex to negotiate and administer and further from general removal of intraregional trade barriers. But that approach can be perceived as mutually beneficial and can build up the export stake of each state in regional trade, thereby easing the route to subsequent trade broadening and reduction of barriers.

The systematic building upon perceived common interests is the only practicable way of extending the scope and depth of regional co-ordination and joint action. The perception is as critical as the underlying reality: unperceived gains do not offset perceived losses. Building from perceived interests is unlikely to be neat and tidy and certainly unlikely to follow the history of any other regional integration process. Still less will it follow any schedule posited by texts on customs unions or economic regionalism. Whatever the defects of these divergencies, they are outweighed by the absolute necessity of producing desired results reasonably promptly, especially at the beginning of the process when willingness to wait for gains is likely to be low. For example, the present Tanzanian/Mozambique trade patterns do not turn on any normal definition of comparative advantage nor on co-ordinated production/trade plans. They arise because Mozambique has temporary production surpluses resulting from an inherited industrial sector tied to the colonial demand pattern and temporary deficits in certain consumer goods and food resulting from similar historic and transitional factors. These complement certain Tanzanian gaps, e.g. in cement, related to delayed implementation of production plans and to specific exportable surpluses. Thus a perceived common interest in trade now, on a planned basis and in specific goods exists. The implementation of that common interest can lead to a perception of mutual interest in broader and longer term trade development including co-ordination of production of certain goods to allow for exports to and to take account of imports from the partner state. A free trade area would have failed to achieve the desired short term results and so would have eroded, not built up, perceived common interests.

Closely linked to the preceding point is the need to start with mutually perceived needs and possibilities. If, for example, the new Botswana vaccine plant produces more effective hoof and mouth vaccine than is available from the UK or RSA and Swaziland needs or wishes a new vaccine source, then hoof and mouth vaccine is the place to begin developing Botswana/Swaziland trade and co-ordinated production. If the insecurity of RSA sources causes Swaziland to seek a regional source for petroleum products and if at the same time RSA state or fertilizer cartel action cripples its fertilizer industry, then petroleum products from the Maputo refinery and fertilizer from the Matsapha plant are central to implementing the

37

Swaziland–Mozambique trade agreement. In practice many of the perceived mutual needs relate to transport and communication. These vary from upgrading or filling gaps in road links through harbour development in, say, Beira to serve interior state needs, to scheduling Botswana, Lesotho and Swaziland air lines to broaden links with states other than RSA. The fact that initially these links may not carry much regional traffic is secondary: the interior states must have effective import/export access to the outside world; as these links remove a barrier to regional trade, successful co-operation in regard to them would tend to broaden to cover new areas. However, transport does pose a problem. During construction, the capital cost to the coastal state is high both absolutely and in terms of national projects foregone: for example Tanzania committed some Shs. 3,000 million or 25 per cent of its total fixed investment to transportation over the period 1967–75. During operation, the cash flow from the interior to the coastal state for port, rail, road, clearing and forwarding and related services, probably of the order of K 100 million a year for Zambia, appears high to the interior state especially if it is facing severe foreign exchange difficulties. In principle the two factors may seem to cancel out, in practice they are rarely perceived in that way and more care in identifying and agreeing to the division of costs from the start would be prudent.

A final key factor in approaching regional co-ordination is retaining flexibility. Nothing is ever permanent; phasing out an arrangement which has served its purpose or modifying one whose specific provisions are out of date is a sign of ability to make progress, not evidence of failure. For example planned trade agreements need annual revisions of goods covered, quantities and prices if they are to remain viable. Now that Zimbabwe is liberated, regional transport planning and implementation will include phasing down of some existing routes as well as establishment of new ones. Many joint educational or research programmes have a limited life expectancy. Flexibility does not imply absence of institutions: it creates a need for bodies able to build, modify and phase out arrangements. What it does imply is the need to avoid massive, interlocked institutional structures in which the institutional frame, not the content of the programme, becomes the justification of continued co-operation and through which problems of co-operation in one field are magnified into a general crisis of regionalism.

INSTITUTIONS, INITIAL ACTION AREAS

Institutions should be designed first in terms of what they are supposed to do, second in their requirements for staff and finance and the availability of this staff and finance and only third in terms of internal institution considerations—the exact opposite of the normal administrative reform approach. In the context of southern African regionalism, the first institutional requirement is national rather than regional. Each state needs to have a senior official in each relevant ministry or parastatal, one of whose major responsibilities is to keep in touch with regional affairs and to consider regional aspects and possibilities of the work of his institution. Unless this is done there will be no ongoing perception of regional dimensions and the possibilities for building regional co-ordination will go by default.

To achieve a coherent national set of data, technical papers and evaluation of proposals on regional issues requires that these officials maintain close contact. That normally requires a chairman solely responsible for national co-ordination of regional issues at official level based in an institution integrally involved in regional affairs (whether State House, Planning, Treasury, Foreign Affairs or Industry, Mines and Tourism will depend on the state).

For the official level staff work to be effective, it must be available to the relevant political decision takers. That normally will suggest a parallel ministerial and, in some states Party, committee.

Regionally there is a similar need to provide forums for official and ministerial meetings. A few should be general but most should be on specific co-operation topics and should have whatever membership, of states and of personnel as is relevant to the particular topic of the meeting.

Beyond that point it is difficult and unwise to generalize on regional and multinational institutions for southern Africa. A few guidelines are possible:

A. The surviving East African Institutions: Development Bank, Management Institute, Standing Committee on Shipping Line (the last two including Zambia), can potentially be enlarged in membership to serve the southern African region;

B. The eastern and southern African preferential trade area can be a useful facilitating measure;

C. Existing multistate (subregional) institutions can be reviewed to see what models and lessons they offer for similar or broader co-operation institutions;

D. Co-ordination may not require, or even be furthered by, the joint institution literally owning and operating the national units (e.g. in respect of airlines or linked manufacturing establishments);

E. In production and commerce, as in government, it is critical to create units or departments with a real interest in regionalism whether via joint ventures, multi-year contractual arrangements or trading companies specializing in regional imports and exports.

The appropriate institutions are likely to emerge once initial and subsequent areas of regional action are more clearly identified and their implementation has begun.

The evident themes around which initial co-ordinated action is likely to turn are: improved transport and communications, especially for the land-locked states; trade diversification especially in respect to non-traditional

39

e.g. manufactured exports; reduction of dependence on RSA and promotion of the economic front of southern African liberation; particular projects of special interest to adjacent states such as border river basin development. In most cases particular projects or programmes can be identified now. The next step is the preparation of pre-feasibility or feasibility studies—indeed, in some cases the basic data and analysis are already in hand or are being prepared.

However, in the case of production/trade regional selfreliance, a case for a more general study can be made. A series of bilateral production/trade agreements would be more limited and less valuable than a regionally co-ordinated approach. Precisely because the negotiation and implementation of such an approach would be lengthy, there is some urgency to start data collection and analysis now, in order to lay the foundation for beginning negotiation on co-ordinated national planning and implementation. The same argument applies to the largest and most complex multi country projects e.g. the Trans-Kalahari Railway with its implications not merely for Zambian, Zimbabwean, Botswanan and Namibian external trade routes but also for Botswanan coal, copper, salt pan and agricultural development and the possibility of Namibian processing and manufacturing oriented to regional markets.

To erect a detailed blueprint for institutions or even a detailed scenario for states of southern African regionalism today would be counter-productive. The growing perception of multinational and regional interests is not yet precise enough nor based on enough information for that. However, the number of areas in which co-ordination could be productive does indicate that southern Africa can be a region in political and economic fact as well as in geography. For the potential to be achieved requires an identification, at political level, of priorities for co-operation and co-ordination, a series of exercises at official/technical level to collect data and construct instrumentalities for achieving the priority targets, and the creation of a workable set of channels and institutions so that these instrumentalities can be used to achieve the targets that have been identified.

Economic Dependence and Regional Co-operation

INTRODUCTION

The African continent is one of the world's poorest areas. Nevertheless the potential of most African countries is substantial. In southern Africa a major blockage to the realization of this potential has been the political situation. Up to the early 1960s all the countries in the region except the Republic of South Africa (RSA) were colonies. One still is. Economic development in the area was designed primarily for the benefit of the European centres, both directly and through RSA. Substantial parts of this colonial type regional co-operation still exists, perhaps most clearly seen in communication and trade links. The southern African peoples' struggle for liberation from an externally imposed and adverse economic order is also complicated by the power and the racism of the regime in RSA.

The liberation of Zimbabwe and the impending liberation of Namibia will alter the situation in the region and mark a milestone in the historical process towards majority rule in Africa. Whatever the near future may bring of mounting conflict between the majority ruled states and RSA one can now see the contours of a fully post-colonial era in the region. The present Conference itself demonstrates that the governments of the area accept the responsibility to shape the future of southern Africa and that they are ready to take the first steps.

UNITY AND DIVERSITY

COMMON AIMS

The ten states do not come together simply because of idealistic principles or even as a reflection of strongly forged historical bonds between them. They do so in order to establish new relationships which cut across the old colonial ties and which they judge to be in their national interest, individually and collectively.

— They face a common long term need for a broadly based increase in the material living standards of their peoples.

41

— They also share a concern for the human dignity and rights of the people of the countries still under minority rule, and they feel a special responsibility to come to the aid of oppressed groups in their own region.

— Having learned the hard way that the industrialized world's solutions to social and economic problems rarely bring benefits to them, they are searching for their own solutions, each country looking to its own experiences and needs but increasingly in a regional context.

The decisive factors for the ultimate failure or success of any co-operation scheme in its first stages are the expectation, perception and experience of the balance between costs and benefits of individual, specific projects and programmes which are undertaken by the countries as part of such schemes. It is therefore important initially to focus on the individual nations; what are or will be their main economic problems and their aspirations in the medium and long term, what are their present problems, and how are these connected? Summary analyses, country by country, are given in Annexe I. Superficial as such summaries must be, they at least serve to stress that identity and unity of economic and social conditions and concerns are not the main characteristics.

The imprint of colonial ties pulls these countries in different directions: Portuguese, British and German influences have put their special marks on the region and have embedded themselves in different trade patterns and different languages. Some countries have been independent for almost two decades, others for a few years or months and one is still to achieve its freedom.

Forms of government include one colony, two monarchies, two multi-party republics and five one-party republics. Ideologically, the region is also diverse, giving rise to a variety of political connections, both on the African continent and beyond.

ECONOMIC STRUCTURES

Economically, the differences between the Ten are striking. In terms of area and therefore potential resources the largest country is Angola, which is 72 times as large as the smallest, Swaziland. As the number of inhabitants bears no clear relation to the size of the country (or for that matter to its natural resources), wide variations in population density result. Although five of the prospective partner states have a higher density of population than the African average, the average for the area as a whole is well below. This reflects the very low densities of Botswana (1.2 people per sq.km.), Namibia (1.5), Angola (4.4) and Zambia (6.6).

In terms of production, the region comprises Namibia with a GDP per head at the level of the Third World's 'middle class' countries, whereas in these terms Tanzania, Malawi, Lesotho and Mozambique are among the 'poorest of the poor'. However, African incomes vary much less. Indeed in purchasing power terms they have been as low, or lower, in Namibia and in pre-independence Zimbabwe as in Tanzania.

In terms of economic structure, most of the countries have a considerable agricultural bias, but the shares of the sector of industry and mining in Namibia, Zimbabwe, Zambia and to a lesser degree Swaziland, are similar to those of some European countries. [1]

The countries are different in their degree and type of dependence on RSA. For Botswana, Lesotho, Namibia and Swaziland, in the short term, this economic dependence manifests itself in overwhelming actual and potential economic and political leverage by RSA over them. In the longer term, the political dominance of RSA will no doubt change and become more manageable, but the problem of economic dependence for these countries, reflecting their localization on the periphery of RSA, is more intractable.

Somewhat more loosely connected to the centre of gravitation represented by RSA are Malawi, Mozambique, Zambia and Zimbabwe. Their economies are in some important respects linked to that centre but hardly to the extent of making them economic appendages as is now largely a characteristic, in varying degrees, of Botswana, Lesotho, Swaziland and Namibia. Geographically, Malawi, Mozambique, Zambia and Zimbabwe form a group situated between the centres of the East African region and of RSA. Somewhat peripherally in the region in this respect and therefore having the weakest dependence on RSA, are Angola and Tanzania.

The above descriptions represent at best a snapshot—a static picture—of the diversities in the region. Quite quickly, the picture can change; economies grow at uneven pace; mineral finds can lead to large and concentrated developments in particular economies; the opening of new railway lines and other means of communication could alter the geopolitical situation; the internal political scene and even the predominance of particular ideologies of individual states will evolve and change; and thus, along with all this there will be changes in context, direction and form of national economic and political interest and in the very basis for co-operation in southern Africa.

THE PROBLEMS TO BE FACED

The short to medium term scenario for the region is not pleasant, six of the countries (Angola, Mozambique, Namibia, Tanzania, Zambia, Zimbabwe), comprising roughly three quarters of the region's productive capacity, are currently in the throes of (or are likely in the near future to go through) severe economic disruptions and/or restructuring. Mozambique, Namibia and Zimbabwe all have, in addition, to contend with their considerable dependency on RSA. For three other countries, Botswana, Lesotho and Swaziland, their dependence on RSA is the major determinant of their economic future; Botswana and Lesotho have the additional handicap of being landlocked by countries with hostile regimes. One country, Malawi, has been dependent not only on RSA, but also on pre-independence Zimbabwe. One country only, Tanzania, is relatively immune from this RSA dependence.

Judging by conventional conceptions of what constitutes the essential ingredients of successful economic co-operation or integration, the odds do not appear favourable in southern Africa. The potential partner states are in fact very dissimilar in terms of size, in economic structure, potential and level of development, and in politics and even philosophies of economic and social systems. Economic and political cohesion internally within individual states, often regarded as a precondition to proceed to stronger interaction with potential co-operating countries, has not yet had the time to develop very far in many countries of the region. Furthermore, as a region the countries concerned, given the diversity of their colonial backgrounds, even lack common experience in the colonial type of co-operation.

The problem of giving form and content to co-operation therefore has to be approached in an unconventional manner: the nature and extent of diversity must be clearly and explicitly recognized and accepted, in order that this very diversity may provide a basis for constructive action, thus turning apparent weakness into real strength. This need not be wishful thinking. It is easy to realize how economic diversity can serve, indeed be necessary, for such a relationship, but it has to be brought to bear with circumspection, lest it be spoiled by narrow considerations of immediate self-interest.

Ideological and political diversity certainly complicates any effort at closer co-operation. Yet it is not entirely a disadvantage. As individual countries struggle to develop their respective new domestic economic orders, they will each search for the most helpful external contacts and relationships. As a result, for the region as a whole, economic and political external relations to different countries of the developed world, to the First and Second Worlds and to different trading areas, will become more diversified and balanced than would be true if the member countries were ideologically similar.

It seems clear that a form of relationship which is to build on the self-interest of partners and yet permit diversity to play a positive role, has to have as a principle a high degree of independence for the individual nation states. Especially at the start of concrete co-operation it would be important to give the relationship a loosely knit form.

The benefits and costs from each part of any co-operative activity would have to be fairly and evenly distributed between the participating members. From the outset, it should not be regarded as a definitive failure if one or more partners were to find that for some activities costs outweigh benefits, and therefore withdrew from certain aspects of co-operation in the region. In the longer term, as the scope of interaction broadens, partner states would gradually come to see the whole set of projects and programmes of

44

co-operation as a totality, and become conscious and confident of the advantages of accepting some costs to their respective countries from co-operative action in one specific area as a worthwhile price to pay for gains derived—immediately or in the next round—from other elements of regional co-operation.

A FRAMEWORK FOR THE FUTURE OF THE REGION

THE ECONOMIC GROWTH RATE

As a guide to what will actually happen in the future, studies and forecasts of the long term future seem to be of limited value. Current conventional wisdom visualizes that in industrial societies economic restructuring and pollution problems will increasingly come to the fore in the coming decades; that world economic growth will perhaps level out; that Third World producers will capture an increasing share of the production of manufactured products; and that global resource problems will gradually become more pronounced and by the early decades of the 21st century will become very serious, with the relative prices of natural resources as a result improving to the advantage of the commodity exploiting nations.

For Africa in general, future expectations are, very broadly, that in spite of relatively abundant and largely untapped resources (in agriculture, as well as in energy and minerals), economic growth will be slow and that poverty and underdevelopment will remain a predominant scourge of the continent—some exceptions notwithstanding. The basic reasons for such a dismal view include the legacy of the colonial drag and the likely persistence of rapid population increase. However, one further important reason is the economic and political fragmentation of the area. Raw materials production, it is commonly asserted, will remain dominant while in-dustrialization will develop only slowly within small domestic markets. The major economic attraction for external capital and entrepreneurship will remain the continent's natural resources. Considering the major division of the southern part of the continent, where RSA is one political and economic entity, it is clear that the major weight of the industrial world's economic interest is still centred on RSA. RSA's exports to the rest of the world are over twice that of the Ten; RSA's imports from the rest of the world are almost three times that of the Ten. Abundant natural resources, ample infrastructure, well-functioning transport and an advanced industrial tradi-tion, combine to make RSA an attractive economic partner, with all the power and influence this implies.

It may be more in doubt, however, whether for major industrial powers of the West this relationship should be—or need remain—economically, politically and militarily strategic to the point of compulsiveness. Although RSA appears to have more than four fifths of the world's reserves of chrome and of the platinum metal groups, about two thirds of the

45

vanadium and half of the world's gold, manganese and fluorspar as well as sizeable deposits of other minerals, alternative sources and substitutes for all these minerals are in fact available. Even a sudden cut-off in the supply to industrial countries of minerals from RSA could be overcome in a relatively short period of perhaps up to three years. However, the experience of the oil crisis and the inability of the world economy to absorb the shock it imposed, deter the industrialized West from accepting a cut-off or a significant reduction in its dependence on supplies from RSA, unless they are compelled to do so by unexpectedly strong sanctions from the Third World, coupled with assurances of increased and sustained supplies from alternative sources.

It is not impossible—given determined and persistent action it is not even improbable—that the countries of southern Africa beyond RSA, could in the long run come to wield an influence commensurate with that of RSA in the world economy. Combined, they are an important economic partner of the industrialized world and potentially they could be a formidable force. With respect to mineral wealth, the vast area, almost five times the size of RSA and largely unexplored, is replete with promising prospects. In spite of the lack of exploration, this sparsely populated region[2] already has a wide variety of economically exploitable minerals, apparently including about one tenth of the world's uranium reserves. The region also produces 28 per cent of the world's gem diamonds, 7.4 per cent of industrial diamonds, as well as sizeable quantities of the world's bauxite, chrome, copper ore, gold, lead, nickel, zinc and asbestos. In addition, the energy potential of this region is much larger than that of RSA. It is clearly not the resource base or economic potential which limits the role which this region plays in the world economy and which determines its bargaining power, politically and economically, with RSA and the rest of the world; it is rather the still nascent state of economic development and political mobilization within individual countries and its comparative fragmentation still as an economic region.

THE REALITIES OF DISPARITY BETWEEN THE TEN AND RSA

The existing dependence of the region on RSA is an economic and political reality of dominating importance. What does the future hold in terms of the balance between the region and RSA?

A merely illustrative but instructive calculation is the following: at present the ten countries, compared to RSA, cover about five times the area, have about twice as many people, but less than half the total GDP (i.e. one quarter of the GDP per head). If serious political controversies and military confrontations between the Ten are avoided, while constructive economic co-operation is built over a decade or more, their economies would most certainly grow much faster than that of RSA, which would be constrained not only by slow long term growth in the West, but also

46

possibly by lack of oil, and potentially even more importantly, by internal unrest. Nevertheless if one assumes, for example, a growth rate of 3 per cent per year for RSA over the coming two decades and twice that rate for the Ten, the GDP of RSA would still be higher at the end of this century than that of the region of the Ten; in these terms RSA would still be the most economically important of the two blocks.

Another indication of the comparative power of RSA is the fact that RSA today means much more economically to the Ten than the Ten do to RSA.[3] This disparity may persist for a long time, even though, as discussed below, it must be a major objective of co-operation among the Ten gradually to reduce this imbalance. Nevertheless, these and other considerations suggest the need for caution and for modest expectations and aspirations by the Ten in their dealings with both RSA and the rest of the world. Specifically it seems reasonable to base policies of the Ten over the next five years or more on these presumptions:

a) that the industrialized world will uphold and even further develop its economic dealings with RSA,

b) that there is no basis today for the Ten to apply economic pressure against RSA successfully and

c) that RSA (more precisely the area of Transvaal), may remain for quite some time the economic centre of gravity in the southern part of the continent.

The last point is very important. It underlines the need to aim simultaneously at the establishment of a measure of balance between RSA and the southern African region as a whole. It equally demonstrates the need to seek to ensure that an eventually liberated RSA does not become the overwhelming dominating metropolitan area towards which economic activity in southern Africa gravitates. Only through determined planning and early action can the group of Ten avoid becoming the victims of economic polarization and peripheral backwardness. A liberated RSA might well, in a spirit of co-operation, accept such a philosophy of balanced regional development, but the economic centre-periphery problems would still be facts of life and would have to be tackled whatever the changing regimes and political dispensations in the area. However, in the interval—be it short or long—until the people of RSA can also achieve majority rule, the political necessity to seek a reduction in the dependence of the region of the Ten on RSA can be used to give impetus to create the foundation for a more even development in the future, more self-reliance and better economic balance in the area as a whole. There is, in other words, a certain degree of complementarity between the aim of reducing excessive economic dependence on RSA over the next few years and of creating the basis for balanced regional development in the longer term.

Economic policy and co-operation, seen as part of the ten countries' struggle against apartheid, can thus be so designed as to contribute towards the long term objectives of equal and balanced development. In its turn, however, such a policy of co-operation derives its meaning and importance mainly from the contribution it makes towards the ultimate objective of increasing material living standards for the broad population groups, and liberating their individual and collective qualities and capacities. From this very general aim, common to all countries of the region, follow the more tangible and specific actions and strategies for co-operation, such as the need for emphasis on manufacturing industries and on a growing and wider exchange of industrial products within the region. The alternative strategies of continued concentration on raw material exports, on import substitution and on self-sufficiency for each economy, are seen by all of the ten countries as having built-in limitations and self-defeating consequences.

Given the strong and varied natural resource base for industrialization, what are the bottlenecks? As should be clear from the brief country analyses in Annexe I, the most pressing common problems today are the scarcity of skilled and educated manpower, and the unavailability of appropriate technology; in other words the absence of such physical, organizational and human resources as spring from industrial development, experience and tradition. Industrial development and experience are best promoted where industry already exists; the idea that the manpower and technology base for industrialization can be planned bureaucratically or forced into existence by administrative or political fiat has been disproved often and decisively.

Because the easiest way to industrialization is to build on to existing industry, the question of intraregional balance becomes critical. While a free market system combined with high factor mobility can have impressive growth consequences, it often leads to polarization and regional imbalances. At some point and in some circumstances there would probably be increasing pressures to give greater weight to the inter and intracountry distribution of economic activity within the region as against the concern for rapid growth in the region as a whole.

AN IMPRESSIVE DEVELOPMENT POTENTIAL

For a strategy of industrial development which does not depend so heavily on RSA to be realistic, the need is to promote new and expand existing centres within the region, aimed at gradually substituting local output of certain goods and services for RSA imports—initially those from RSA and thereafter from outside i.e. mainly Europe and America. A strategy framework for discussion within the region on the distribution of economic activities and functions needs to be hammered out.

Within the vast geographical area of the region there are at present a few small and scattered centres of substantial economic activity. However, the contours of a relatively densely populated and industrialized area, with the potential to emulate the economy of Transvaal in RSA, can be delineated by the Bulawayo–Salisbury area in Zimbabwe, the surrounding copper-belt of Zambia (stretching into Zaire), the relatively advanced parts of southern Malawi, the areas around the harbours of Beira and Maputo in Mozambique, the economy of Swaziland, as well as the Francistown area of Botswana. Add to this the mineral and other resource potential of Botswana, Angola and Namibia and we have a very impressive development potential. The realization of this potential would help enormously to lessen the present overwhelming dependence on RSA. The further development of this potential would serve as an important element in creating the basis for a viable economic balance in southern Africa in the long run.

The interaction, indeed, dependence between this area and other main areas would be apparent. First, the Dar es Salaam–Moshi–Tanga and Dar–Mwanza–Mbeya triangles (which in turn provide a link to the rest of the former EAC area) would be of immediate and strategic importance, both as a market outlet and transit port for the products of the area and as a source and channel of supply. Second, the Walvis Bay–Gobabis–Francistown axis could be an important alternative line of supply and, even more importantly, eventually a more logical route for Botswana's exports and for opening up its north–central agricultural/mineral and eastern coal potential. Third, both immediately and in the longer term, coastal Angola could become an important and even indispensable source of oil and certain industrial goods for the development of the whole new region.

It must be readily admitted that this overall sketch of a possible regional framework needs to be subjected to more detailed sectoral considerations and further study. Given that modifications will be needed, a framework of future regional development as we have here suggested could provide a much needed sense of direction for co-operation in the region, in a manner that may give the countries concerned a shared vision of a common future in which each individual country can see tangible benefits to its own people. Such a strategy based on a common vision would be decisive for the co-ordinated development of the whole area.

WHERE TO START? SOME CONCRETE PROBLEMS OF THE NEAR FUTURE

As argued above, it is important and realistic to spread economic activity in the region away from RSA gradually but decisively. Under the present circumstances, such a strategy might in its early phases concentrate on establishing better trading links both internally in the region and externally by developing direct links with foreign supply areas, thus reducing transit through RSA and bypassing RSA as an intermediary.

Most of the facets of co-operation, be they concerned with multi-nationals, markets, communication, oil, finance, construction or imports of capital goods, may well be considered by RSA as being adverse to its

49

interests. When co-operation in the region goes beyond reviews and studies into specific and active common policies of gradual disengagement from RSA, it is more than likely that RSA will feel compelled to take retaliatory action. At the political level, the Ten will no doubt take an increasingly strong stance against apartheid and colonialism; they will also use a strengthened position of regional co-operation and co-ordination to encourage the world powers to take a stronger stand against the present regime in RSA. Action oriented co-operation in some other fields, like the issue of migrant labour, may have to proceed carefully. Military confrontation may—indeed already does—occur from time to time and border states are accused by RSA of harbouring guerillas. In such situations, the dangers of escalation of the conflict are real and could be very serious. Such risks of confrontation and escalation are taken largely at the cost of doing great harm, in particular to the economies of the bordering states. Strengthening the unity of the ten could make such an escalation scenario less probable, in that the economic or political response to adverse action by RSA against any one of its bordering states would be met by supportive and co-ordinated action by the whole region. Assistance to the region from the international community for such purposes might be slow in coming, but if the countries of the region demonstrate ability and political will to act together, assistance to meet aggressive economic action by RSA would be more likely to come from the world community. At some point the countries of the region in co-operation with the world community might consider the establishment of a 'Southern Africa Contingency Fund', possibly in conjunction with the proposed Southern African Development Bank.

There are some particularly important areas where RSA retaliation is possible and where the existence of contingency plans would make retaliation less likely to occur, but if it does occur more bearable for the countries directly affected. In these areas, policy oriented research, review and action should take place without delay, drawing on work already done. It would seem advantageous to do this within an institutional setting such as the Southern African Contingency Fund suggested above.

(a) For Botswana, Lesotho and Swaziland an immediate, unplanned break up of SACU would probably be financially disastrous and have very severe consequences for their balance of payments. This is certainly true for Lesotho. Because SACU payments are based on past, not current, import levels, the cash flow effect on Swaziland and Botswana revenue is much more problematic. A study of this arrangement should seek to determine the minimum amount of resources needed to compensate the three states in the event of a break up. Plans could then be formulated and agreed within the region and with friendly countries elsewhere as to how such resources could be provided. Also the long run costs and benefits of SACU need to be assessed, including the possibilities within the treaty for the three states to derive further benefits, and the legal and other aspects of the treaty as they

50

bear on the expansion of their trade co-operation with non-SACU states.

(b) The prevalence of large scale labour migration in the area—particularly to RSA from the countries closest to it—carries potential for both adverse action by RSA and for cartelization by the labour supplying countries. Analysis is needed of the basis for and probability of action by RSA, as well as of the amounts of resources that would be required to compensate the affected states if such action is taken. Studies are also called for of long term perspectives regarding the effect of migration on the economies of supplying countries in the region.

(c) Even more complicated, but possibly of greater importance, are the problems of import suppliers and of exports of the countries which would be affected by an RSA decision to curtail or stop the flow of goods through that area. In the present situation, the most severely affected countries would be Botswana and Lesotho. The financial consequences of such action and the possibilities of finding other sources of supplies and other markets for exports need to be studied from technical as well as economic points of view, and contingency plans for quick remedial action prepared and agreed.

The achievement of independence by Zimbabwe has altered the scenario. A look at the map suggests that the emergency supply situation is now easier. However, capitalizing on this potential requires urgent rehabilitation of the Zimbabwean, Mozambican and Zambian rail systems.

For an independent Namibia the maintenance of links with RSA could be critical. If there is an immediate break of all ties the economy as it is today might collapse. As it is not out of the question that RSA might take such action against an independent Namibia, this scenario needs to be studied to decide what other states in the region could do to prevent or to counter such a situation. Concrete planning could start immediately.

An early and successful start for future regional co-operation depends crucially on what happens in Zimbabwe. Disruption to the country's economy proceeded quite far over 1976–9. If, however, Zimbabwe's productive capacity can be restored and kept running, the release of demand from the neighbouring states presently held back by sanctions, border closure and war could have a stimulating effect on its economy. True, post-independence boomlike conditions in Zimbabwe, including—by repercussion—stimulation of economies in the whole region, could also initially increase the pressure of demand on supplies from and through RSA. However, a shift of trade with RSA, initially (by necessity rather than preference) to outside Africa, later to some extent to trade within the region, must be the lynchpin of the strategy for regional development, as described above.

ORGANIZATION AND INSTITUTIONS

Some facets of the regional approach outlined above are already being

51

handled by other regional or worldwide organizations and institutions. The countries of southern Africa promote their special interests in various sectors by membership in organizations within Africa and beyond.[4] The institutional framework for regional development in southern Africa should as far as possible build on and closely relate to existing institutional structures.

The establishment of a few common institutions has already been suggested. It is important to strive to make these institutions as flexible as possible, since the central issues of co-operation may vary considerably from time to time. As interaction between countries of the region develops from a beginning of case to case co-operation to perhaps more comprehensive integration, the institutions must also be adjusted and developed.

Before a measure of explicit political consensus for the scope and direction of regional co-operation has emerged, there would be little point in proposing detailed outlines of an institutional structure. However, some suggestions and ideas for a minimum organizational framework may be given:

A CO-ORDINATING BODY

There would seem to be a definite need for a high level political body, which by its very existence would manifest the political will to keep the region together. It would debate and determine major policy directions; it could possibly also be used as a high level institution for mediation in conflicts of view and policy as between member states.

In line with the intention and the need for co-operation to build on the perceived national interest of the partner states, such a co-ordinating body would have to be structured so as to give equal scope for participation and ultimate sanction by each individual state. As is the case in other such bodies a consensus principle might be applied in respect of major decisions.

One conceivable form for such a co-ordinating body could be an annual meeting of Heads of State, perhaps with an alternating venue and president, in the manner of OAU or the group of non-aligned states. In addition, quarterly or semi-annual meetings at ministerial level could serve to focus and relate ongoing projects and to plan further co-ordination activities.

THE BUREAUCRACY

The major development constraint for the region is educated manpower. To secure efficiency in the use of manpower and also to minimize the disadvantage of having international bureaucrats who lose touch with their home country, the bureaucratic functions might be carried out by arranging for each of the member countries to assign to certain individuals centrally placed in their respective national bureaucracies (Ministry of Foreign Affairs and/or Finance and Planning) a regional co-operation portfolio. Their task would be to ensure that all information on projects and programmes in their countries which have regional implications is made available to them, so that they are in a position to inform their respective opposite numbers in the other countries of the region and discuss and agree co-ordinated action. While some committees or institutions at the regional level may become necessary, much of the work of co-ordination could be done ad hoc and informally. A mode of operation of this nature would minimize the need for bureaucratic institutions, and for regional conference and meeting infrastructure.

Only a small secretariat or body of experts may be needed to ensure that the various elements of co-operative action are judicially and carefully designed in such a manner that the partners are well aware of their respective rights and obligations. An important role for some kind of secretariat would be to monitor the execution of co-operation agreements, so that the early corrective action can be taken if imbalances and conflicts are beginning to make themselves felt.

The core of the central secretariat could be quite small. It should be given ample opportunity to form groups doing ad hoc studies. In such studies the prime function of the central secretariat would be to give policy direction to working groups composed, as and when needed, of administrators or other specialists from member countries and of outside experts. Such might be the case, for instance, for the studies of manpower, multinationals, communication, trade matters, river basin development projects etc. suggested above. At a later stage, when needs have been clearly demonstrated and experience gained, steps could be taken to institutionalize the work in special fields of policy or within given sectors.

Another main task of the core secretariat would be liaison between the members, especially with a view to dissemination of the results and proposals derived from the work of the various ad hoc groups and, when appropriate, to bring together decision makers and specialists from member countries to discuss such matters with a view to decisions to take concerted action.

A MEDIATING BODY

A main feature of the organization from its start would be to provide a framework for co-operation between two or more partner states within the region and also between members and non-members. The history of bilateral and multilateral co-operation (not only in Africa) points clearly to the need for co-operative projects and policies, individually and as a package, to be designed to give a fair balance of costs and benefits as between the parties. Another lesson is that it is vital to establish, in advance, institutions and procedures for mediation when conflicts arise.

A mediating body would have to be given substantial authority in the settlement of conflicts. [5] This could be done by setting up a council with high level members from all the ten states, e.g. at the level of attorney-general or the like. In some cases when conflicts between any two—or a few only—of the Ten are at issue, other members of the council could play a mediation role.

A SOUTHERN AFRICAN DEVELOPMENT BANK (SADB)

This might be built up much along the lines of EADB and perhaps be some sort of an extension of it. If found desirable, the proposed bank could have some additional functions.[6] It could seek to mobilize and undertake to administer the proposed Southern African Contingency Fund to provide quick financial relief to states in the RSA periphery if they are actually exposed to adverse action by RSA in the economic and financial field. The Contingency Fund should seek to dispense such relief in the light of the agreed overall framework for regional development, and in that way could co-ordinate its activities with those of the Development Bank. The SA Contingency Fund's first task might be to initiate the three proposed contingency studies regarding SACU, southern African labour migration, and the supply problems of RSA's 'hostages'.

THE ROLE OF EXTERNAL AID

What external aid could do or ought to do in assisting the countries of the region in their efforts to build southern African co-operation, is a question which involves much more than technicalities. Before the countries of southern Africa themselves decide the extent to which, in their effort to increase co-ordination of their policies and activities, they will wish to use foreign technical assistance for human, material and financial resources, and how they will do it, they have to assess and agree the political implications of available options.

When a measure of consensus on these matters has been achieved among the countries of the region, they have to agree on some sort of action programme for co-operation and development. Only then can foreign governments and international agencies be properly involved in the mobilization of external resources for regional development. At the moment, the area as a whole receives somewhat less aid per head than does the rest of Africa, although the economic problems in southern Africa are as great as elsewhere. In addition, the Ten have got some political backing from industrialized countries for their struggle against racism and minority rule in southern Africa. Commercially, the natural riches of the area should augur well for increased investment flows to southern Africa. The proposed Southern African Development Bank and SA Contingency Fund might be well suited to deal with both concessionary assistance and more commercial investments in the region.

Industrial countries and international agencies would have to meet new challenges. They would have to work with multicountry host governments on individual regional projects; this is seen as a complicating factor of project assistance by many donor institutions. On the other hand, the fact that these governments would be partners within a regional framework would serve as some assurance that project proposals have been thoroughly considered and accorded high priority.

In 1975 about one quarter of total investment of the ten countries of the region was financed by foreign aid. Since a very large part of all capital goods are imported into the region through RSA, this means that a substantial part of this financial assistance was used in RSA. Some donors have tried to bring an end to this, or at least to limit it, by prohibiting purchase in RSA of project inputs which are aid-financed. This has in certain cases created grave difficulties for the recipients and severely reduced the value of the aid received. A more constructive attitude would be to allow purchases in RSA, but with incentives for purchase in other countries, especially those of the region. This approach would also be in support of the objective to increase intraregional trade.

As the policy to decrease the dependence on RSA becomes more explicit, detailed and concerted, countries outside the region may also be required to play a more positive and active role. Many foreign governments have condemned RSA's racist policies. One of the motives behind many of the aid programmes in the independent states of southern Africa has been to demonstrate an interest in encouraging and assisting the majority-ruled regimes in a peripheral relation to RSA to become less dependent on RSA. It will be important to win wide international recognition and support for a major commitment by the Ten to promote their own co-ordinated development in ways that will make it possible for them to resist RSA's economic and political measures. It should also be possible to win that recognition and support.

Annexe I

Some Characteristics of the Countries of Southern Africa

ANGOLA

In the medium term Angola, like her former sister colony Mozambique, will go through a period of post-independence crisis. It is partly the absence of a unifying national movement like FRELIMO and partly the great economic importance of Angola which has led to severe factional strife and stepped it up to guerilla warfare. Even more significant in this respect has been the RSA intervention, both direct and through arming, supplying and financing rebel groups. This has meant that as yet only a limited start has been made on MPLA's socialist reconstruction programme.

MPLA's short term aims reflect the disrupted state of the economy. The central problem is to secure food supplies for the towns and thereby bring consumption up to a reasonable level. In the rural areas, subsistence agriculture hardly produces enough to feed the population properly. In spite of excellent conditions for agriculture, Angola imports food. Health and education are other sectors of particular national priority.

Like Mozambique, Angola aims to restore pre-independence production levels as a first step. This aim is not likely to be met before well into the eighties, much depending on the political situation and the extent of the continuing war.

No complete geographical survey has ever been undertaken but some sources argue that Angola is richer in minerals than any other area in southern Africa. The main minerals exploited have been diamonds, iron and petroleum. At present, iron ore production is at a standstill and diamond production has dwindled to perhaps 15–20 per cent of 1973 levels. Crude petroleum, produced in the Cabinda enclave by Gulf Oil Corporation has reached pre-independence levels of about 140,000 barrels a day and now provides from 60–80 per cent of government revenue. The oil sources of Cabinda are the ones nearest to the southern African region. Other important exploitable minerals include copper, lead, zinc, gold, phosphate, bauxite, uranium and cobalt.

Only a fraction of Angola's hydro power potential has been exploited. The political situation has prevented further development of the Kunene

56

project in cc-operation with RSA/Namibia.

Unlike Mozambique, pre-independence Angola has a substantial industry (18-20 per cent of GDP) with an extensive range of products concentrated around Luanda. The major lines of products were processed foods and textiles. The industry presently works at less than half capacity, due to the loss of skilled manpower, as well as to loss of the markets provided by the pre-independence European population.

On the whole, the existence of varied and abundant natural resources and—at independence—a relatively well developed economy, indicate the highest growth potential of any of the countries in the region (annual GDP growth 1970-2 was over 11 per cent). The constraints in the long run will relate to technology and skilled manpower.

BOTSWANA

Botswana has experienced phenomenal economic growth since its independence in 1966. The major source of growth since the beginning of the seventies has been exploitation of minerals and favourable climatic conditions for the country's traditional economic mainstay, beef. The discovery of diamonds and copper nickel and the subsequent construction of mining and social infrastructure caused a major boom in the tiny economy. The boom was further fuelled by the additional government finance from a successful renegotiation of SACU together with Lesotho and Swaziland. External aid also increased and now constitutes some two thirds to three quarters of the public capital budget. After 1974-5 the tendency has been for the economy to level off.

The growth pattern of Botswana has been shaped by an export oriented mining enclave. This has raised GDP and given the country a relatively sound fiscal and balance of payments position, but the interconnected problems of employment and income distribution are still largely unsolved. This is in spite of the pronounced policy of using mineral surpluses to create sustained employment and economic activities, especially in the rural areas. This could remain as a main problem for quite some time. Work has already started on a further sizeable diamond mine which is expected to start operating in 1981/82 and additional mineral discoveries are not unlikely.

There are major external and domestic limitations to the country's ability to create economic activities which can absorb its surplus labour. Of a labour force of about 332,000 only 46,000[7] are employed in the Republic of South Africa or in wage earning jobs at home. Externally the problem is the same as that facing Lesotho, Swaziland and Namibia and is essentially a periphery problem; because of better developed infrastructure, industrial tradition, and proximity to the large markets, virtually all sorts of manufactures can be produced more efficiently in RSA, so that the periphery industries are not able to compete without protection. A protection strategy, however, would be hampered by Botswana's membership of SACU (together with Lesotho, Swaziland and RSA).

Other constraints to indigenous economic activity include the lack of water, not very favourable soil conditions for arable agriculture, the very high cost of power, the lack of educated manpower and the fact that a substantial proportion of the business sector is owned by RSA nationals whose main centre of interest is their home country.

The large export industries' problems are mainly connected with the political uncertainties in the region. Diamonds, copper nickel and beef are exported to European and North American markets. The outlet for beef and copper nickel are, however, dependent on the smooth operation of RSA and Zimbabwean railway systems. The railway line also carries 70 per cent of Botswana's imports, including important inputs and capital goods for the mines. Foreign corporations' uncertainty about the safety of their investments has had a major negative influence on their decisions whether or not to locate in Botswana.

LESOTHO

Its geographical characteristics also describe Lesotho well as an economy; a small exposed mountainous area, relatively high density of population (about twice the average of SA) and completely landlocked by a country with a hostile regime.

Despite its disadvantages Lesotho's GNP has grown since independence at an impressive rate. However, this growth has been based on increased emigration to RSA, where over 30 per cent of the country's economically active population of 200,000 people presently find their employment. The wage earnings of these migrants—to a large extent miners—rose quickly in the first half of the seventies. Migrant workers' salaries now constitute about 40 per cent of GNP. The pronounced growth of the public sector and, through its investment, of the construction sector has been based on improved incomes from SACU, which presently contributes about 40 per cent of total government revenue. The growth in the GNP therefore has very few roots in economic development *within* Lesotho.

Important obstacles to a materially better future for the Basotho are: apparent lack of natural resources, difficulties in mobilizing human resources and heavy economic dependence on a country with a regime whose political ideas are clearly incompatible with those of the Basotho and with which co-operation therefore must be minimized.

Only 10–15 per cent of the country's area is considered suitable for crop production. Most of this is in the lowlands where about 70 per cent of the population lives. The major indigenous source of income, i.e. agriculture, has declined in absolute terms since independence. The actual area under cultivation for five major crops declined by a third from 1973 to 1976. More encouraging has been the growth of livestock industry, especially mohair goats and sheep, which is said to have the potential for further expansion.

Except for a small and high cost diamond mine no extractive industry of any size exists. Prospects for further mineral discoveries do not seem bright, but search is going on for coal, uranium and oil. A certain potential for a hydroelectric scheme is present. Realization of this could mean reduction of dependence on energy imports from RSA; but the project would be virtually totally dependent on RSA as the dominant purchaser of Oxbow water power. Since the Orange is an international river the downstream state, Namibia, might query Lesotho's diversion of a substantial portion of its headwater to the Transvaal.

Like Botswana and Swaziland, Lesotho started from a very low base as regards skilled and semiskilled manpower, but has to a greater extent experienced an outflow of skilled and semiskilled workers to the more rewarding labour market in RSA. This outflow creates a vicious circle in that while it is caused by lack of economic activity at home it has a detrimental effect on the creation of such activity.

Only political will has prevented Lesotho from becoming fully part of the RSA economy. In spite of the fact that all external transport links must go through RSA or its air space, that virtually all trade links are with that country, that RSA nationals dominate the private sector, and that the two countries are parts of the same monetary and customs area, it still constitutes a distinct economy. In the long run, with majority rule in RSA, the potential for friendly co-operation and integration will need to be exploited to improve the living conditions of the Basotho. Until such time the only possible way forward for Lesotho is to try to achieve greater economic independence through regional co-operation with the other independent African states in southern Africa.

MALAWI

Malawi is a small (94,300 km^2 in area), densely populated (5.2 million people in 1976) country round the shores of Lake Malawi. Ninety per cent of the population derive their livelihood from agriculture.

So far no sizeable mineral resources have been discovered. There is some potential for hydropower on some of the country's swift running rivers and for thermal power based on coal. The resource base however must on the whole be characterized as narrow.

In spite of this narrow base, fluctuating prices and a break in labour exports to RSA, Malawi has achieved fair GDP growth rates viz. 5–5.5 per cent during 1973–6.

A main factor behind this was the strong increase in the major export crops—tobacco, tea, sugar and groundnuts. The agricultural strategy has been twopronged. The small holders grow mainly maize, groundnuts, cotton and tobacco while estates produce tea, tobacco and sugar.

Malawi is self-sufficient in foodcrops. The livestock industry has in recent years satisfied the local market in beef and pork and exportation has started. A small, but fast-growing manufacturing industry (13 per cent p.a. 1964–73) has mainly been processing agricultural goods and supplied inputs.

Malawi has adopted a fairly liberal and pragmatic approach to its external trade and finance relations. In the latter years imports from RSA have constituted an increasing percentage of total imports. Imports from pre-independence Zimbabwe have dropped as a result of the closure of the Mozambique/Zimbabwe border and the war situation in the latter country. Several larger capital projects have been financed from RSA and other external sources. Malawi's main trading partner however, remains the UK (46 per cent of exports and 22 per cent of imports in 1976).

The southern parts of Malawi are heavier populated and more developed than the northern parts. National planning has taken this into account by stressing balanced regional development.

The instability of agricultural markets, regional imbalances and the present political upheavals in southern Africa form three important areas of Malawian concern for future economic development.

MOZAMBIQUE

Mozambique is another country in the region which for quite some time will struggle with all the problems of a newly independent country.

Colonial rule left exceptionally little on which Mozambique could build. The country had largely been used by the colonial partner as a cheap source of raw materials, a market for Portuguese manufactures, and a transit route for RSA. At independence, Mozambique imported about twice as many goods as it exported. The external balance was ensured by foreign exchange earnings from tourist traffic, transit traffic, rail and harbour charges and remittances from migrant labour to Zimbabwe and RSA.

Many of the present problems in the economy are related to the events which took place as the country got its independence. Even though the unfavourable trade agreements with Portugal ceased, the effect of the oil crisis and unfavourable world market developments on the prices of Mozambique's main exports led to deterioration in the balance of payments position. The exodus of 150,000–200,000 Portuguese just before and after independence meant a severe loss of skills which was strategic to the smooth operation of the economy. As the drop in gold prices reduced the level of activity in RSA mines and black unemployment there soared, migrant labour from Mozambique was severely curtailed. The advantage of the Mozambique Convention[8] decreased with the gold prices. In 1976 on closing the border with Zimbabwe, further losses to the economy were sustained. The adverse effect of this action was a staggering deficit of US$100–150 million on the balance of payments, the loss of about 10,000 jobs and additional contingency capital expenditure.

Mozambique now faces the difficult twin tasks of restoring pre-independence levels of production and changing the structure of the economy with the aim of alleviating inequality and poverty. With the industrial production presently only half and agricultural production significantly below what it was in 1973, these goals will probably be the predominant ones in the medium term.

The border closure to pre-independence Zimbabwe and the breaking of colonial ties increased Mozambique's dependence on RSA. Briefly, these are the major points. The foreign exchange and employment situation will be seriously worsened if access to the RSA labour market is curtailed. Important foreign exchange is derived from RSA's transit traffic through Maputo.[9] The independence of Zimbabwe should, as soon as rail routes can be rehabilitated, reduce the degree of dependence on RSA transit traffic and strengthen the balance of payments. The Cabora Bassa hydroelectric scheme would not be economically viable for a long time if it were not based on extensive power transmission into RSA's grid. No supplier of important capital goods and industrial inputs could compete with the RSA suppliers. These considerations explain Mozambique's pragmatic economic line towards RSA.

Despite all disruptions, important progress has been made in several sectors, especially health and education. In the long term, Mozambique's natural resources base indicates excellent potential for economic growth. With more stable and peaceful relations in the region, its excellent harbours will no doubt regain their importance as an outlet for the landlocked states to its north.

The vast hydroelectric power potential in combination with minerals (coal, iron, bauxite, titanium, gold, asbestos, copper, phosphates and natural gas) will give opportunities for base metal production and a basis for manufacturing industry. Agricultural (50 per cent of the soil could be cultivated) and fishery prospects are also very good. Educated manpower, technology and markets are the constraints.

NAMIBIA

Of the countries most closely linked to RSA, Namibia is the biggest in terms of population, area and GDP. With its vast mineral resources, its fisheries, cattle and karakul sheep rearing, it is a rich economy, having a higher GDP per head than any other of the Ten.

At present Namibia is under RSA rule with grave consequences for the exploitation of the country's natural resources and the distribution of the returns.

For a country which still has not achieved its political independence it is more than hazardous to try and assess what the major economic problems will be. Immediately after independence, which must surely come soon, Namibia will have to cope with all the internal problems that newly independent states have always experienced. Because of the extraordinarily

61

low level of indigenous manpower development, the high degree of technical and managerial sophistication of the economy and some sectors' international importance, Namibia's transition problems could be substantial. The abolishment of the contract labour system which would probably be an early initiative of any majority-based popular government, will cause pressure for housing and facilities in urban areas as the workers' families, at present compulsorily settled in homelands, move to settle with the workers.

SWAPO's present political bent indicates that in the medium and long term the dependency problem both with respect to RSA and European and US based multinationals will come to the fore. In the case of RSA much will depend on that country's willingness to concede majority rule in Namibia and on its responses in the early period after independence. The extent to which at present consumer goods, capital goods, important industrial inputs and technical expertise are supplied from RSA would make it possible for that country to strike crippling blows to the Namibian economy. If there is not to be immediate chaos there will need to be no more than a gradual switch of connections away from RSA. The achievement of Namibian sovereignty over Walvis Bay, the linking of Namibia's rail system to Botswana's and better access to the Angolan industrial centre will be vital issues during this slow transition.

Both in the short and long term the lack of manpower will be crucial. It could take considerable time before the more economic problems of structural transformation and growth in the economy come on the agenda. The achievement of a fair distribution and of an increased internal integration in the economy will be more difficult than in most developing economies.

For continued industrial and mining development, power supply questions will have to be handled. In addition to this, agricultural expansion and the interconnected distribution and employment issues will be difficult. Depending on the scenario with respect to RSA, development of manufacturing industries might face problems similar to those of Botswana.

SWAZILAND

Swaziland has, like Botswana, enjoyed rapid export-led growth until the mid seventies, mainly in agrobased commodities (sugar, woodpulp, canned fruits, citrus, meat and products) and asbestos. However, that growth seems to have faltered since 1975.

With its mining activities, agriculture, forestry and a sizeable manufacturing sector, the Swaziland economy is quite diversified, and has a relatively high GDP per head. Nevertheless, the economy is closely integrated with that of RSA. Virtually all imports come from RSA, which supplies a major part of Swaziland's water and power, operates major outward transport links and absorbs 20 per cent of Swaziland's exports. On the human resources side, 25,000 Swazi migrant workers are employed in RSA and key technical and managerial experts in both public and private sectors are white RSA nationals.

In addition to the usual periphery symptoms in evidence, an obstacle to real Swazi participation in the economy is the ownership pattern. Major parts of industries as well as over 40 per cent of the land is owned by expatriates. Historically the Swazi economy has been based on independent expatriate activities in agriculture and mining. National planning efforts have not yet reached a very high degree of cohesion.

About three quarters of Swazi exports go overseas, mostly to UK, Japan, USA, but also to Europe and South America. To African countries the main exports are coal and sugar. A main problem in exports, apart from the vagaries of international sugar and woodpulp markets, is the dependence on shipping access. What secure export outlets mean to Swaziland is underlined by the fact that although the Maputo harbour is the natural access harbour, construction is completed on a linkage to the RSA system via Golela. This line makes it possible to export via Richards Bay and Durban.

Institutional consequences of Swaziland's dependence on RSA is its membership (as Botswana and Lesotho) of SACU and (together with Lesotho) of the Rand Monetary Area. Even though Swaziland has its own currency, the lilangeni, monetary management has little scope as the lilangeni is wholly backed by the rand and both currencies circulate in the country.

After the liberation of Mozambique, steps were taken to increase trade and co-operation between the two countries. A trade co-operation agreement has been signed. A major problem both for bilateral or wider treaties e.g. Swaziland's membership in a prospective southern and eastern African preferential trade area, is the relation to SACU and the balance of costs and benefits between the two directions of economic interaction.

TANZANIA

Tanzania's population of over 17.5 million constitutes about one third of the total population of the Ten. In terms of GNP per head it ranks low, just a little over the level of Malawi and Lesotho, and like those countries, its economy is predominantly an agricultural one. Seventy-five per cent of the households earn their livelihood from this sector; its contribution to total exports is about 80 per cent and to GDP some 45 per cent.

After almost 20 years of independence, the struggle for structural transformation and creation of independent economic strategies is not over in Tanzania. However, much has been achieved and the country has brought inspiration and ideas for independent economic strategies to many countries on the continent. Search and experimentation might well have affected

63

overall economic growth rates, which were at a low of 3.4 per cent in the 1971–5 period. For 1976–8, however, the average was over 5 per cent.

The great emphasis given lately to productivity generally, but especially in agriculture, might have been part of the reason for the satisfactory growth in this sector in the later years. However, bad rains in 1979 and 1980 (following a relatively good 1975–8 period) have caused new and very serious setbacks.

The product range of the manufacturing industry has been greatly expanded, but the sector as a whole still only contributes one tenth of GDP. Industrial protection has led to high costs and poor competitiveness in some lines of production. Presently there is also underutilization of existing capacity. Some main problems are disruption in the flow of inputs like water and power, in the supply of spare parts, and lack of skilled technicians and experienced management. Further development of industries has been given high priority in national planning. The strategy emphasizes industries which can meet the population's demand for food, clothing and shelter; can process agricultural raw materials for export; are basic industries, like woodpulp, cement, iron and steel.

Tanzania from its colonial start has been considered economically as part of the East African area. Its most important transports and trade links on the African continent have been with Kenya and Uganda. Although there is some economic logic for the attachment to the north, the historic reasons weigh heavily and one could conceive of Tanzania as a bridgebuilder of economic links between the East African area and the centres of economic activity to the south.

One may consider the break-up of the EAC as a major setback for regional co-operation. Taking the positive angle, it has, however, provided Tanzania with valuable experience which could benefit a wider and different type of regional co-operation. The liberation of Uganda from Amin and Tanzania's co-operation in that struggle should help create political and material conditions for renewed co-operation.

Tanzania has been active in promoting co-operation with neighbouring states. Its commitment to assist in the anti-colonial struggle in southern Africa has been marked by its co-operation with Zambia on the Tazara railways and a close co-operation with Mozambique (a Joint Commission for Co-operative Action in Economic and Social Development has been set up). Co-operation agreements with Rwanda and Burundi as well as with the Seychelles have been signed. Tanzania is a member with Rwanda, Burundi and Uganda of the Kagera Basin Development Commission.

ZAMBIA

Zambia's economy until 1973 was closely interlinked with those of pre-independent Zimbabwe and RSA. If the closing of borders to Zimbabwe had not taken place, the economy would probably have still been a well-functioning copper enclave system appendaged to the RSA system.

The border closure in 1973, coupled with the RSA/UNITA insurgent severing of the rail route to Lobito Bay in Angola, had some positive effect on forcing into existence a little manufacturing industry. Nevertheless these events were severely damaging to the economy. In a country where one third of GDP and about 90 per cent of export earnings originate from exported copper, major disruption of the export channels has had grave consequences. Large parts of the revenue from the exceptional copper prices at the time of the closure had to be used for strategic investment and emergency measures in the transport sector. Little reserves were therefore built up to cushion the collapse of copper prices which came in 1974.

The policy of redirection early in 1978, including devaluation and substantial fiscal and monetary tightening is likely to be continued into the eighties. A main worry in the shorter term will still be the export outlets. With Tazara damaged by UDI rebel action, with declining rail efficiency and a congested harbour in Dar es Salaam, with many Tazara wagons used as warehouses and with a weak clearing and forwarding structure, the Tazara system must be supplemented. However, there are also severe difficulties in handling cargo flows through Beira, Maputo and Francistown in a manner consistent with not creating warehouse congestion. Mozambique's and Zambia's internal rail systems are badly in need of rehabilitation and reorganization and their rail and rolling stock is severely inadequate. Steps must be taken therefore if traffic flows are to be restored on the Bulawayo–Salisbury–Beira route. Finally, another possible route, the Benguela line, is obstructed by insurgents. Zambia's transport problems continue to be the greatest single obstacle to a real and sustained revival of her economy.

Beyond the present emergency one would expect some reorientation in Zambian economic policy. A constant and worsening problem since independence has been that average GDP growth rates are below the population growth rates. In fact, from 1974 to 1977 real income per head decreased by 33 per cent. Diversification of the economy is high on the agenda of the Third National Development Plan. The country's agricultural potential could be exploited to a greater extent. At present Zambia imports food. Increases in the productivity of traditional agriculture should be possible and is necessary to improve the living standards of Zambians in the future, but the resource input to help this process will have to come from the mining sector.

Foremost among Zambia's manpower problems are some 5,000 key posts in the mining sector held by expatriates. Lately the problem has become acute as some of them have been leaving because of the current circumstances with respect to salaries, income tax and remittances. A smooth transition to a stable and efficient local staff in the mines is crucial for Zambia to master the short term problems and to lay foundations for reaching the target growth rate of 4.8 per cent p.a.

Zimbabwe has the biggest, most modern and cohesive economy of the Ten. In Africa south of the Sahara, it is second to only the Republic of South Africa in industrial production, though on a much lower level.

A product of its history, Zimbabwe's economy was export and settler/colonial oriented. The latter has had familiar distributional effects both on incomes and the ownership of land. The commercial agricultural sector is run by small numbers of companies and individuals on 45 per cent of the best land which is reserved for Europeans. Modern agriculture is not the biggest sector in terms of GDP (about 16 per cent) but it employs nearly 40 per cent of those in cash employment and contributes about 50 per cent of foreign exchange receipts. Main agricultural exports are tobacco, maize, beef, cotton and sugar. The subsistence side of agriculture is mainly located in the Tribal Trust Lands (TTLs), (45 per cent of the area) where 4.4 million of Zimbabwe's 6.5 million people live, partly off the land, partly functioning as a labour reserve for the modern sector. (In the TTLs, 38 per cent of the population are men, 62 per cent women.)

Mining, presently contributing about 7 per cent of GDP and 40 per cent of total foreign exchange earnings has grown rapidly since 1965. The major mining export products are gold (30 per cent), asbestos (30 per cent), copper (15 per cent), chrome (5 per cent) and nickel (20 per cent). Coal and coke are mostly consumed domestically. Three quarters of the gross output in the mining sector is produced by foreign and multinationally owned mines.

The degree of internal integration achieved in the Zimbabwe economy has not been reached by any other of the 10 prospective partner states. The agricultural and the mineral sectors supply major shares of the inputs for the manufacturing industry which is the biggest sector of the economy—in 1977 21.9 per cent of GDP. UDI and the subsequent bans on economic relationships played a positive role in diversifying and increasing the degree of self-sufficiency in the economy, with multinationals playing a central role in many subsectors. The strongest growth has occurred in such relatively complex subsectors as plastics, iron and steel, paper products, industrial chemicals and machinery and metal products. Pre-independence Zimbabwe in fact produced some of the rolling stock for its own railway system. The main difficulties for the manufacturing sector lately have been due to the deterioration of machinery, lack of spare parts and the curtailment of export opportunities which have all been a result of the war and the UN-sponsored blockade. With independence, Zimbabwe should soon be able to clear those away.

The blockade naturally led to a greater economic dependence on RSA, but there are several factors which will limit the future importance of this. First, the openness of the Zimbabwean economy is not excessive: in relation to GDP, exports were 25 per cent, imports only 16 per cent.[10] Second, at present about 40 per cent of imports come from RSA, but this was reached after the blockade by switching from UK imports, which makes it just credible that a reversal could be achieved. Of the exports only 16 per cent go to RSA,[11] the rest mainly overseas. Third, Zimbabwe has diversified transport links with the outside world, especially rail and air, and cannot be said to be dependent on RSA for the major strategic import—oil. Fourth, although connected by the Central African Power Corporation grid with RSA, Mozambique and Zambia, Zimbabwe is (with the Kariba and Wankie generating capacity) practically self-sufficient in power. An important point of dependence on RSA is, however, the financial sector.

The country suffered from war and partial international blockade with severe effects on the economy. Transitional problems will be dominant in the short and medium term. The structural (distribution of income and assets) and dependency problems are in principle similar to those of Namibia. Zimbabwe has a very complex economy and even if the absolute number of educated and trained manpower is quite high, rapid outflow of key expatriate personnel would effect the economy severely. Rebuilding the economy to its pre-war strength on a quite different structural basis might take the better part of the next decade. This is by no means to say that some structural changes—in access to land, jobs, education, health—cannot be achieved rapidly nor that regional co-ordination programmes must wait until 1985 or 1990. It is to warn against unrealistic hopes that Zimbabwe's independence can transform either its own economy or the entire region overnight.

OTHER MAJORITY-RULED STATES BORDERING THE REGION

Regional interdependence does not stop at the regional borders. There is no such thing as *the* natural region e.g. ECA includes in its East African region most of the 10 states dealt with and in addition Rwanda, Burundi, Uganda, Kenya, Ethiopia and Somalia. As mentioned, Tanzania's membership in a southern African region naturally also ties in with the former EAC: *Kenya*, as the industrial centre with a GDP comparable to that of Zimbabwe and a well developed and competitive manufacturing sector; *Uganda*, presently disrupted, but with considerable agricultural and industrial potential. *Rwanda* and *Burundi*, two very small landlocked agricultural states, are wholly dependent on transportation of their overseas exports through other countries, today dominantly Tanzania.

Zaire links naturally with both Angola and Zambia, its Shaba province having the transport problem and other problems of mineral production in common with Zambia. *Madagascar*, a relatively large island economy, definitely belongs to the South and East African orbit.

Mauritius, *Comoros*, *Seychelles* and *Sao Tome e Principe* also have historic and current economic links with the coastal states of the region.

ANNEXE II

Some International Organizations in Southern African Member Countries

Name of Organization	Members from the region (The Ten)	Other Members
Organization of African Unity (OAU)	All except Namibia	All other African countries, except RSA
African Development Bank (ADB)	All except Namibia. (Zimbabwe will presumably join)	All other African countries, except RSA
Lomé Convention	All except Namibia, Mozambique and Angola. (Zimbabwe has applied to join)	All other African countries, except Algeria, Djibouti Egypt, Morocco, RSA, Tunisia
Economic Commission for Africa (ECA)	Namibia (SWAPO) is an associate member	All other African countries except RSA. (Suspended 1963)
Southern Africa Customs Union (SACU)	Botswana, Lesotho, Swaziland	RSA.
African Timber Organization	Tanzania	Algeria, Ivory Coast, Libya, Morocco, Senegal, Tunisia, Upper Volta, Zaire
Desert Locust Control Organization for Eastern Africa	Tanzania	Ethiopia, France, Kenya, Somalia, Sudan, Uganda
International Red Locust Control for Central and Southern Africa	Botswana, Lesotho, Swaziland, Zambia, Malawi, Tanzania	Kenya, Uganda, Zaire, Rwanda, Burundi
Lakes Tanganyika and Kivu Basin Commission	Zambia, Tanzania	Zaire, Rwanda, Burundi
Regional Centre for Services in Mapping and Surveying	Malawi, Tanzania	Kenya, Uganda, Somalia
Association of African Central Banks	Malawi, Tanzania	Kenya, Zaire, Burundi, Ethiopia, Ghana, Mauritius, Sierra Leone, Somalia, Sudan, Zaire
African Centre for Administrative Training & Research for Development (CAFRAD)	Botswana, Swaziland, Zambia, Tanzania	22 other African countries

Name of Organization	Members from the region (The Ten)	Other Members
Conference of East and Central African States	Zambia, Malawi, Tanzania	Central African Republic, Chad, Congo, Equatorial Guinea, Ethiopia, Gabon, Kenya, Somalia, Rwanda, Sudan, Burundi, Malawi, Uganda, Zaire
African Postal and Telecommunications Union	Angola, Namibia, Botswana, Lesotho, Swaziland, Zimbabwe, Malawi, Mozambique	RSA, Zaire, Burundi, etc.
Inter-African Coffee Producers Organization	Angola, Tanzania	Benin, Cameroon, Central African Republic, Congo, Ethiopia, Gabon, Ivory Coast, Liberia, Malagasy, Nigeria, Sierra Leone, Togo
Association of African Airlines	Air Zambia, Air Tanzania	Kenya Air, Uganda Airlines, Arab Air, Tunisair, Air Maroc, Ghana Air, Air Afrique
Southern African Regional Commission for the Conservation and Utilization of Soil (SARCUS)	Angola, Namibia, Botswana, Lesotho, Swaziland, Zimbabwe, Malawi, Mozambique	RSA, Sao Tome
Southern African Regional Tourism Council (SARTOC)	Lesotho, Swaziland, Malawi	RSA, Mauritius
East African Joint Shipping Line	Zambia, Tanzania	Kenya, Uganda
Union of National Radios and Televisions in Africa	Zambia, Tanzania	Algeria, Cameroon, Chad, Congo, Zaire, Dahomey, Ghana, Guinea, Ivory Coast, Liberia, Mali, Mauritania, Morocco, Niger, Nigeria, Egypt, Senegal, Sierra Leone, Togo, Tunisia, Upper Volta

Source: Africa, South of the Sahara, 1978–79 Yearbook of International Organizations.

NOTES

1. Extractive industries, especially mining, form the predominant parts of industry in Zambia, Swaziland and Namibia.
2. Nine people per sq km compared to a world average of 30, 14 for Africa as a whole, and 21 for RSA.
3. One clear illustration of this is given by the trade patterns: the 10's exports to and imports from RSA, as percentages of their total exports and imports, are respectively 5.5 and 28.8. The equivalent percentages for the trade figures of RSA are only around half of these levels,

although excluding gold perhaps a quarter of RSA's exports are to African states (including Namibia).

4. A list of some of the more important of these organizations is included in Annexe II.

5. Major conflicts would, of course, have to be discussed by meeting of the governing body i.e. the Heads of State.

6. Eventually, a division of such a bank might take up the function of a clearing house.

7. About 14 per cent of economically active population.

8. Convention whereby part of the miners wages was paid directly from RSA to the government in gold at the official gold price.

9. The operation of the harbour itself is also dependent on RSA expertise.

10. The figures are from 1977 and the percentages could for tactical reasons have been deflated.

11. See 10.

Transport and Communications

I. TRANSPORT LIBERATION

ERODING THE RSA CONNECTION

Transport and communications are the most immediate and highest priority sector for economic liberation for six reasons:

1. Zambia and Botswana are severely limited in their struggles to support political liberation and to achieve national development by their continued dependence on the transport and communications system of the Republic of South Africa;

2. Consolidation of genuine independence in Zimbabwe and (later) Namibia will require their delinking from the RSA transport and communications systems and their linking with a southern African system;

3. No serious degree of economic integration can be achieved within the region as a whole until it becomes significantly easier, faster and cheaper to move messages, persons and goods than it is today;

4. The economic health of the region requires sustained and increased exports to economies outside southern Africa to secure the foreign exchange to finance nationally oriented structural change. Therefore, dependable, prompt and economical movement of goods to and through ports is essential;

5. Because six of the region's states are landlocked and four have ports suitable for serving one or more landlocked states, regional co-ordination of capacity and cargo allocation, handling of rolling stock, organization of clearing and forwarding as well as processing of documents, in addition to joint planning of new transport facilities, is essential to pursuing economic liberation in respect to transport and communications.

6. The achievement of internal integration in several states depends on long new truck routes. These are very expensive and often can be viable only if a substantial through traffic can be obtained to bolster revenues

until development-based traffic builds up over time. For example, Tazara is a major development inducing factor for the Kilombero Valley and Mbeya region in Tanzania but its revenue for at least a decade will be basically from Zambian transit traffic. Another example is that a linking of north, central and western Botswana into the present north-south (Francistown/Gaborone) economic axis depends on a railway linking Sua Pan, Ngamiland and Ngami Ridge. This would be a viable proposition only if it was then extended further to Gobabis thus linking with the Namibian system and allowing coal exports through, and imports via, Walvis Bay.

COUNTRY CAPSULES

ZAMBIA

The most urgent challenge confronting the Front Line States in transport and communications is that of ensuring that Zambia is not crippled by inability to meet its transport requirements. In the slightly longer term it is essential to regain the possibility for Zambian external trade to pass wholly over routes within the genuinely independent states of southern Africa. This is not Zambia's problem alone—it is the problem of the region. The recent past situation in which Zambia found itself increasingly tied to RSA and pre-independence Zimbabwe routes hampered both the economic and political liberation efforts not just of Zambia but of every state in the region.

The need is not to apportion blame for the problems but to overcome them together. The exodus of experienced expatriate personnel after Zambia's independence, the shocks and costs imposed by the neighbouring UDI rebellion, the weakness of interim expatriate management, the disruption of service to Lobito Bay by RSA-promoted insurrection, the devastating impact of low copper prices on foreign exchange and finance to replace and repair rolling stock as well as to maintain track and roadbed, and the UDI rebel commando raids, are facts imposed on Zambia from outside. They have made the Zambian transport system slow, undependable and fragile. This has greatly increased the strain on port, road and rail systems seeking to serve Zambia. The cumulative results have been disastrous for transport systems in Zambia and serious for her neighbour. Major rehabilitation is needed not only in Zambia but also in Zimbabwe, Mozambique, Angola and Tanzania in order to overcome these barriers to the development of Zambia and the region as a whole.

BOTSWANA

Botswana's rail system is formally a branch of Zimbabwe Railways. During UDI Botswana switched the direction of trade, so this line now primarily links Botswana to Capetown. With the genuine independence of Zimbabwe,

72

Botswana now has a route to the sea free of RSA control. Building a major rail link through a genuinely independent Namibia is still needed to give access to the Atlantic because a domestic east-west link is critical to tie together a series of major mineral and agricultural potentials. The plans for Botswana to take over the domestic rail line together with the training of Batswana to operate it and the acquisition of rolling stock and maintenance facilities are still relevant—but perhaps less urgent with Zimbabwe's independence. Top priority now turns on the negotiation of medium term arrangements between Zimbabwe Railways, Mozambique Railways and Beira Port and the mobilization of support for the rehabilitation of the three railway systems and the expansion of Beira's capacity.

ANGOLA

Zambia, Angola and Zaire face a joint challenge to achieve full restoration of service on the Lobito Bay-Shaba-Copperbelt line. Domestic communications and revenue considerations make this critical for Angola. For Zambia and Zaire it is integral to reducing their dependence on very long, uneconomic and dependence-intensifying routes to ports in the Republic of South Africa. This may not be possible until the liberation of Namibia cuts off RSA training and support for UNITA's insurgents.

In the medium term, issues arise as to the potential addition of a branch of the Lobito Bay line direct to Zambia. Similarly the southern Angolan system could be linked to a northward extension of the Namibian line and/or to the proposed Trans-Kalahari line.

MOZAMBIQUE

Mozambique had in early 1979 restored and taken full control over its transport system despite the loss of expatriates and the damage from neighbouring rebel commando raids. The major transport destruction raids in late 1979 created major new rehabilitation and replacement needs. It has also faced difficulties in meeting somewhat unpredictable demands for capacity from its neighbours and in planning future expansion of its harbour, rail and road facilities to serve them.

The colonial economy of Mozambique was first made dependent on RSA through the creation of Maputo to serve the mining and industrial area. Later dependence on pre-independent Zimbabwe was centred on the building of Beira port facilities to serve that colony. Economic liberation requires a reorienting and expansion of transport facilities to serve Mozambican, Zambian, Malawian, Swazi and Zimbabwean traffic. In particular Maputo and Beira are wellplaced and can be developed to serve as major coal ports (say five million tonnes at Maputo and 13–20 million at Beira) for Mozambique, Swaziland, Zimbabwe and perhaps Botswana, while improved facilities at Nacala could serve increased Malawian and Zambian trade. The phasing of the harbour, road, railroad track and rolling stock for these services needs to be co-ordinated with the potential users to avoid both unused facilities and unforeseen bottlenecks.

ZIMBABWE

Zimbabwe's genuine political independence creates immediate needs for its relatively new dependence on RSA transport to be disentangled so that it begins to use the Mozambican links again as much as possible. Until this can be achieved the economic liberation of Zimbabwe (and of Mozambique) will be very seriously constrained.

Major transitional problems face Zimbabwe and the region in respect of deferred maintenance, rolling stock replacement and—above all—training of Zimbabweans to handle technical, supervisory, managerial and executive positions. During 1980/1 keeping the system rolling may in itself be a major challenge, judging by past experience in several other newly independent states in the region.

Over a slightly longer period it is likely that Zimbabwe will seek to increase coal exports sharply. This will require increased capacity on rail lines to and in harbour facilities at Beira. It may also envisage use of Windhoek to give access to the Atlantic for some general trade and coal trade directed to northwest European markets.

NAMIBIA

At attainment of genuine independence Namibia will face an immediate problem: delinking its rail and road systems from those of RSA. Personnel constraints and the near total absence of heavy maintenance and headquarters facilities will be particularly serious.

A link with Botswana would be useful to Namibia both in providing a land route to the rest of the southern African region and in affording access to Botswanan coal to replace the RSA coal now used in the critical smelting industry. Road—or perhaps rail—links to Angola would also be of value especially as they would have the internal effect of improving transport and communications between the northern and central regions of Namibia. They would be even more important if at independence Walvis Bay remains in hostile RSA hands. If Walvis Bay remains occupied at the independence of the rest of Namibia it will be critical to reactivate Swakopmund (possible but costly), make more use of Luderitz (problematic), link to Angola's southern ports of Moçâmedes and Puerto Alexandre (possible but costly). To do this requires both national (SWAPO) contingency plans and regional co-ordination by Angola as well as Zambia and Zimbabwe which could provide highway access from the main Windhoek/Katima Mulilo route.

LESOTHO

Lesotho is land-locked by RSA. Therefore its options for loosening transport and communications dependence are limited to a regional standard

74

(Hercules, 737) airport to allow direct cargo and passenger flights to Lusaka, Salisbury and Maputo and to an earth satellite station to end routing of telecommunications via RSA. Limited as they may seem these projects would significantly reduce Lesotho's isolation.

SWAZILAND

Swaziland faces severe problems in rehabilitating its railway, acquiring its own rolling stock and securing additional specialized terminal facilities in Maputo. Its railway used to be in practice a branch of the Portuguese colonial Mozambican line. Mozambique—which lost its Portuguese skilled rail personnel—has been unable to continue in that role and, in any event, neither state desires that it should. However, the transition is proving difficult for Swaziland especially as it has led to an enforced (though Swaziland hopes temporary) need to rely more heavily on RSA personnel and equipment. In addition Swaziland needs and plans to build a tarmac highway to Mozambique and an earth satellite ground station.

MALAWI

Like Botswana, Malawi requires additional regional links to strengthen domestic economic integration. A heavy duty highway or a railway extension linking the existing system to Tazara would strengthen Malawi's access to the region and allow more balanced internal rural developments. Additional possibilities include joint lake service on Lake Malawi/Nyasa by the three lakeside states of Tanzania, Mozambique and Malawi.

TANZANIA

Tanzania has a relatively well articulated set of main communication links. The major gaps relate to Rwanda, Burundi and Uganda—its northern and western regional neighbours—and to land communication with Mozambique in the south east. A rail link to Uganda and a highway/Ruvuma River bridge to Mozambique are under active consideration with preliminary studies completed. Construction is proceeding on road and bridge links to Rwanda and on restoring and upgrading the Lake Tanganyika rail ferry terminal and lake service linking Zambia, Zaire, Burundi and Tanzania. However, much of Tanzania's existing railway/highway network is in urgent need of rehabilitation. Heavy use, old age (except for Tazara and the Tanzanian Highway) and lack of foreign exchange have taken a heavy toll. The weaknesses were increased by abnormally heavy rains and floods in 1979. While re-equipment and reorganization in 1979 cleared congestion at the Port of Dar es Salaam, the programmes on main railway, highway, rolling stock and lorry fleet rehabilitation and buildup have not progressed equally rapidly. Because of Tanzania's role as a transit country for Zambia, Zaire, Rwanda, Burundi and Uganda (and a potential route for southern Africa/Kenya trade) the rapid completion of these programmes and

75

resolution of tonnage and facility guarantee questions is of major concern, regionally as well as nationally.

ACTION NOTES

This sketch of national transport needs demonstrates clearly that co-ordinated action is required. While bilateral arrangements—such as the subcommissions linking Mozambique and her neighbours and the Zambia-Tanzania joint corporations—are a first step, regional action is also needed. Many issues involve more than two states; for example, the allocation of total Zambian traffic and the development of facilities to handle it logically requires co-ordinated planning and decisions by Zambia, Mozambique, Angola, Tanzania and Malawi.

It would therefore appear desirable to create a Southern African Transport and Communications Commission—initially involving all the independent African states in the region, with SWAPO participating as an observer and with Lesotho's participation limited by its geographical position to air transport and telecommunications. This Commission would not need a large permanent secretariat. It would require a small one to maintain communications and organize meetings. It would also require that each participating state designate one or more senior transport personnel to oversee regional aspects of national transport systems as a major portion of their duties in their own states.

Areas in which the Commission could facilitate economic liberation through improved regional transport and communications operation include:

(a) identification of major transport and communications projects—including rehabilitation—with regional implications for which regional initiatives would raise external finance;

(b) agreed multilateral allocation of landlocked state cargo to coastal state routes to allow effective use of existing capacity and to limit bottlenecks and pileups;

(c) joint efforts to meet the rolling stock and hauling power needs of rail systems with especially tight constraints, perhaps through joint use of certain maintenance facilities and/or limited loans of equipment and personnel;

(d) co-ordinating and simplifying clearing, forwarding, transit and documentation arrangements to limit pileup of delayed or unclaimed cargo;

(e) making transport and communications training facilities available to meet regional needs and in particular those of Botswana and SWAPO in respect to building up initial citizen rail cadres;

76

(f) co-ordination of national airline schedules and landing points to make air travel within the region faster and easier;

(g) study of ways in which the external communications buildup by national satellite ground stations can be used for regional telecommunications—perhaps via the Dar es Salaam or the Rift Valley station.

The short and medium term investment needs which include expanding Beira, Maputo, Nacala; rehabilitating Zimbabwean, Zambian, Mozambican, Swaziland and Angolan Railways; creating an independent Botswana Railways; building the Trans-Kalahari and establishing lesser road and rail links, are likely to be of the order of $1.5 billion. Unlike the training needs which can and must be met primarily nationally and regionally, the fixed investment requirement will entail securing very substantial external resources. A regional strategy for raising these resources should have a good chance of success. The region is a significant supplier of base metals. In the 1980s it will become a critical supplier of coal. Industrial economies have a clear interest in availability of base metals and coal and therefore in co-operating in southern African initiatives to improve regional transport capacity.

II. TRANSPORT AND DEVELOPMENT

INTRODUCTION

This second part is addressed to the potentials for and problems of developing a rational, co-ordinated southern African transport and communications system conducive to reducing dependence on RSA, decreasing transport costs and encouraging regional economic interaction. It hopes to set the identification of immediate objectives (which constitutes the first part) into a wider framework of analysis. One of the difficulties experienced relates to the availability of reliable and comparable data for the 10 countries. This applies with especial force to Zimbabwe and Namibia. Moreover, the effects of the Zimbabwe liberation struggle and of sanctions against the UDI regime make the interpretation of past freight and passenger traffic figures unreliable for the purposes of projecting future trends. Estimates of the pace at which traffic from Zimbabwe, Zambia, Botswana and Namibia now routed through RSA could be rerouted through independent African states are difficult to make with any pretence of accuracy.

In other economic sectors as well, co-ordination can be advanced further now that Zimbabwe is liberated. Zimbabwe has a fairly well advanced industrial sector which could easily substitute for some of the goods imported both from RSA and from outside the region. But it is very difficult to be at all precise about what may be possible. More specifically, the volume and flow of freight and passenger traffic depend on growth and structure of the economy; economic, institutional and legal arrangements for co-operation between the countries concerned, and strategies adopted for development. It is difficult to make traffic projections without having clear ideas about each of these factors. This paper will examine various scenarios up to the year 2000 before estimating traffic flows. Since the main object of the co-ordination exercise is fundamentally to change relations among the southern African economies, it is clear that a mechanical extrapolation of existing traffic flow trends without constructing new scenarios for the future would be of limited value, except as a first and rough approximation.

Nevertheless, the situation in southern Africa is such that it is possible to make suggestions for rerouting without the aid of quantitative information. Some of the suggestions require only a certain amount of intuition and common sense. It is for instance obvious that if these countries are to increase trade with each other there must be some rail and road network connecting them. Many of the suggestions made in the following pages are of this kind, and designed to help set a framework for identifying areas in which co-ordination is likely to prove fruitful. At a later stage when definite action is to be taken, it will be essential to obtain more detailed figures and projections.

BASIC CONSIDERATIONS

Transport and communications is a key sector for the development of any country or region. Development entails a greater movement of goods and people for which an efficient system of transport and communications is essential. Greater structural complexity and higher levels of output both require and justify increased transport and communications facilities. This does not mean that the existence of an efficient network of transport and communications is a sufficient condition for development to take place. The contribution of transport and communications to development depends crucially on appropriate policies in other sectors as well, such as agriculture, industry and mining. The existence of an adequate and efficient transport and communications network can facilitate development only if it is combined with strategies and policies for the development of the economy as a whole.

The strategic importance of this sector lies in the adverse impact on development of inadequate or expensive transport and communications facilities. For instance, in a situation where one has to travel long distances in order to effect a transaction instead of making a telephone call, development is bound to be slow and the cost of production very high. Canada and Australia are often cited as countries whose development is partly attributable to efficient systems of transport and communications. Similarly in Botswana, cattle marketed to cattle herd ratios are closely related to the very different availabilities and costs of transport in different parts of the country.

Transport and communications services also satisfy a final consumer demand, and are therefore directly related to welfare. For instance, taking a pleasure ride on a train or telephoning a relative are events related to the satisfaction of final demand and the standard of living. This aspect of transport and communications tends to be overlooked because planners are more preoccupied with bottlenecks in the production process attributable to inadequate means of transportation and communication. It is also the kind of demand more easily suppressed in times of difficulties because it is usually exercised by individuals and the cost of not satisfying it falls on the same individuals. In the absence of telephone services, many individuals may have to travel long distances to get up-to-date news about their relatives, and thus waste time and money to achieve what they could have accomplished at a lower cost.

In the case of most southern African countries the fact that communication between the various countries, by air and telephone, is through RSA, limits the ability of the general public to take advantage of these services, and accordingly detracts from the sum total of their welfare. Further, it limits the closeness of official and personal contact which is critical to building up the levels of trust and mutual understanding needed for the steady development of regional co-ordination and for effective waging of the southern African liberation struggle.

The transport and communications network of southern Africa was designed to integrate these countries with the metropolitan countries and with RSA rather than with one another. Thereby it facilitated external economic integration and national as well as regional economic fragment-ation and hindered the growth of southern African regionalism. By facilitat-ing contact between people with various cultures, beliefs and history, transport and communications can foster the feeling of national and regional cohesion and understanding. Indeed modern administration, as we know it, would be difficult without adequate means of transport and communica-tions. The development of this sector is therefore crucial for the promotion of nationhood as well as regional co-operation in this part of the continent.

COSTS, BENEFITS, FORWARD PLANNING

By and large, transport and communications services are public goods and as the initial investment of providing these services is usually high in relation to operating costs, it is usually governments which can afford to mobilize the large sums of money involved in such ventures. In term of international relations this makes this sector suitable for development through official assistance to the developing countries of southern Africa. It also raises critical questions regarding pricing and management of these services in order to attain the broader objectives of development.

Transport and communications projects take a long time to be completed, and they render services over a very long period. Long term planning is therefore essential to ensure that inadequacy of these services does not retard development. In particular, transport and communications services must in many cases be developed in anticipation of demand, taking into account the long term perspective of the economy or region concerned. It is for this reason that an attempt is made later in this paper to examine the pattern of demand for transport and communications in southern Africa up to the year 2000.

NATIONAL AND USER COST CONSIDERATIONS

The operation of the transport and communications sector is also characterized by external economies and diseconomies. Improvement of transport and communications services may reduce the price of certain commodities—in some cases literally make their availability of production in certain areas possible where it was not before—and thus confer advantages to consumers and producers. This was amply demonstrated in the nineteenth century with the development of sea transport between Europe and the Americas as well as rail transport in USA and Canada. This development made it possible to provide food at lower prices to many countries of Europe and indeed boosted trade between the two groups of countries.

On the other hand the provisions of transport and communications services can result in serious external diseconomies unless carefully planned. Recent spills of oil from oil tankers with the consequent adverse impacts on fish and scenery are only some of the glaring examples of these external diseconomies. But it is well known that the siting of airports and the operation of diesel vehicles create diseconomies which do not enter into the balance sheets of the operating enterprises but are borne by the general public. This is an important consideration in the planning, management and control of transport and communications services.

This then raises the question of cost of transport and communications to the user and the society as a whole. The cheapest means of transport to the user of the service need not be the one that is cheapest to the society. It is traditional for railway officials to claim that road transport is unfairly competitive with the railway network because road transporters do not meet the full cost of constructing and maintaining roads, whereas the railway authorities are forced to meet these costs in respect of rails and railway stations. How valid this argument is depends on whether fuel and vehicle taxes plus licence fees do or do not cover recurrent spending on roads, locally procured capital spending and debt service on externally funded highways. The carrying out of road revenue/cost analyses might be a useful first step in determining to what extent the state is subsidizing one mode of transport and, if so, which. (E.g. in Swaziland it is probably rail, not road which is subsidized.) However the important point to note is that where alternative means of transport and communication exist, and state subsidies on or revenues from different modes are similar, the cheapest means of transport can only be decided by the user of transport. The user of transport and communications will take into account not only the tariff of each mode in deciding which service to use but will consider such factors as terminal costs, e.g. godown to airport and airport to godown costs, the time element especially in case of perishable commodities, ability and willingness of his customers to pay for increased speed, decreased spoilage etc. In terms of cost it may be more expensive to telephone somebody than to send a telegram or write a letter, yet the circumstances of the situation may be such that one is prepared to incur the higher cost involved and that may in fact represent the cheapest means of communication at that particular moment of time.

The existence of various modes of transport and communications offers an opportunity to the user of these services to choose the cheapest mode given the circumstances in which he finds himself. The mere fact that the tariff per ton-mile of one mode of transport or communication is lower than another does not render such a mode the cheapest to the user under all circumstances. At the same time planning of this sector must aim at minimizing the external diseconomies to the society.

It is useful to recapitulate some of the major theoretical considerations relating to the transport and communications sector. So many fuzzy recommendations have emanated from technical and journalistic circles that it is necessary to outline the conceptual framework relating to this subject. It is often assumed, often without adequate justification, that railway transport is cheaper than other modes of transport. This position is usually based on the tariff per ton-mile charged by the railway compared to those set by road or air transporters. This of course overlooks the important point that the tariff is just one of the considerations a user takes into account in deciding on the mode of transport to use. The user is also concerned about terminal costs, reliability and speed of delivery, safety in transit etc. It is therefore important to bear these points in mind when planning the provision of transport and communications services in a country or region. On the other hand many technical studies begin from an equally fallacious general assumption that road transport is always less expensive. It is necessary to identify the makeup of traffic, average length of journey and tonnage on a route and the revenue/cost impact on the general government budget to determine the true low cost of most transport.

EXISTING TRANSPORT SYSTEM

The transport and communications sector in southern Africa is oriented towards RSA and is also designed to integrate the countries of southern

81

Africa into the economies of the developed countries. This is a feature commonly found in developing countries where the former colonial powers laid more emphasis on improving communications with the mother country and less on promoting national or regional integration. For instance, the railway system of the southern African countries was geared to the exploitation of mineral deposits for export to the outside world and the importation of consumer and producer goods from the developed countries—including, in this region, RSA. This mainly explains the existence of economic enclaves in southern Africa which have stronger linkages with developed countries and with RSA and less with the rest of the economies of the region.

RAILWAYS

For clear reasons the railway system is historically the most highly developed mode of transport. This group of countries produces a variety of minerals whose transport to the sea is better effected by rail and is also characterized by long hauls of bulk agricultural commodities, another area in which rail tends to be cheaper than road. The critical immediate importance of the Tazara railway to Zambia is that it makes it easier for that country to transport her copper and import essential goods such as fertilizers, rather than that the railway promotes trade today between Zambia and Tanzania. One cannot lose sight of the limited current capacity of Tanzania to export to Zambia, and vice versa. However, in the context of collective selfreliance the future development of transport and communications infrastructure in this region should be undertaken against the background of promoting trade and other contacts between the countries concerned. After all, the lopsided development of this sector and its orientation to RSA is due to the ability of RSA to supply goods to these countries, not simply because it produces them but also because it has the routes to deliver them. The reorientation of transport and communications services must therefore be seen in the wider context of increasing production and trade between the countries of the region to meet local needs.

Transport within the region faces critical problems. These centre on the need to improve the effectiveness of southern African routes to Zambia and of transport within Zambia. The causes of the deterioration of service are multiple and largely caused by external factors. The result is increasing Zambian dependence on the goodwill of RSA, a result which is deeply damaging not just to Zambia but to the whole southern African liberation struggle. It is not useful to assign blame as opposed to identifying bottlenecks—whether in cargo handling at Dar es Salaam, track maintenance and wagon unloading in Zambia or godown facilities at Beira. What is needed is co-ordinated action to overcome them. Until Zambia receives regional and external assistance to increase its personnel, maintenance, godown and clearing and forwarding capacity and to augment or repair its rolling stock, no amount of argument will make it possible for her to disengage more fully from RSA routes. This is desirable for economic as well as political reasons, as it is normally expensive, both in terms of direct cost and time, for Zambia to import or export goods via RSA. Similarly, Botswana's logical routes to the sea are via Namibia and Zimbabwe/ Mozambique not RSA, but an independent Namibia and co-ordinated action to build the Trans-Kalahari are necessary to make action based on that logic possible.

The core of RSA's railway system is a set of lines linking Cape Town-Durban-Johannesburg. Major external links run to Walvis Bay, Maputo, Gaborone and Bulawayo. Secondary external links exist to Matsapha and Maseru. Zambia is reached via Zimbabwe.

The glaring gap in the southern African main line railway net is that from Zimbabwe through Botswana to Namibia. On paper the rest of the main lines exist. The rebel regime in pre-independent Zimbabwe limited Zambian and Botswanan regional transport choices. They are still constrained. The Benguela Railway, following RSA's invasion of Angola and continued support of insurrection there, cannot be used. Further, many of the lines have suffered from overcapacity use, the desertion of expatriate staff before citizens could be trained, the general financial constraints imposed by the external economic crises facing most of the regions' members since 1974 and the sustained transport destruction raids into Zambia and Angola in late 1979.

The railway system has been of tremendous value to the exploitation of the natural resources of the region, mainly minerals. These bulky, long haul commodities are suitable for rail transport. Indeed, for the landlocked countries of the region, further exploitation of their natural resources will very much depend on selective extension to and upgrading of the railway network.

HIGHWAYS AND ROADS

Outside RSA the road network in southern Africa is very unsatisfactory. This is a matter of great concern. Road transport not only supplements other modes of transport, but is also crucial if efforts to increase domestic production, both in agriculture and industry, are to succeed. In order to change the existing patterns of production by promoting industrialization and selfreliance in the production of food, improvement of the rural road network must be accorded high priority. An important highway linking southern and eastern Africa is that running from Zambia to Kenya through Tanzania. After the imposition of economic sanctions against the UDI regime this road was Zambia's major surface link to the outside world.

The Economic Commission for Africa is busy encouraging the construction of three Trans-Africa highways. One would link Mombasa with Lagos; a second is to run from Tripoli to Windhoek; the third will run from Gaborone to Khartoum and on to Cairo. The 1980s have been declared by the United Nations General Assembly as a Transport and Communications

Decade for Africa. The countries of southern Africa, especially Botswana, Namibia, Zimbabwe and Zambia stand to gain from such ventures provided effective co-ordination of road user rules (including weight limits and licensing) and of transit traffic regulations can be achieved. However, the immediate need is to build those sections of these routes which are urgent for national and regional development over the next decade e.g. Ruacana-Moçâmedes, Gaborone-Livingstone and Mtwara-Mozambique rather than to view the long term through-routes as modern variants of Cecil Rhodes' Cape-to-Cairo rail dreams.

AIRWAYS

It has already been pointed out that for several of the countries of southern Africa, air transportation is often effected between them via RSA. This is a most unsatisfactory state of affairs, for the countries concerned and for the travelling public, and is a constant reminder to these countries of their heavy dependence on RSA. The underlying problem facing these countries is the lack of infrastructure. Most of the airports are not equipped to receive large jets. Passengers on international flights have to make connections in RSA and change to smaller aircraft. But this does not explain why small aircraft cannot be used to provide better interstate service among these countries. Mozambique and Zambia appear to have effective international airlines (DETA and Zambia Airways respectively) with direct scheduled flights to European and regional points. Tanzania has a regional airline with links to several neighbours and to India and will presently fly to Europe. The smaller national airlines do link up with these larger networks. A co-ordinated system of scheduling and transfer could be devised by the national airlines for passengers, mail and air freight with considerable gains in airline revenues, passenger convenience and reduction of dependence on RSA.

Moreover, in the field of air transport and communication considerable cost reductions can be effected by substituting direct flights among independent states for indirect ones. This particularly applies to the countries surrounding RSA such as Swaziland, Lesotho and Botswana.

PORTS AND HARBOURS

Only four of the Ten countries, Angola, Mozambique, Namibia and Tanzania, have direct access to the sea. Mozambique is in a good position to serve five landlocked countries (Zambia, Zimbabwe, Malawi, Botswana and Swaziland). More traffic through the ports of Beira and Maputo will require major expansion at Beira. In addition, expanding the port of Nacala would be critical for Malawi traffic. Tanzania's main port of Dar es Salaam caters for Tanzania and Zambia and for Rwanda, Burundi, Zaire and to a lesser degree Uganda. Once Angola recovers from the RSA invasion and its continued support for insurrection, Angola's Benguela Railway can be expected to resume its historic role in providing a major external trade route for Zambia and Zaire and in giving Angola effective access to the other states of the region.

Namibia should become an important provider of external transport links to Zimbabwe and Botswana. This, however, depends on the liberation of Namibia (including its main port and second city, Walvis Bay) and the construction of a heavy duty line from Windhoek to Selebi Pikwe. This line could also serve to link Namibia to the region—thereby giving it access to Botswanan coal to replace coal from RSA in its mineral smelting, and it would also make practicable the development of Botswana's western copper prospects, Okavango delta irrigated agricultural potential, Sua Pan soda ash and 1,000 million tonne coal reserves near Marapa in the eastern part of the country.

TELECOMMUNICATIONS

Telecommunications services in southern Africa are far from fully developed and are characterized by (a) their dependence on the telecommunications network of RSA and (b) their strong orientation to the urban centres. In the countries bordering on RSA international telephone calls and telexes are routed through it. The inadequate internal services that exist are concentrated in the urban sector, with the rural areas being poorly served. The immediate task facing these countries, therefore, is not merely to reduce their dependence on RSA in this subsector but also to expand the telecommunications network to the rural areas. Earth satellite stations to allow direct links abroad—via Intelsat—are a priority for those countries not now having them. Cost, including shares and training, is in the $3–4 million range. Even in a country as small as Swaziland traffic and revenue estimates suggest they would be surplus generating. Regionally there is need to co-ordinate direction of stations to allow direct or indirect communication among the countries' stations.

In this regard the complementarity between the various modes of communications should be underlined. A good system of telecommunications can, to a certain extent, compensate for poor means of communication by other modes. In practice there is a tendency for planners to concentrate resources devoted to transport and communications along particular routes leaving other areas without good roads, railway or telephone services. This must be one of the factors leading to polarized development with a few areas having all the facilities while others have none; it is usually those areas which are inaccessible by road during the rainy season which also do not have reliable telephone services or all weather air strips. In a situation where resources are particularly scarce and the need exists to integrate all parts of the country into the mainstream of development, an equitable distribution of transport and communications facilities must be attempted in the context of overall development planning.

85

The outstanding characteristic of transport and communications in southern Africa is the inadequacy of these services. For instance, the length of rail per 1,000 square kilometres of territory in this region is too low to meet the development needs of the area. This length per 100 km^2 ranges from zero for Lesotho to 6.8 km for Zimbabwe. [1] The corresponding figure for RSA is 16 km and for developed countries 60 km even though they have in addition alternative and better means of transport and communication. Admittedly, southern Africa is better provided with rail transport than most of Africa but this infrastructure consists mainly of single track lines of limited capacity built with the primary objective of exploiting the mineral potential of the region. Accordingly, the railway usually traverses large undeveloped areas with little impact on the intermediate territory, partly because of a lack of feeder road or rail connections to serve a comprehensive long term development strategy. This tends to raise the cost of transport. Given the market structures for exports and imports, these costs are borne by domestic producers in the case of exports and by the local consumers of imports. The producers of export commodities cannot realistically expect to influence the world prices of their products on account of transport cost considerations; still less can consumers bargain successfully for transport costs to be partly met by the exporters in the developed countries.

In some instances the geographical structure of the country is largely responsible for the high cost of transport. This is particularly so in the case of Tanzania and Zambia, many of whose transport routes go through areas with low production potential thus increasing the cost of transport since very little traffic is picked up in those areas. However, in Tanzania, development in the Kilombero Valley and Southern Highlands and the creation of a southern metallurgical and heavy industry complex over the next two decades would radically alter Tazara traffic patterns and reduce real unit costs sharply.

This underscores the need for overall development planning geared to the utilization of each country's production potential, and designed to achieve a network of interlinked modes of transport which would increase the flow of traffic and hopefully reduce the unit cost of transport. Transport may well be the starting point for economic co-ordination in southern Africa. To be a springboard to structural change, transport co-ordination must not merely serve present trade and production but be directly linked with new production and trade co-ordination efforts. It is necessary to co-operate with other countries in the region to utilize to the full the transport facilities available and, so far as possible, maximize complementarity between the various modes of transport and communications. Political will is needed to bring about meaningful co-operation if transport and communications facilities are to be used to the optimum in the interests of the region. This is a good moment to begin this greater co-operation. Zimbabwe will again want to use the rail route leading to Beira in Mozambique as it is the shortest surface link to the sea. This will allow gradual reversal of the diversion of traffic to RSA routes started during the UDI period. Without political will among the ten countries, unutilized facilities may well exist alongside an acute shortage of transport capacity and heavier dependence on RSA routes, as is the case today with Botswana, Zimbabwe and Zambia. Because it was impossible to maintain the rail system adequately during the UDI period (for over a decade) and Zimbabwe may face departure of many key personnel, the revival of the Zimbabwe rail system is not just a national but a regional priority.

Special attention must be made of the problem Lesotho and to a lesser extent Botswana and Swaziland are likely to face with increased isolation of RSA. Lesotho is completely surrounded by RSA, while the other two countries are heavily dependent on its transport system, although they have alternative routes. These countries have little option but to deal with RSA while at the same time participating in a programme of co-operation with the surrounding countries to reduce their dependence. This is not an easy task; the possibility that RSA would take retaliatory action against these countries cannot be ruled out.

RAILWAYS

In order to provide an additional outlet for Botswana it is proposed that a line be constructed to link with the Namibian system. This will enable Botswana to exploit her mineral and agricultural resources more fully and to use the nearest deep water port for external trade. It will also connect Namibia to the main railway network of the region and give access to Botswanan coal. Zimbabwe would also benefit from access to the Atlantic. A spur line linking with the Zambia–Angola–Eastern Zaire–Tanzania system at Livingstone might also be desirable.

To deal with increased traffic on the Ngwenye to Maputo line (Swaziland to Mozambique) the capacity of this single track line may need to be increased. This line constitutes Swaziland's main access to the sea. Improved service could reduce the dependence of Swaziland on the RSA railway system, to which an extension was connected last year by linking Phuzumoya on the Ngwenye line to Gollel in RSA.

Consideration could be given to extending the Zambia section of the Tazara railway to Nacala in Mozambique by building a 200 mile track in Zambia to its border with Malawi. Zambia would then be able to make greater use of the port of Nacala following completion of the line under construction from Salima in Malawi to the Zambian border. It will also give Malawi better access to Zambia and Tanzania.

The line from Tanga in Tanzania should be extended to Musoma on Lake Victoria linked by rail ferry to Uganda and Bukoba (for traffic to Rwanda). The main direct impact would be on Uganda–Rwanda–Burundi traffic, but by increasing the usability of Tanga this line would lessen pressure on facilities at Dar es Salaam to the benefit of Zambia and Zaire as well as Tanzania.

ROAD TRANSPORT

Because of its flexibility, road transport is more suited to many aspects of national and regional economic integration than rail transport. Roads also supplement the other modes of transport by providing feeder services to them. For example, air cargo traffic depends on reliable roads penetrating the countryside to collect exportable commodities and to distribute those imported by air.

Unfortunately roads in southern Africa are in a very bad state. Main trunk roads are usually of a higher standard but in many cases they run more or less parallel to the railway. While this means that such roads offer an alternative to railway transport for long haul traffic, it has to be remembered that the integrative effect of road transport can be better realized through a well co-ordinated road system, related to other modes of transport. In this sense the development of feeder roads must receive priority if development is to spread beyond areas through which the main roads and railways pass.

A main focus of road development programmes should be the promotion of trade among the 10 southern African countries with links to the other neighbouring independent states. There should therefore be at least one road link with each neighbouring country, especially where no railway connection exists at present. This is one of the objectives of the Trans-African Highway network initiated by ECA. Botswana lies at one end of the Cairo–Gaborone Highway. On this particular highway two sections still to be completed are found in southern Africa.[2] These are:

(a) Tanzania: Makuyuini to Dodoma   350 km
(b) Zambia: Zimba to Livingstone   76 km

It will also be necessary to construct a bridge at Kazungula on the Zambia–Botswana border to complete the route. The bridge alone is a regional priority to provide a dependable link removing the bottleneck in the Botswana–Zambia road link.

AIR TRANSPORT

Air transport will play a critical role in the economic and social development of those countries of southern Africa which are landlocked, especially Lesotho which is completely surrounded by RSA. For this reason it is urgent for Lesotho to build up a network of direct flights with Botswana, Zimbabwe and Zambia and to sustain the new services to Maputo and Matsapha in order to replace the present routes through RSA airports. While Maseru is most unlikely to attract many intercontinental flights, a situation can be envisaged whereby traffic originating from overseas destined for Lesotho and vice versa would transit through Lusaka, Salisbury or Maputo transferring there to a smaller regional flight.

In the case of Swaziland, a number of air links with her neighbours have been developed albeit not, to date, with Botswana or Tanzania. One obstacle which Swaziland and the other countries bordering RSA still face is that air connections with countries further north in Africa and in Europe are routed through Johannesburg. One way of dealing with this would be to increase the frequency of flights from Salisbury to Lusaka and Maputo to countries further south to cater for transit passengers from Europe and East Africa. Another would be to institute a service between Botswana, Swaziland, Lesotho—following completion of its new airport—Dar es Salaam and Nairobi.

It will be easy, by using present traffic figures, to argue that the volume of transit traffic through Lusaka, Dar es Salaam or Maputo is unlikely to attract international airlines to land at these points instead of Johannesburg. However a good deal of transit traffic is routed through Johannesburg for lack of other transit facilities to Gaborone, Maseru or Matsapha. Regular flights between these cities and Maputo, Dar es Salaam and Salisbury would boost international traffic to Lusaka.

Joint airlines pose a number of problems and may not be desirable ventures to attempt during the early stages of regional co-ordination. But even if joint airlines are not contemplated, co-ordination among national airlines can be developed through pooling of traffic, equipment, training and repair facilities, granting of liberal traffic rights to each other, meshing of regional service schedules and possibly sharing of intercontinental services. This would mark an important development in the process of economic integration of southern Africa.

It is worth emphasizing that without co-ordination the region is likely to be saddled with surplus capacity for air transportation while at the same time demand for these services goes unsatisfied. Aircraft can fly half full while passengers and freight are stranded at airports because of traffic rights problems. This is an area in which the African Association of African Airlines (AFRAA) and the regional office of the International Civil Aviation Organization (ICAO) as well as UNDP can play an important role in promoting co-operation and offering technical assistance.

SHIPPING

Kenya, Uganda, Tanzania and Zambia own and operate the Eastern Africa National Shipping Line. Other countries in southern Africa could become partners in this venture to reduce dependence on foreign shipping companies to transport their goods. In terms of regional co-ordination coastal shipping could play a significant role, possibly with one line to serve the Walvis Bay–Dakar range and another for Maputo–Alexandre plus a more limited inter ocean link. Such trade would be greatly facilitated by improvement and expansion of a number of ports on the eastern and western coast including Tanga, Nacala, Lobito and Luderitz.

Apart from the development of existing physical infrastructure, there is an urgent need to improve the efficiency of port operation. The key obstacle to improvement is the scarcity of citizen managers, foremen, artisans and pilots. In several specialized fields co-ordinated development of training facilities and of programmes geared to students from several countries could speed loosening of the manpower bottleneck.

TELECOMMUNICATIONS

Three main problems confront the countries of southern Africa in the field of telecommunications. The first is the inadequate availability of equipment and physical facilities for telecommunication. This reflects the low levels of overall investment and also the low level of effective demand. The second is the huge gaps in the networks both to rural areas nationally and to other southern African countries regionally. The third is the routing of several external links via RSA.

The countries of southern Africa can reduce their dependence on RSA if they agree to share the services of expensive equipment such as microwave and satellite stations. There are already plans to improve telecommunications services between a number of southern African countries such as Botswana and Zambia (Francistown to Livingstone), Tanzania to Malawi and Zambia to Malawi, while Swaziland has plans to reroute some of its external traffic via Maputo. The Pan African Telecommunications project (PANFTEL) could provide assistance to these and similar ventures in collaboration with the International Telecommunication Union. In telecommunications as in ports—and indeed transport in general—upgrading of serving personnel and training of new citizen personnel could be expanded and hastened by regional co-ordination of programmes and exchange of students.

TRANSPORT: KEY TO REGIONAL CO-ORDINATION

Transport and communications are critical to the achievement of development co-ordination in southern Africa for four reasons:

1. Without them the landlocked states, and especially Zambia, will be unable to sustain their present levels of support for the liberation struggle much less to increase them and to set in motion a steady reduction of links with RSA;

2. However future structural changes affect extraregional trade, today such trade is vital to every economy in the region and consequently so are improvements in service and reduction of costs;

3. Clear possibilities exist for reduction of dependence on RSA and

building of regional interaction and many could be utilized fairly soon and with economic gains as well as economic dependence reduction and political gains;

4. Mutual interests in cost reduction, revenue generation for coastal states and making possible development of isolated areas are clearly perceived by southern Africans and therefore one major precondition for co-ordination programmes is met more clearly than in some other sectors;

Initially, the trade creation and production co-ordination impact may be low. However without better transport links—which are in the short run fully economically justified by external trade and national development considerations—it will always be 'too hard' to build up trade, 'too soon' to embark on selective production co-ordination, 'too difficult' to identify other complementarities. If people cannot communicate easily and cheaply, nor goods move rapidly, smoothly and at reasonable cost, economic co-ordination will be very hard indeed to develop.

This sector, like others, offers a wide diversity of projects and programmes in which co-ordination among two or more regional states could be fruitful. Some, e.g. the Trans-Kalahari, are both massive in terms of costs and gains and would require up to a decade to complete. Others such as a regional working group to identify the problems limiting the efficiency of transport to, from and in Zambia and to propose co-ordinated regional action (including joint approaches to external sources) to overcome them, are no less broadly critical but could be implemented more speedily. Yet others, for example, co-ordination of training and building up Lesotho's and Swaziland's air links to other states in the region are not, taken individually, of major significance but are immediately practicable at low cost, would provide quick evidence that co-ordination can both reduce economic dependence and provide short term economic gains and, collectively, could help build a network of multistate and regional programmes to create a dynamic toward fuller economic co-ordination in southern Africa.

NOTES

1. *Transport and Communications Decade in Africa (1978–88)*, UNECA (E/CN.14/ECO/138 and E/CN.14/TRANS/136, p. 38).
2. *Op. cit.*

Financial Institutions and Mechanisms

INTRODUCTION

The object of this paper is to suggest ways in which the southern African states could co-operate more closely on financial and monetary matters. What follows is deliberately tentative and exploratory. Also, the availability of data for some countries leaves much to be desired. This is, therefore, a sketch of the main issues and a series of proposals for further investigation. This can serve as a useful beginning to be built upon by those closer to and more directly involved in southern African financial and monetary affairs.

DEGREES OF ECONOMIC CO-OPERATION AND THEIR IMPLICATIONS

The most complete form of economic co-operation is a common market in which all trade barriers between the ten states would be removed as would all restrictions on factor mobility. The implication of this is that national fiscal policies would need to be very closely harmonized to prevent intraregional flows of goods or factors in response to fiscal discrepancies. This degree of harmonization is not required in a customs union or free trade area in which trade between members is unimpeded by tariffs, quotas, etc., but capital and labour movements are subject to control. The basic requirement of this degree of co-operation is the absence of inter-member state restrictions on trade and the presence of a common external tariff.

The first main problem with common markets or customs unions is the growth of regional inequalities, i.e. regional distribution of benefits and costs of co-operation. Unless mechanisms can be developed to offset differential gains and losses there will, inevitably, be pressures created in the less well off countries to opt out of the agreement and to seek an alternative status that will improve their position. A basic requirement, therefore, for this degree of co-operation is political, that the participating states be prepared to forego a degree of autonomy in decision-taking for the common good of all partner states, and that the political will exists on the part of states who benefit most from the union to develop mechanisms to transfer part of their benefits to the not-so-fortunate countries.

The second problem is that a standard common market is based on a free trade/market controlled outlook not on a planned/interventionist approach. Either an absence of national planning of any seriousness or a high degree of joint regional planning (including a common determination of taxation, credit and investment policy) would appear to be required to reconcile a laissez-faire common market and national development strategy.

These are also very demanding political requirements which are very often unattainable or undesirable.

Even less ambitious degrees of co-operation, such as those of joint infrastructure projects or of industry agreements, raise essentially the same distributional issues. Being less all-embracing and more specific it is possible that these difficulties can be resolved more easily than would be the case if co-operation were more extensive. This is consistent with the arguments of the chapter on 'Instruments, Institutions and Instrumentalities' that a middle road between full integration and completely ad hoc bilateralism is required. [1] This approach envisages a limited degree of co-operation focussing on a number of key sectors backed by a small centrally located planning and financing capability. The initial commitment to co-operation would therefore be limited in terms both of resources and of loss of national autonomy in policy making. Over time, as the planning efforts bore fruit, more extensive linkages could develop, building on and contributing to greater commitment to the idea of integration.

EXISTING INSTITUTIONAL ARRANGEMENTS

Historically the monetary systems of Angola and Mozambique were integrated into those of Portugal. To a large extent they still reflect Portuguese law and practice. The other states have systems based historically on British banking practice but with ties to three quite distinct regions of monetary co-operation: Tanzania to the East Africa currency area centred on Nairobi; Zimbabwe, Zambia and Malawi to the Central African monetary area centred on Salisbury (up to independence a satellite of the South African area), and the remaining states to the South African currency area centred on Johannesburg/Pretoria.

Today the ten states have differing monetary systems reflecting their actual or aspiring degree of economic independence, and their commitment to state intervention in the economy. The banking and credit institutions of Tanzania, Mozambique and Angola are essentially state owned. Those of Zambia are partly state owned and partly private while those of Zimbabwe, Malawi, Lesotho, Swaziland, Botswana and Namibia are dominantly privately owned.

Zambia, Tanzania, Angola, Mozambique, Zimbabwe, Botswana, and Malawi have their own separate currencies while Namibia, Lesotho and Swaziland are members of the Republic of South Africa's Rand Monetary Area. Swaziland has its own currency, the lilangeni, and Lesotho now has the loti; both are backed 100 per cent by the rand and both currencies circulate. Namibia to date does not have a separate currency.

Tanzania, Zambia and Malawi maintain the value of their currencies externally against the Special Drawing Right (SDR) of the International Monetary Fund. All countries operate, however, on the basis of fixed exchange rates supported by monetary reserves. Changes in these rates have occurred fairly frequently since 1970 but the currencies of Zambia, Tanzania and Malawi have remained within 12 per cent of each other relative to 1970 values—except in 1974 when the Zambian kwacha appreciated significantly relative to the other currencies. (See Table below.) The increasing spread between the rand and other African currencies since 1976 reflect the devaluation of the dollar relative to the SDR.

Relative Value of Selected African Currencies in SDR's 1970–78.
1970 = 100

	1970	1971	1972	1973	1974	1975	1976	1977	1978
Zambia	100	92.1	92.0	92.0	90.7	94.8	77.5	69.7	69.7
Tanzania	100	92.1	92.1	85.8	81.7	73.9	73.9	73.9	73.9
Malawi	100	99.8	89.8	81.5	81.0	79.1	79.1	79.1	79.1
LS (Rand)	100	86.3	84.4	88.6	81.9	70.5	71.0	67.9	63.3
Botswana	100	86.3	84.4	88.6	81.9	74.0	74.5	71.3	66.5

Source: Derived from International Financial Statistics IFM, 1978–79.

Tanzania, Botswana, Lesotho, Malawi, Swaziland and Zambia are members of the International Monetary Fund and Zimbabwe proposes to join. Angola and Mozambique are not members.

Tanzania, Mozambique, Angola, Zambia, Zimbabwe and Malawi exercise fairly rigid exchange controls and the first three also practice strict import licensing procedures. Tanzania undertakes fairly detailed credit and foreign exchange planning and budgeting and, on a rather different model, so does Zambia. Mozambique and Angola have begun to institute planned allocation systems.

The members of the Rand Monetary Area practice freedom of current and capital payments within the area and have a uniform exchange control policy towards transactions with non-member states. Botswana is a member of the South African Customs Union but not of the Rand Monetary Area. It therefore reserves the right to pursue an independent exchange control policy towards neighbouring countries which are members of the RMA.

DEGREES OF MONETARY CO-OPERATION
AND THEIR IMPLICATIONS

Varying degrees of monetary co-operation are possible but there is no simple, direct relationship between these and the varying degrees of economic co-operation. For instance, a common market could be serviced by a single common currency or by separate national currencies. Exchange rates relative to the outside world could be fixed or flexible in either case. At the other extreme, complete monetary integration could be accompanied by only a modest degree of economic integration. The literature on the subject is divided on whether monetary integration should lead to or follow from economic integration.[2] The experience of the East African Common Market suggests it should follow or at least accompany economic integration and that the possibilities of using monetary integration to stimulate greater economic (or political) integration are severely limited.

COMMON CURRENCY

The most extreme form of monetary co-operation is that of a single common currency with pooled external reserves. Normally this presupposes a single central bank, but in the debates preceding the dissolution of the East African Currency Board, Erwin Blumenthal developed a proposal which combined a single central bank issuing a common currency with separate, but in many ways subordinate national central banks.[3] At the same time this was correctly dismissed as a high cost branch banking system and as a compromise loaded with potential for dispute.[4] It was a compromise because it sought to capture the benefits of a common currency while at the same time retaining a degree of national autonomy in matters of monetary policy. If, however, a common currency system is to be effective and stable it must necessarily entail a surrender of national autonomy in the area of monetary policy in order to ensure balance of payments equilibrium in the long run. Similar arguments apply to a lesser degree to fiscal policy. A common currency reduces the ability of any one member government to deficit finance its expenditures. The group as a whole would, however, retain that discretion and the problem would then be one of apportioning the proceeds of money supply expansion among member governments.

The benefits of a common currency are:

(a) Foreign trade between co-operating states becomes internalized so that the availability of foreign exchange of itself ceases to be a bottleneck to trade expansion. This is not to say that unequal income flows cannot arise or that aggregate demand cannot become grossly out of balance between co-operating states—just as it can among regions in one state. All it means is that there can be no foreign payments problem as such if domestic money is available for transactions between member states, except to the extent that intraregional trade flows stimulate imports from outside the region.

(b) External reserves are pooled providing each individual member state with access to a greater volume of reserves than its own contribution, i.e. pooled reserves hold out the possibility of one or more members deriving greater domestic stability than its/their foreign trade position would dictate if the common currency did not exist. This can be described as an insurance benefit.

The magnitude of these insurance benefits would depend very much upon the extent to which movements in the terms of trade of co-operating states offset rather than complement each other. In case of the four countries for which data was available—Malawi, Tanzania, Zambia and Zimbabwe—only a limited degree of offsetting took place between 1972 and 1976. If data were available for Angola and Namibia, which rely much less on non-mineral primary products, one would in theory expect a much greater degree of offsetting movements in the terms of trade and, therefore, greater benefits from reserve pooling than the chart indicates.

(c) There will be economies of scale to be derived from pooling reserves and administering a common currency, in the form of the need to hold fewer foreign balances, reduced management costs and commissions, possibly higher interest rates on foreign assets, reduced printing costs of currency, etc.

(d) Commercial calculations are made easier both within the area of the common currency and between that area and outside countries, thereby facilitating trade.

(e) Within the currency area possibilities would exist for various types of payments credits to be offered to both economic enterprises and to the states themselves. There is nothing inherent in common currency systems that necessitates immediate payment for goods or services or the immediate settlement of national common currency liabilities.

The implications of a common currency area are, as stated, that individual national members must sacrifice autonomy in certain policy areas if overall balance of payments equilibrium for the region is to be achieved. This could have far-reaching implications for unemployment and/or inflation resulting from trade or investment imbalances between member regions—problems that might otherwise have been dealt with by exchange rate adjustment between national currencies of member states, by tariffs or by exchange control. Given the realistic assumption of labour immobility, such intra-regional demand imbalance problems will be difficult to tackle.

Establishing a common currency requires highly developed political co-operation. Historically, this has been imposed by colonial authorities. With the coming of political independence monetary integration has tended to collapse rather than expand. The surviving joint central banks are still heavily French influenced by credit lines and personnel. In short, independent African countries have been reluctant to establish common currencies because of the autonomy costs entailed. There is little or no possibility that the southern African states could undertake this degree of monetary co-operation in the foreseeable future.

Several of the advantages of a common currency can, however, be achieved with a lower degree of co-operation in the form of a currency area. In this case individual national currencies are maintained but member states agree to peg the value of their individual exchange rates relative to other currencies in a fairly rigid, semi-permanent way. There is no common currency as such and no single central bank, but for the exchange rates to be held constant against non-member currencies domestic monetary and fiscal policies still need to be harmonized. In the East African case W. T. Newlyn suggested that such harmonization could be achieved by the creation of an East African Reserve Board.[5] This proposal was not accepted and instead, once separate central banks were established, co-ordination was achieved in East Africa, quite successfully for a decade, by quarterly meetings of the Finance Ministers and of the Governors.

In the East African case there was no pooling of reserves, although theoretically this could have been provided for. There were provisions for limited credit facilities, for exchange of currency notes at cost, and for freedom from exchange control barriers to current account transactions.[6]

Due to political differences between partner states and to structural inequalities (the metropolitan nature of Kenya vis-à-vis Uganda and Tanzania) the overall economic community, and therefore the currency area, collapsed. Given the very divergent ideological and political positions of the 10 states now seeking greater economic development, the lessons to be learned from the experience of the East African monetary arrangements are clear. A currency area is an unsuitable form of co-operation to aim for at this time.

CLEARING AND CREDIT ARRANGEMENTS

More modest degrees of monetary co-operation would seem to be needed. One possibility is the institution of a clearing arrangement for the settlement of net indebtedness among participating states. Such a mechanism would be crucial for any significant expansion in trade between them and could be located either in one of the existing central banks or else in the proposed Southern African Development Bank. The former location would be the simplest; the latter not much more costly nor more difficult to arrange and having the potential advantage of being tied into an intraregional credit system. Wherever located, the clearing unit would hold working balances in foreign currencies and would settle net indebtedness between countries by transferring balances from one national account to another.

A credit element could be built into the system quite easily. This could be effected by allowing net debtor states to delay settlement over a period of time, either on a regular short term basis, or on a seasonal basis. The former might require meeting previously agreed conditions with regard to the debtor nation's overall foreign reserve position and its balance of payments position with the partner state from which it borrows. The latter would require a careful analysis of seasonality in international and intraregional payments. The extent to which such 'foreign currency' credits are possible will depend upon the overall balance of payments position with the outside world of countries enjoying a creditor position within the region. If the creditor is experiencing balance of payment deficits with the outside world this will severely constrain the extent to which such foreign currency credits can be extended within the region of co-operation.

This type of credit need not simply be bilateral. Being in foreign currency form it could quite easily be extended to cover multilateral relationships, i.e. if A is indebted to B, and B to C, then C could extend credit to A. In effect the co-operating states would be undertaking a limited pooling of reserves but on a strictly temporary, repayable basis. The problem with such a system is in ensuring that credit actually revolves. This is particularly difficult if all, or almost all members face severe extraregional payments problems.

Other credit arrangements are possible. For instance co-operating states could agree to accept a limited amount of other national currencies in settlement of clearing debts. This would have the effect of expanding the foreign reserves of the co-operating states by the amount of the domestic currencies so exchanged. These balances could be used bilaterally or multilaterally as agreed. Since they represent, ultimately, national liabilities of debtor states they are in effect the equivalent of loans, albeit in inconvertible currency.

A variation of this latter theme was embodied in the Treaty for East African Co-operation whereby, under stringent conditions, countries experiencing balance of payments problems externally as well as with the partner state, could borrow from that partner state in the local currency of the lender. This was a highly restrictive form of inconvertible currency credit, and one which in practice was never utilized even though two states in fact could have done so.

It was restrictive in that credit arrangements were purely bilateral; borrowing countries had also to have serious problems on their external balance of payments (must have used their first credit tranche at the IMF) before they could use the credits; the allowable amount of credit was fixed in terms of the recent value of commodity trade rather than of total payments between partner states and the maximum amount of credit permitted was quite small and somewhat arbitrarily arrived at. Mark Segal has argued quite persuasively that the credit ceiling could have been rendered less arbitrary and more generous if it had been tied to the local value-added content of intraregional balance of payments transactions.[7] This would seem to be a reasonable rule of thumb for the southern African states to follow in planning any credits of this kind. However, given the special nature of transit transportation charges—and their large size relative to trade in goods—these would need to be treated separately in any credit arrangements.

In spite of the restrictive nature of the credit provisions of the Treaty for East African Co-operation, they do constitute a useful precedent for the introduction of medium term settlement credits in the larger regional grouping under consideration. Also, it could be argued that a sensible way to proceed in instituting such credit arrangements is to start conservatively, relaxing the restrictive nature of credits as economic integration itself becomes more advanced.

TRADE, PAYMENTS, CREDIT

Ultimately the desire and ability to engage in these types of credit arrangements will depend on the importance of intraregional trade and payments relative to extraragional trade and payments, and on the magnitude of extraregional transactions. While the relatively low degree of economic integration between the Ten implies that the scope for such credits is quite limited, it may also mean, ironically, that the principle of reciprocal credits could be built into a clearing arrangement with relatively little difficulty, since it would imply no immediate large scale call on the resources of surplus credit countries.

Consideration might also be given to the co-ordination of exchange control regulations and policies between the ten countries. Clearly, given the very divergent ideological and political positions of the states involved and their varying degrees of dependence on both private and foreign capital, it is highly unlikely that agreement could be reached on a common set of regulations and policies. Recognizing these differences, it would perhaps be inappropriate to seek such an agreement.

There would, nevertheless, be a great deal of value in the ten states co-operating closely on all matters relating to exchange control. Many problems, such as evasion, are common to all these countries but the administrative experiences in dealing with them differ greatly. The advantages of such co-operation would, of course, be greatest for newly liberated countries. These can be expected to have the most acute problems and the least experience in dealing with them. Also an expanded volume of intra-regional trade would predictably bring with it expanded opportunities for exporting capital illegally. An awareness of this likelihood and of the channels through which capital might flow under the guise of trade would be a necessary prerequisite for any co-operative action to deal with the problem. This would seem to be an area where joint staff training programmes might be developed to the benefit of all ten states.

More particularly a case can be made for preferential exchange control among participating states as an integral part of preferential trading. At the least, exchange and payments control should not be more favourable for intraregional than for regional transactions.

Close harmonization of monetary policies generally would be essential if exchange rates of co-operating states were to be fixed in fairly stable relationship to outside currencies, or if pooling of reserves were to take place on any significant scale. This would entail some agreement on rates of inflation and on rates of monetary expansion. Likewise, if capital were to flow relatively freely between partner states, then close co-ordination of interest rates and of exchange control regulations and policies would be required. In practice this degree of co-operation is not desired or possible at this stage.

Nevertheless, even limited programmes for economic co-operation in the fields of production and trade may require some harmonization of monetary policies. Thus the planned introduction of industries, power facilities, agricultural production or transport units catering for regional markets will have implications for national credit plans, for foreign exchange plans and for import licensing priorities (often administered by central banks and therefore classified here, somewhat loosely, under 'monetary policy').

Where such detailed plans do not exist, i.e. in the more private enterprise oriented economies, there will still be the need to ensure that the policies of the monetary authorities do not unwittingly impede co-operation in the production and trade spheres.

The creation of even limited credit facilities for interstate payments implies some constraints on the extent to which domestic monetary policies of borrowing states can be allowed to move out of line with those of 'creditor' partner states. The ability of the borrower to repay the credits will depend upon its ability to earn surpluses on its overall balance of payments and this, of course, is not unrelated to the rate of domestic monetary expansion. Thus some minimal degree of consultation and co-operation in general monetary policy is implied if the credit system is to work smoothly.

There will be a particular need to ensure that interstate trade is not impeded by inconsistencies, ambiguities or lack of reciprocity in the terms and conditions of documentary letters of credit, bills of exchange, collections etc. This will also require close co-operation and consultation among the southern African states.

COMMERCIAL BANK ASPECTS

Closer economic co-operation will require not only more contact between central banks but also a review of relationships between the respective commercial banking systems. At the very least this will require that the banks of each state hold nostro (foreign currency) balances with at least one bank in each of the other partner states. Such direct links already exist between Zambia, Tanzania and Mozambique but will probably need to be created between them and other states, especially with Zimbabwe and Namibia. Surpluses or deficits on these nostro accounts will be dealt with through the clearing mechanism discussed above and all day to day payments transactions will pass through these accounts.

100

It is of course possible for a credit element to be built into these accounts as well as, or instead of, in the central bank clearing accounts. Where both commercial and central banks are state owned the precise location of bilateral clearing credits is academic, but central bank clearing credits would facilitate the administration of multilateral credits. Where commercial banks are owned privately, foreign credits (overdrawn nostro balances) would normally require central bank approval, are not common and can be expected to be costly.

These working balances should be kept to a minimum and would need to be closely related to payment patterns. Initially their appropriate size would need to be established by trial and error and at this stage, temporary overdraft facilities would simplify the process.

Interstate trade could be encouraged by the extension of bank credit in exporting countries to individuals or institutions in importing countries. This could be achieved in the normal manner through export bills whether or not these are drawn under letters of credit. The net effect of this nationally is similar to that of the limited pooling of reserves or of the extension of credit through the clearing mechanism. The difference is that the credit worthiness can be ascertained. It is conceivable that state banking institutions could agree on a scheme whereby trade in certain specified strategic commodities intraregionally might be encouraged through favourable credit terms. Such a scheme could operate quite independently of any clearing credit agreements.

Finally, in terms of closer co-operation in the international banking sphere, the ten states might wish to consider establishing a jointly owned foreign bank with branches in Europe, North America and Japan. The benefits to be derived from such a move would take the form of reduced commissions on collections for export proceeds now paid to foreign banks, where such proceeds are not covered by a foreign letter of credit—in which case commissions go entirely to the issuing bank i.e. the foreign bank. Most export transactions with Europe are conducted under foreign issued letters of credit but a minority are not and the pooling of these collections might go a long way towards making a foreign bank pay. A second type of benefit is involved which is likely to be more decisive in the calculations. This concerns the pooling of commercial bank nostro balances in a number of banks in a given foreign centre. By establishing a joint bank it should be possible to pool the balances of the banks of the co-operating states and to locate them in one bank only, thereby economizing on them. The foreign exchange savings flowing from this would be equal to the difference between any interest now paid by foreign banks on these balances (at best an overnight rate but frequently nothing at all) and the average foreign rate that can be earned by central banks on the amount by which these reserves are economized.

The southern African states might wish, therefore, to pursue this idea further to determine whether or not the likely savings from commissions and interest on balances would offset the likely capital and operating cost of establishing such a foreign presence.

A SOUTHERN AFRICAN DEVELOPMENT BANK

It has been suggested by other consultants that a Southern African Development Bank would be a useful financial institution to facilitate co-operation in the region and that it might be created by extending the membership of the existing East African Development Bank.

Such a bank would be desirable and might be an acceptable proposition to the southern African states provided its role and operating principles are laid out clearly and are not overly ambitious. It would be consistent with the maximum degree of economic co-operation envisaged as initially feasible in the first section of this paper and would help stimulate that co-operation. Such a bank might initially draw in part on the staff, procedures and charter of the East African Development Bank. Simply enlarging the membership of the EADB may not however be the best way to proceed. First of all neither Kenya nor Uganda are southern African and while Uganda might now wish to be included in future discussions concerning closer co-operation in southern Africa, Kenya might well have different views. The absence of Kenya, for whatever reason, would rule out creating a Southern African Development Bank by merely expanding the EADB.

Second, while the charter of the EADB would provide an excellent starting point it would, even as amended to allow for new members, undoubtedly need some adjustment in terms of objectives, capital funding and operating principles. The objectives of the EADB are at once too narrow and in other respects too broad for the proposed Southern African Development Bank.[8] They are limited to financing 'industrial development' and although this term is defined broadly to include processing in the agriculture, fishing and forestry industries it specifically excludes the building and transport industries and appears to exclude pure farming ventures, all three of which are crucial to the first stage of southern African integration. It also excludes tourism but this is unlikely to be a priority area of co-operation. Transport and communications are central to southern African development co-ordination and are likely to be the main early users of jointly raised finance.

At the same time the objectives of the EADB appear to be in other respects somewhat broader than those envisaged for a Southern African Development Bank. Thus the first two functions of the EADB are to promote industrial development of the partner states and to reduce industrial imbalances between these states by giving priority to the relatively less industrially developed states.[9] Only the third function stresses the desire to increase economic co-operation by making the economies more complementary. This ordering of priorities reflects the historical fact that the EADB was set up partially to help rectify imbalances that had developed between partner states as a direct result of a high degree of economic co-operation over a long number of years. A Southern African Development Bank, on the other hand, seems to be justified largely as a mechanism for initiating broader economic co-operation. It is seen primarily as an instrument to deal with industrial imbalance between the Ten and the outside world rather than as one to concentrate first on unequal levels of development within the ten states. This difference in emphasis will have profound implications for the operating principles of a Southern African Development Bank relative to those of the EADB.

The capital funding provisions of the charter of the EADB are satisfactory in general terms, providing for an authorized capital stock subscribed to by partner states in both local and convertible currency, for the raising of loans and guarantees from within and outside the partner states and for the management of special funds. But the authorized capital and the principles of subscriptions underlying it would need to be altered. Initially the EADB called for a capital of £20 million to be subscribed over a period of time in equal amounts by partner states. A Southern African Development Bank would need a much larger initial authorized capital of, perhaps, between $250 and $300 million. These figures are arrived at by expanding the original EADB authorized capital by an allowance for inflation in the price of investment goods since 1967 and by a factor reflecting the much higher total GDP of the ten states relative to that of the three East African partner states. This would be called up over a period of time as the Southern African Development Bank required funds and once more the EADB charter provides useful guidelines in this respect. How might this authorized capital be distributed among the ten contributing states? Here a major departure from the EADB charter[10] would be called for. Given the very unequal sizes of the countries in question and their uneven levels of development, equal subscriptions would be out of the question, for this would entail countries like Swaziland and Lesotho contributing the equivalent of over 10 per cent of their annual GDP, while Angola and Zimbabwe would contribute less than 1 per cent of their annual GDP. It might therefore be preferable to allocate subscriptions in proportion to domestic product or, perhaps more practically, domestic exports.

Since a Southern African Development Bank is not seen as being primarily a redistributive mechanism, contributing states would need to be guaranteed an investment by the bank equal, over a period of time, to the value of their capital contribution. And unlike the EADB,[11] a Southern African Development Bank should fund only those projects which contribute clearly and unambiguously to the economic integration of member states. Building greater equity within the region would, at best, be a secondary objective subject to these constraints and the extent to which it could be pursued would depend largely on the ability of the bank to raise additional funds from aid donors or from other foreign or regional sources, in addition to capital subscriptions. The bank might, for instance, be successful in raising special funds for this purpose in the manner of the Caribbean Development Bank.[12] These radical divergences from the present EADB charter would raise problems for using it as a foundation institution. However, as the EADB's charter has already been amended once to allow it to continue to operate, and could presumably be amended further, they may not be insuperable.

SOUTHERN AFRICAN DEVELOPMENT BANK FUNCTIONS: A PROPOSAL

In terms of functions the bank should be more than a financing vehicle. The bank should be the planning centre for southern African co-operation and apart from its normal banking, evaluation and review functions should have sections dealing with industrial, agricultural, infrastructural and financial integration. These sections would liaise with national planning bodies and could draw up five year integration plans for submission to policy making bodies. On approval of these plans bank personnel would be empowered to enter into negotiations with bilateral and multilateral donors for financial assistance to planned projects.

Each of these planning sections would also be responsible for drawing up suggested policy positions in their respective sectors for submission to the policy makers. The bank, if so organized, could serve as the planning, policy and secretariat centre for co-operation between the ten states.

A Southern African Development Bank should not seek to monopolize the flow of foreign aid for regional projects. If it does, it will assuredly fail and be destroyed by the strains caused by the attempt. Situations will arise where member states wish to arrange their own aid bilaterally for projects which fit into agreed plans for integration. It would never be desirable or politically feasible for the bank to attempt to interpose itself between the two parties to all aid transactions. Likewise, member states might wish to take advantage of African Development Bank/African Development Fund funding and to have funds channelled directly without the intermediation of the Southern African Development Bank. The essential point is not that the bank be the sole body through which aid for regional projects is channelled but that the projects receiving aid are consistent with approved plans and policies for integration. To the extent that the bank is successful in drawing up meaningful plans and in administering its own and others' funds efficiently, one can expect its intermediation function to assume more importance over time. It would serve no constructive purpose to seek to give the Southern African Development Bank a monopoly of aid administration from the outset.

Relationships between the ADB/ADF and a Southern African Development Bank should present no problems. The ADB has already signed agreements of co-operation with the OAU, the UNDP, UNESCO, FAO, ILO, and WHO and has worked closely with a number of national development corporations. It could be requested to assist the Southern

African Development Bank in terms of technical assistance and later a formal agreement of co-operation might be signed between the two bodies. Initially, however, informal co-operation would suffice and the ADB/ADF could decide on a project by project basis whether its funds should be channelled via the proposed bank or now go directly to the recipient state(s).

The Southern African Development Bank should have a board of directors with representatives drawn from each of the subscribing states. The board should meet at least quarterly in the offices of the bank.

The bank would have two main sections, one dealing with operations and one dealing with planning and policy. Each section would have its own director and both would be responsible to a managing director who would report to the board. Bank relationships with other bodies created to assist co-operation are dealt with in the last section of this paper.

A SOUTHERN AFRICA REINSURANCE ARRANGEMENT

Very little is known about reinsurance arrangements in most southern African countries but the likelihood is that the bulk of local risks in the fields of fire, marine and miscellaneous accident are reinsured in Europe and to a lesser extent in the Republic of South Africa. One can expect between a half and three quarters of local premiums to be remitted overseas for reinsurance purposes. The total amount involved for the ten countries is certain to be significant.

Three quite separate considerations are relevant here in seeking ways to reduce these outflows. First, economies of scale are important in the insurance business. Thus many relatively small private insurers would tend to lay off i.e. reinsure, a higher proportion of total risks, and therefore remit a higher proportion of premiums, than would a single national company—private or public. Second, private profit reasons for reinsuring risks are likely to diverge from social reasons for reinsurance. Thus a single state company should probably have as its goal the minimization of foreign exchange losses and should therefore reinsure only the foreign exchange content of risks.[13] If this is accepted it will probably mean a significant reduction in reinsurance outflows and will certainly entail a change in the types of reinsurance contracts negotiated. Thus in East and Central Africa the historical tendency has been to use a combination of reinsurance contracts covering the following types:

Facultative: where each individual risk is laid off on an optional or obligatory basis
Quota Share of Surplus Treaty: where certain proportions of risks are laid off automatically
Excess of Loss: where reinsurance claims become operative above a certain figure for losses actually sustained.

The dominant categories, historically, have tended to be those of Quota Share and Surplus Treaties.

A shift to the foreign exchange content of risks would entail a much greater use of facultative treaties for risks with large foreign exchange contents and perhaps a limited use of excess of loss treaties for numerous small risks, the exchange content of which is significant only when they are combined.

The third consideration is that even if the first two institutional changes are implemented, there is scope for confining a proportion of reinsurance outflows within the region formed by the ten states, reducing the overall foreign exchange loss on this account. This could be achieved by the reciprocal laying off of business between the national companies or branches operating in the region so that the new flow of reinsurance-premiums is reduced. Initially this type of co-operation could be carried out relatively informally by regular direct contact between companies and would have the greatest appeal to those states which already have state insurance agencies (e.g. Tanzania, Zambia, Swaziland, Mozambique and Angola). Private companies will see little benefit in this arrangement and would need, in all likelihood, to be directed to participate by their respective Ministries of Finance. As the volume of reinsurance business grows, a regional reinsurance agency would need to be considered with its own staff and office accommodation.

Insurance and reinsurance is a field in which it would make sense for the regional states to co-operate in terms of manpower development.

A special case arises in respect of regional transport (goods and vehicles) insurance. As with bank credit, the absence or inconsistency of national arrangements can deter trade. There is no reason to suppose a co-ordinated policy frame operated by national companies would prove unprofitable, so that an early meeting of national companies to exchange views towards this end would appear appropriate.

THE SPECIAL PROBLEMS OF THOSE COUNTRIES TIGHTLY INTEGRATED INTO THE MONETARY SYSTEM OF THE REPUBLIC OF SOUTH AFRICA

NATURE OF THE PROBLEM

Namibia, Swaziland and Lesotho are members of the Rand Monetary Area and, together with Botswana, are also members of the South African Customs Union. As such they are tightly integrated into both the monetary system of the Republic of South Africa, and the RSA economy generally. RSA acts as a metropolitan centre with respect to these countries and the monetary system serves to channel foreign exchange and surplus flows to it. [14] All domestic currency is backed by the rand and financial institutions in Lesotho and to a degree, Swaziland, invest surplus funds in RSA. There is no exchange control between member states of the RMA and therefore profit, interest and capital can and does flow freely from the peripheral countries to RSA.

Economically, therefore, these states are appendages to RSA and the monetary system reinforces this status. This is an unenviable position for the politically independent states of Lesotho and Swaziland but one that is understandable given their geographical position and their size. Botswana's position is equally dependent in respect to trade and tariffs but she is not a member of the Rand Monetary Area.

Namibia is at present a colony of RSA. Its integration into the economy of the latter is, as has been argued,[15] a totally artificial one based purely on the gains that RSA enjoys from that forced union.

A SUGGESTED COURSE OF ACTION

Reducing dependence on the Republic of South Africa will be no easy matter for any of these states, but it is likely to be easiest for a liberated Namibia. Namibia has a lower dependence than the other three countries on RSA both as a market for export products and as a source of imports, as the figures below show. Further, it has direct access to the sea.

	% Imports from RSA	% Exports to RSA
Lesotho	94	90
Swaziland	87	20
Botswana	81	15
Namibia	60	10

Source: 'Economic Dependence and Regional Co-operation' SADCC Sectoral Paper, (in this volume) Table 7.

Namibia has numerous real possibilities for restructuring its economy away from RSA dependence. As Namibia establishes its own central bank and its own currency it could leave the RMA with little difficulty, invest its foreign assets in currencies of its own choice, introduce its own exchange control regulations and conduct an independent monetary policy. There is no question that this can or should be done; the only issue is how soon? An important problem is likely to be that of capital flight when liberation looks imminent, but there is little that can be done about that. Capital flight and manpower shortages after genuine independence will also be real problems and the Liberation Movement should prepare now, to the extent it can, for dealing with them. They are, however, likely to be shortlived problems if proper recruitment and training programmes are planned in advance. A related difficulty might be that of repatriating to Namibia foreign assets that are lodged in RSA. These comprise the counterpart of rand in circulation and the claims of the financial institution branches in Namibia on their RSA regional or head offices.

The monetary integration of Lesotho and Swaziland and to a lesser extent Botswana, will be more difficult to deal with since it is an extension of the extreme economic integration of these countries, including integration of the labour and capital markets. In the long run a liberated RSA is the real solution to their problems.

In the interim it must be recognized that their continued participation in SACU would rule out their use of tariffs against RSA imports in favour of goods obtained from any southern African regional grouping. For Lesotho and Swaziland continued RMA membership would also prevent preferential or even equal treatment for regional goods in respect of import licensing and exchange control.

The answer might lie in the co-operating states establishing a special fund in the proposed Southern African Development Bank to promote, simultaneously, greater integration within the region and greater independence from RSA. This fund, which might attract some multilateral, e.g. UN, and bilateral (from non-aligned and socialist countries?) financing could be used to speed up investment and, possibly, trade with a regional focus. Bilateral or multilateral clearing credits might also be established on preferential terms for these states.

Disengagement from RSA is likely to be a slow process for these countries. There is little that could be gained from reducing monetary integration except as part of broader restructuring of the numerous basic economic relationships with RSA production, trade, ownership, capital and labour flows.

Several of the EEC countries, in particular Britain, France and West Germany, have substantial investments in the Republic of South Africa and considerable trade benefits. It is difficult to reconcile the concern they express for the dependence of the peripheral states on that country with their reluctance to disengage from such relationships. The same can be said of USAID's southern African regional studies and proposed strategies.

STAFF TRAINING IN THE MONETARY FIELD

NEEDS

Training of staff for monetary institutions is an ongoing requirement in all countries of the world but the need will be particularly acute in newly liberated countries because of the discriminatory staffing policies of colonial and white minority regimes. Zimbabwe needs, and Namibia will need large numbers of commercial and central bankers, insurance staff and staff for specialist financial institutions. Within these general categories there will be a crucial need for certain types of skills in fields including exchange control, credit appraisal, foreign exchange transactions, bank inspections, reinsurance.

Angola and Mozambique also face acute staffing problems in their financial institutions. Dependence on expatriate staff appears to remain high in the smaller economies bordering RSA. At the same time Tanzania and, to a lesser extent, Zambia have long experience in financial institution staff training and development. It would appear, therefore, that close co-operation might be particularly rewarding on the manpower front.

POSSIBILITIES FOR CO-ORDINATION

Possibilities for co-operation in the training field should be examined in a systematic manner.

The first step should be a review of present and foreseeable future manpower needs in the monetary/financial institutions area.

The second step should be an analysis of the kinds of training required for each of the categories determined in the first step.

The third step should be a review of training facilities now available in the region, of the appropriateness of their curriculum and practical content and of the capacity of these facilities.

The fourth step should be to assess the extent to which existing facilities could absorb students from other states.

The fifth step should be to ascertain which of the existing institutions might be expanded in order to absorb students from other states and which new institutions serving more than one state might be created.

Finally, a number of purely national training facilities would be needed in some countries and the exercise might identify these.

It is envisaged that purely national training schemes will be needed for low skill requirement, fairly routine jobs. Here co-operation could take the form of the borrowing of experienced instructors from neighbouring states and of access to teaching materials and teaching systems. These latter would need adjustment to suit local circumstances i.e. translation, at least, in the case of co-operation between Angola and Mozambique on the one hand and English-speaking African countries on the other. In the case of newly liberated countries, developing of training courses for even low skilled staff should be accompanied by the review and standardization of banking and insurance procedures and again staff from other parts of the region could be extremely helpful in this regard.

For middle and high level staff in commercial banking, central banking and insurance a higher degree of co-operation would seem warranted. Apart from placing staff in existing training institutions, as suggested above, arrangements should also be made for the secondment of staff for in-service training in institutions in neighbouring countries. Thus, a co-operative, on-the-job training programme could be developed, supplemented by periodic short formal training courses in local training institutions.

High level training courses in banking and insurance should be arranged to cater for staff on a regional basis. The Institute of Finance Management

109

in Dar es Salaam has had experience in this area, having arranged several courses in the finance of foreign trade, credit appraisal and aspects of insurance policy and practice for a multistate student body. There is simply no need for staff of southern African countries to look outside of Africa for this type of specialist training.

INSTITUTIONAL ARRANGEMENTS

We recommend that the review of manpower needs and training facilities proposed above be conducted by the Financial Integration Section of the proposed Southern African Development Bank in conjunction with the relevant financial and training institutions of member countries. Initially the states could appoint a working committee specifically to deal with the task.

As far as possible it is desirable to avoid creating new regional financial training institutions. It is preferable that existing ones be extended and existing programmes amended to meet the needs of neighbouring states. If, however, the suggestion for a broadly regional Management Training Institute is accepted, then an arm of this institute could be used to offer middle and high level practically oriented courses in banking and insurance.

It should be possible to develop training programmes which could be offered regularly in different centres each year. This would cut down the need for costly infrastructure and might permit the development of more appropriate teaching materials which could be catalogued and stored in one central training institute and made available to all southern African financial training institutes and units.

The minimum initial step toward co-operation in this area should be the exchange of information on policies, practices and procedures between financial institutions and of training methods and teaching materials between financial and/or training institutions.

PROPOSED STRUCTURE FOR REGIONAL CO-OPERATION

The most important immediate tasks in building greater co-operation within the southern African region will consist of:

(a) review of existing policies and how they might be changed to facilitate greater integration, and

(b) identification of specific areas in which closer co-operation would make most sense and of the manner in which that co-operation can be achieved.

In organizational terms there is, therefore, the need for at least a minimal capacity for policy formulation and planning. Without this it is unlikely that much progress will be made in the immediate future. These tasks cannot be carried out efficiently solely at the national level. There is need

110

for a small central body liaising closely with national policy and planning bodies but on the whole seizing the initiative, creatively, in terms of analysis and proposals for progress.

A case can be made that this body should be located in the proposed Southern African Development Bank. This would have a number of advantages. First, it would ensure that plans for co-operation are not widely out of line with available financial resources. Second it would ensure that investment projects financed by the bank are fully consistent with plans for integration. These could be achieved of course with a planning body separate from the bank. However, as both availability and need suggest there will be relatively few staff at this stage then, on balance, it would make sense to have the banking function and the planning and policy functions performed under the same roof.

Similarly a small secretariat with responsibility for organizing ministerial and senior official meetings could also be housed in the proposed bank. This would act as a liaison between the policy and planning staff and the national political representatives. It would also help organize, co-ordinate and service the various technical committees established to foster greater co-ordination in specific technical areas. Thus, in the monetary field, a committee composed of national representatives might be established to examine the question of co-operation in the area of reinsurance. The secretariat, drawing on staff from the financial co-operation section of the bank, would help facilitate the work of that committee. Likewise, regular meetings of the governors of the various central banks could be arranged and serviced by the secretariat.

Given the selectivity and flexibility of the co-ordination envisaged at this stage a good deal of reliance would be placed on technical committees, some permanent and some ad hoc and temporary. This would reduce the bureaucratic expense of co-operation and would enable concentration on matters deemed to be most urgent.

The political input into this process could take the form of an annual Heads of State meeting and meetings at the ministerial level every six months.

It is clear that there is a need for formal regional co-ordination at ministerial level for aid negotiating and monitoring. Aid for regional or multi state projects, however the funds are formally transmitted, is likely to be substantial. Ministers advised by the directors of the Southern African Development Bank once it is created should meet with aid donors on an annual basis. The core staff of the proposed bank, for all sections including the secretariat, could be found from within the region without relying heavily upon foreign personnel, so that aid need not be a factor in its formation. The exception to this might be the technical assistance from the ADB, mentioned above. This relative independence from foreign personnel would help make the bank a useful advisory secretariat to ministers on regional aid strategy and practice.

111

The question of co-ordinated national policies in respect of external assistance and foreign enterprises is somewhat separate. This is broader than funds for specifically regional projects and may, as in the case of the Andean Pact, provide a focal point for the early stages of co-ordination. It too could be serviced by staff located in the Southern African Development Bank.

NOTES AND REFERENCES

1. 'First Steps Toward Economic Integration', SADCC paper.
2. H. G. Johnson, 'Problems of European Monetary Union' *Journal of World Trade Law*, July-August 1971, 5, pp. 377–87.
3. E. Blumenthal, *Tanganyika-East Africa: The Present Monetary System and its Future*: Government Printer, Dar es Salaam, 1963.
4. P. G. Clark, 'The Role of a Central Bank in Accelerating Economic Development' in East African Institute of Social and Cultural Affairs *Problems of Economic Development in East Africa*, Nairobi: East African Publishing House, 1965.
5. W. T. Newlyn, 'Monetary Systems and Integration' *East African Economics Review*, June 1964.
6. *Treaty for East African Co-operation*: Government Printer, Nairobi, on behalf of the East African Common Services Organization, 1967.
7. Mark D. Segal, 'A Survey of Monetary and Fiscal Co-operation in East Africa' Paper presented to the Third East African Central Banking Seminar organized by the Bank of Tanzania and the Institute of Finance Management. Dar es Salaam, July 1974.
8. *Treaty for East African Co-operation, op. cit.* Annex VI The Charter of the East African Development Bank, Chapter 1.
9. *Ibid.*
10. *Ibid*, Chapter III.
11. A. Hazlewood, *Economic Integration: The East African Experience.*
12. In the Caribbean Community (CARICOM) Trinidad and Tobago has used revenues from oil to provide a special fund to enable the poorer members to meet their counterpart contributions to loans extended them by the Caribbean Development Bank. See W. G. Demas: 'Essays on Caribbean Integration and Development', Institute of Social and Economic Research, University of West Indies, Jamaica, 1976, Chapter 10, p. 115.
13. J. Loxley, 'Monetary Policies Towards Socialism' ERB 69.6 University of Dar es Salaam, 1969.
14. David Jones, *Aid and Development in Southern Africa*, Croom Helm, London 1977, page 24.
15. R. H. Green, *Namibia: A Political Economic Survey*, Institute of Development Studies, Sussex, Paper No. 144, 1979.

Agriculture

INTRODUCTION

This paper is mainly concerned with the agricultural sector of the economies of southern Africa. This regional definition does not preclude considerations pertinent to either subregional issues, for example Botswana's, Lesotho's and Swaziland's links related to the Southern African Customs Union Agreement (SACU), or bilateral questions, for example, current Mozambican/Tanzanian arrangements and possible Zimbabwean/Zambian ones; nor should it exclude extraregional issues, e.g. those connected to mainland/island relationships embracing, say, Madagascar, Mauritius, Kenya, Tanzania and Mozambique or between southern African and other neighbouring states such as Angola/Zaire or Tanzania/Uganda—Rwanda—Burundi (Kagera Basin subregion).

The paper seeks to relate directly to the underlying objectives which the leaders in the region have already identified as having a very high priority: to reduce economic dependence on the Republic of South Africa; to maximize regional co-operation in southern Africa; to minimize disruption during the period of reconstruction and development of southern African economies; to evaluate current problems and alternatives; to suggest contingency options and technical assistance requirements; and to identify protective measures for majority ruled states in the event of external pressures being applied to RSA.

This paper seeks to relate these objectives to broad regional and country-specific problems concerning the agrarian sectors in the context of the natural resource base of the region. Before moving to this stage, however, it is necessary to bear in mind some signficiant data limitations which apply to the analysis of southern African agriculture (see below). In subsequent sections of this paper the background natural resource base upon which the agrarian sectors are dependent is briefly noted: the agrarian sector itself is identified (by size, structure, character and subsectoral balances—in regard to key trends and the main operative constraints on policy); selected aspects of forestry and fisheries industries are commented upon. Thereafter some sectoral, national, regional and international policy issues are briefly reviewed and some alternative proposals are noted.

Data limitations make difficult, or render impossible, analysis of certain aspects of agrarian development in southern Africa. Some are common to all economies, others are more specific.

First, inherited national accounts systems—based on the prerogatives of colonial recording (a somewhat different experience for Mozambique and Angola than for ex-British colonies)—generally retain all the wellknown weaknesses regarding the rural household sector.[1] Hence for Zimbabwe, Lesotho, Swaziland and Mozambique subsistence sectors have generally been treated as residual categories. Consequently, output/income valuations have been much dependent on arbitrary methods of imputed estimation. Mozambique presents special difficulties even from this perspective in that the national accounts make little attempt to cover non-modern sectors systematically.

Second, not all countries have as yet tried to remedy these inherited deficiencies by use of regular and/or nationwide rural household income and expenditure surveys. Tanzania (1967–76), Botswana (1976) and Malawi (1969) have collected such point-in-time data—which reflect a major advance over other countries. But it is nonetheless difficult even in these economies to construct trend analyses around such evidence, no matter what its quality. Additionally, there are also uneven data available in different economies which derive from micro studies of areas, regions, villages and even subsectors; but these are no substitute for detailed overall surveys.

Third, data collection has at best been focussed on income or expenditure flows. Little data exist on rural agrarian assets and capital or investment structures. Even those countries better off in data terms suffer serious limitations.

Fourth, available national data are not necessarily consistent between countries. This makes international and regional comparisons complicated and difficult or subject to error. Perhaps this is most strongly evidenced in different assumptions used to define the production boundaries for the subsistence sector. It is greatly compounded by the significant effect on regional incomes of the international monetary flows in the form of remittances (and even real commodity flows) which are crucial in economic systems heavily dependent on migrant labour including Lesotho, Swaziland, Botswana, Malawi and Mozambique. For the most part these go unrecorded. These problems add to normal difficulties induced by the use of a variety of currencies, variations in exchange rates and problems of ensuring consistency in terms of purchasing power parities.

Fifth, there remains a strong bias in statistical planning against comprehensive recording of the transactions in the rural sector, notably its non-commercial components. The National Development Plans for almost all countries still rest heavily on expansion of, and diversification within, the modern sectors; and so, to some extent understandably, these elements command the bulk of statistical and planning attention. Beyond this, it could also be claimed that not all states have been aggressivly interested in exposing their economic condition either to internal or external scrutiny. This has been particularly so with regard to estate employment. Thus, local, nationwide and independent efforts to highlight disquieting development trends are often not encouraged. In certain instances they have even been penalized. Yet without such critical stimulation, policy is likely to change more slowly and less effectively than otherwise.

Furthermore, the eruption of war and social crises in many rural parts of the region in the 1970s—in northern and eastern Mozambique, Namibia, Zimbabwe, eastern Botswana and several parts of Angola—have hampered planning and analytical work, thereby making it impossible for reliable data to be obtained.

NATURAL RESOURCE BASE AND CAPACITY

The southern African region encompasses a potentially rich base of land, minerals and water resources. The main feature of the resource base is that it is nowhere utilized at full capacity.

Ample land exists in the region. Only a fraction has been fully exploited. There still remain vast tracts of fertile soils, grazing and forage lands, natural forests, wildlife and fisheries. But significant problems also exist in bringing scarce technical and economic inputs to bear on these resources so as to increase their capacity for yielding viable long term benefits, including means of subsistence, for all the peoples in the region. On the one side there are imbalances in resource allocation, access and use; on the other, social and political difficulties limit the full utilization of potential capacity.

The scope for increase in arable land capacity remains large even though no land inventory yet exists for the area as a whole. At the same time, there are land areas (e.g. the Tribal Trust Lands of Zimbabwe and the southern Namibian Karakul zone) where there has been significant soil deterioration and overgrazing. Other problems—such as drought, shallow soil depth and excess water—also affect parts of the region, but even when these are taken into account a general situation of land adequacy still remains.

Much of the region, however, is lacking in adequate water supply. There are desert areas of Namibia, parts of Botswana, the lowveld in Mozambique, Swaziland and in much of central Tanzania. By contrast, achieved permanent irrigation capacity is still relatively small in size. To alter its dimensions significantly would be expensive. This places a premium on proper conservation measures and sound groundwater management.

The coastal and even several of the landlocked economies such as Malawi can sustain viable fishing industires. Internal lakes and rivers can also be used for fishing and the stocking of freshwater varieties. It is probably true that large manmade lakes, for example, Kariba and Cabora Bassa, are not fully exploited for aquatic resources.

Forestry industries already flourish and could be much expanded in some countries (e.g. Zimbabwe and Swaziland). Indeed, most of the region needs additional development in this sphere—not only for timberbased industries but for domestic fuel requirements and housing needs. Afforestation has a major role to play in conservation and ecological balance.

Wildlife conservation, and its use for protein and tourist-based sectors, also deserves attention. The area faces the prospect of severe constraints on these forms of natural resources in the future, some of which arise out of conflicts with human habitation needs while others derive from land policies.

In sum, it could be said that there is little reason—from a resource perspective—why southern Africa should not have a flourishing agrarian sector. There is even less reason why it should not be capable of sustaining and further developing such an asset for the future.

RECENT TRENDS IN THE AGRICULTURAL SECTORS OF SOUTHERN AFRICA

Here the main focus is on the agricultural (arable and pastoral) sectors as distinct from forestry and fisheries. The latter are dealt with more briefly later in this paper.

This section highlights the following: growth in GDP and production in the region; the size and structure of the agricultural sector as a whole and in respect of different economies; rural labour absorption and employment; patterns of land availability and use; aspects of capitalization; food production and supply trends in the 1960s and 1970s with special reference to nutritional and dietary needs; specific features of regional and country-specific crop specialization and livestock holding; and finally, economically active population (EAP) trends and projections as they affect the various economies and patterns of labour supply allocation to agriculture.

GDP GROWTH AND RECENT SECTORAL CHANGES

Basic Data Table 4 provides data on GDP/sectoral growth rates and the structure of production for eight southern Africa economies over the periods 1960–70 and 1970–6. A few key points deserve special mention. First, the growth rates of aggregate output in the region have been uneven and declining in most cases. Botswana and Malawi are the two exceptions, with Botswana's very high and rising growth rates (16.1 per cent annually over 1970–6) being closely linked to mineral development. All the other economies have experienced a fall in overall growth rates. There has even been an absolute decline in GDP over 1970–6 in the case of Mozambique and Zimbabwe and a decline in per head real GDP in those of Angola and, since 1974, Zambia. These latter effects have had special origins and been associated with liberation wars, international recession and the effects of sanctions (of a primary kind in the case of Zimbabwe and in the form of secondary effects in the case of Mozambique and Zambia). More recently, Zimbabwe's GDP has fallen even further in real (inflation adjusted) terms. Today, the economy's real output per head level approximates that of 1970.

This set of overall trends has had massive implications for the rural population, especially the poor and in particular marginalized groups in the rural sector. Declining growth rates and falling levels of output have also made more critical the existing problems in the field of resource allocation, equity of access to means of subsistence and the domestic generation of savings and investments. These problems have been especially accentuated in rural sectors. Until positive GDP expansion is recorded, and overall per head growth rates much improved, it is difficult to envisage major and successful rural development over the long term. This is not to say that certain reconstruction policies and transformations—which often have high costs in terms of foregone output and short run adjustments—are not necessary. However, in order to make them workable and sustainable over time, these policies need to be situated in a context of expansion and development.

Second, even in certain high growth economies such as Swaziland, there has recently been some dimunition in agricultural sector growth rates. Only Malawi, Zambia and Botswana have recorded rising growth rates in the agricultural sector between 1960–70, and 1970–6. There have however, been large falls in agriculture growth rates in Angola and Zimbabwe, and no improvement in Mozambique (over 1970–6). Thus the larger economies have experienced more severe difficulties than the smaller ones and those not subject to the disruption of colonial wars.

Third, the changes recorded in the structure of production over 1960–76 were also uneven. Only in Zambia, Swaziland and Namibia did the share of agriculture in total output rise; and it may have done so in Zambia only because of severely depressed conditions in the copper market. Sizeable falls in agrarian/GDP shares resulted for other countries, notably Angola.

Further, FAO data on per head domestic food production show significant gains over 1965/7–1974/6 only for Tanzania, Malawi and Zambia with absolute falls for Angola and Mozambique. Namibia also had a per head decline because the agricultural output increase was in export oriented meat and fish, not locally consumed crops or dairy produce.

The general trends reflect a number of deep, broad determinants apart from war, recession and the country-specific effects of sanctions. It would probably be accurate to state that no country has really yet resolved the agrarian problems inherited at independence. Moreover much of the growth which has been recorded has derived from non-peasant households i.e. the plantation/estate subsectors of agriculture; and in the smallholder sectors (e.g. in Malawi and Swaziland) there has developed a growing income

117

stratification between rural households. A relatively small proportion of the rural population now produce a relatively large marketable surplus. Even fewer would appear capable of marketing their surplus production under conditions enabling sustained, long term viability. Most must still have recourse to economic activity in other sectors or in the national or international migrant/contract labour market either in RSA or in the region as a whole. Hence changes outside the agricultural sector tend to affect most, if not all, rural inhabitants.

The trends which have emerged have also reflected planning choices, realistic constraints and efficiency of performance. Much emphasis in the 1960s was placed on modern sector growth e.g. copper in Zambia, estate export crops in Malawi, minerals in Botswana, large scale production schemes in Swaziland, migrant-labour export policies in Lesotho (and Mozambique under colonial rule), mining, plantations and industry in Zimbabwe. A certain imbalance was thus encouraged in the southern Arican economies. These difficulties have not been effectively redressed in the 1970s and they pose major problems for the 1980s.

A switch in sectoral emphasis has been made more problematic by the international economic recession since 1973, with higher import costs and deteriorating difficulties of regional integration. At the same time, the latest National Development Plans of many countries still give considerable preference either to the non-agricultural sector or to the modern components of the agricultural sector. The share of investment allocated to agriculture has often been relatively low and mostly located in the large scale or foreign owned private sector. There are recent exceptions to this, however, e.g. Mozambique and Tanzania.

From these economic conditions have emerged problems of adequacy of domestic food production, of local food supply, and where the latter are found wanting, of inflationary tendencies. In most economies, the overall inflation rate (measured on the All Items index) has risen over the 1965–70 and 1970–5 period as follows: 2.0 per cent to 8.9 per cent in Malawi, 3.7 per cent to 10.5 per cent in Mozambique and 3.7 per cent to 13.1 per cent in Tanzania.[2] More crucial is the fact that growth rates in food prices have been set at a higher level and appear to have risen even faster than the general index, e.g. 3.4 per cent to 10.7 per cent for Malawi, 4.7 per cent to 11.1 per cent for Mozambique and 2.5 per cent to 17.7 per cent for Tanzania. This pattern may have deteriorated even further over 1975–9.

However, the trend exhibited may not necessarily be wholly attributable to domestic agricultural production problems, sectoral performance, or shortages of locally-produced goods. Import costs and physical availability problems have also played a part, as have transport factors. Further, it may in some cases, for example Tanzania, represent a deliberate shift of urban/rural terms of trade in favour of peasant incomes. Nonetheless the real issue is that domestic agrarian systems have not yet achieved a level of performance capable of wholly meeting domestic needs and export requirements.

POPULATION, EMPLOYMENT AND THE STRUCTURE OF AGRICULTURE

Data on population, rural wage employment and agrarian population are found in Basic Data Table 5 for southern African migrant labour exporting countries as well as, for international comparison—RSA. The population of the region has increased relatively rapidly over 1950–75.

An important trend is that of a rising population growth rate, evident in most economies and notably the large ones. This has ramifications for employment growth requirements and subsistence needs, rural sector absorption and the future demand for essential foodstuffs.

In all the independent majority ruled states of southern Africa and in Namibia as well, the rural population constitutes a high percentage of the total population. This is unlikely to be radically altered by rural urban migration in the next 10 years (except perhaps for Namibia). Even if the share is reduced further, the aggregate numbers in rural areas will still be increasing sharply in absolute terms. Furthermore, rising urban populations will still need a viable domestic agricultural system to support their food demands. So too will agro-allied industries for inputs and other industries which are dependent on imported commodities financed from primary product export earnings (a common characteristic of manufacturing in the region, especially in the non-mineral economies).

An important feature of the region is the size and distribution of wage employment on large scale, often foreign owned, estates. Estate employees are particularly numerous in Zimbabwe (360,000 workers), Mozambique (150,000), Namibia (50,000) and Malawi (140,000). They are less significant in other countries. Typically, these groups are amongst the poorest of the rural poor. They are for the most part weakly organised. The estate labour force in several cases includes a high proportion of women and children. Their earnings have not risen much in real terms in the last two decades; indeed certain groups of estate workers have probably experienced a decline in their earnings in real terms. The expansion of estate/plantation agriculture appears as a major cause of the emergence of rural wage-labour; but this is linked with surplus labour generated by the non-development of peasant agriculture and by the marginalization of growing numbers of households within the latter sector. Thereby a system of cheap labour has been developed.

At the same time in all economies the labour force in agriculture (peasant and estate) is large in absolute and relative terms (see Basic Data Table 5, col. 6). Hence there exists a fundamental and direct dependence on agrarian activity. Performance in the agrarian sectors is therefore a major influence on standards of living and on the overall economic welfare of the majority of households in the states of the region.

The conditions of life of the population are partially illustrated by life expectancy data (Basic Data Table 5, col. 7). Life expectancy at birth is still relatively low. This reflects historical processes, generalized poverty and contemporary underdevelopment. It also results from the strong pressure of slowly falling but still high birth rates and more rapidly declining but still high death rates. Conditions for the rural population are likely to be even more unfavourable than the national aggregates shown in the Table.

Population balance in relation to land size is also uneven. Thus, considering agricultural population per hectare of arable land, it is found that Mozambique and Lesotho fared worst of all countries in the region, although Mozambique was far better placed. Hence new settlement schemes, even on a regional basis, could play a major role in changing the present population/arable land balance. On this issue Namibia's position looks relatively good in theory; but this does not take account of the country's arid conditions and the high cost of largescale irrigation.

It is probable that almost all these economies are encountering some form of landlessness, despite traditional tenure mechanisms of generalized usufruct and access to land. Landlessness has taken various forms and has a number of manifestations: smaller plots as population pressure lead to fragmentation; unviable units, as cropping and technical requirements alter; higher ratios of population to arable land; the growth in non-agrarian petty production; an expanded supply of workseekers drifting towards the towns; the growth of a sizeable reserve pool of cheap labour willing to enter the exploitative RSA contract labour market, both conditionally and under agreement with The Employment Bureau of Africa (TEBA)—the international recruiting agency for the RSA Chamber of Mines.

These general tendencies highlight the critical need for successful development programmes in the rural sector. They also point to the need for higher rates of (productive) employment growth, and necessary restructuring in investment allocation between sectors and towards less capital intensive projects.

LAND SIZE AND USE OF THE AGRARIAN RESOURCE BASE

Because the region's population is large and growing, manpower questions will present no serious difficulty as long as agriculture is well organized, resource frontiers are still not fully extended, and viable long term projects can be successfully implemented. Much then depends on the disposition of land resources and their current use. Data on these issues are shown in Basic Data Table 7. They illustrate that there exists both a varied pattern and substantial future potential in the region.

It is patent that the region's land area is large in relation to total rural population. Southern Africa covers an area equal in size to Europe. Problems of land scarcity, such as exist in South East Asia, do not yet exist in a generalized form, though in certain districts there is land scarcity. In regional terms, the area under arable and permanent crops is still very small and remains for all countries at a small fraction of land size. The region's arable land is little larger than that found in Spain and is smaller than the

120

arable land area in France. Hence scope for considerable expansion exists—resources permitting. At the same time, there is some noticeable concentration in the distribution of arable lands (e.g. in Mozambique, Zambia and Zimbabwe) and probably even greater concentration in terms of already developed and highly productive lands.

Most countries have access to sizeable areas of permanent pasture; hence the region could support a major expansion in its livestock industry. To some extent it already has such an industry but in certain areas (e.g. Zimbabwe and Botswana, though for different reasons) expansion has been held back in the last two years. Expansion in this subsector could undoubtedly occur in both quantitative and qualitative terms over the medium term. However, some national and local livestock industries, notably in parts of Botswana, Namibia and northern Tanzania, may already be at stock levels which are ecologically dangerously high.

The resource base for a natural and/or cultivated forestry industry is also sizeable, albeit heavily concentrated in three or four countries. Lesotho and Zambia appear to be least advantaged on this score. But even in these countries, considerable improvements could be expected under planned policies allied to a greater sufficiency of technical and economic resources.

Another significant feature relates to the availability of irrigated lands. In general terms, the region is poorly provided with present irrigation capacity. These resources are highly concentrated and are obtainable only at high capital and recurrent costs. As a whole they are probably only 15 per cent to 20 per cent of the irrigation capacity found in RSA. New programmes for lower unit cost irrigation schemes deserve attention.

PROMINENT RURAL ASSETS

Irrigation capacity represents an important capitalized asset on the land; but there are other indicators of the degree of capitalization which bear critically on arable agricultural development. The most commonly used indicator of the degree of rural asset formation relates to tractors (on which some data are shown in Table 1). Such data helps provide crude measures of the sophistication of agrarian sectors and their general orientation to modern forms of production. At the same time, care must be taken in using such indicators.

The numbers of tractors in use has risen sharply in all countries over the period 1969/71–6. This has been most noticeable in growth rate terms for Lesotho. However, the distribution of tractors is highly skewed towards Zimbabwe, which has the largest commercialized agrarian sector in southern Africa (excluding RSA). In 1976 the region had around 31,242 tractors in use compared to 188,000 in RSA. Of the former, 19,000 were reported as being in Zimbabwe.

These data may also conceal other important aspects indicating the region's low level of development, e.g. tractor horsepower, size, quality, capacity utilization and efficiency. When these facets are taken into account, it is probable that there is an even greater inequality of distribution between RSA/Southern Africa, between Zimbabwe/Others, and between (although not shown in the data) modern/non-modern subsectors.

The issue of tractorization is a complex one. For the future, it is important to create employment. An increased use of tractors may, but not necessarily will, displace rural labour without necessarily creating industrial jobs, as most tractors are imports (often from RSA). Tractors moreover are impossibly high cost items for the average farmer and are most often acquired by large estates or by small numbers of successful smallholders. Very few are in the control of co-operative production units. Nevertheless, in Zimbabwe and Namibia, it will be vital that tractor capacity is retained as much agricultural production depends on this installed capacity. Attention should thus be given in these countries to ensure that these assets are not removed at independence, to ensure the quality and efficiency of their operations after independence, and to ensure that they are used to maximum capacity, especially under co-operative production schemes. On the latter, it may be necessary to guarantee better access to, and allocation of, tractor capacity amongst productive units. Various schemes might be devised to achieve this end.

The data also illustrate a further point: the fact that large numbers of tractors in a country is not in itself an adequate indicator of the relative situation. Tractor/arable land ratios also need to be taken into account. When this is done, Swaziland comes out close to RSA. But it would not do so if ownership and use by large scale units (in particular sugar plantations) were omitted from the calculation. Malawi and Zambia would seem worst affected in the region vis-à-vis adequacy of supply of tractors.

It also needs to be emphasized that a measure like 'tractors in use' is only one indicator of the adequacy of rural assets. Others also need to be weighed in the balance: credit volume and supply, on-farm infrastructure, rail and road facilities, transport and trucking capacity, the supply of more simple implements, grain and crop storage capacity, etc. Equally, technical skills, managerial expertise, bureaucratic supports and extension services play a vital role in output expansion, in improved growth rates and higher levels of agricultural efficiency.

AGRICULTURAL PRODUCTION, FOOD SUPPLY AND NUTRITIONAL BALANCE

Compared to Africa as a whole, the southern Africa region fared relatively well in terms of recorded average annual increases in food production over 1960/61–70 and 1970–6. Rates of growth were 3.1 per cent and 4.2 per cent respectively as against 2.5 per cent and 1.2 per cent for Africa as a whole.[3] However, this provides little room for complacency given a closer examination of trends. Nor, in the context of post 1973 world price changes, is food production growth an automatic guide to external balance trends. Among the countries listed as 'most severely affected' (MSA) by the UN are found Tanzania (+3.7 per cent food production growth for 1970–6), Lesotho (0.0 per cent) and Mozambique (–1.0 per cent).

More detailed data on these points are shown for 1966–77 (for seven migrant labour exporting economies) in Basic Data Table 8. A few points of relevance need to be highlighted.

First, overall food production levels have risen over 1970–7, except in the case of Mozambique. They have been rising very quickly in Botswana (a relatively small producer). In several other countries growth rates were higher than was achieved in RSA. But this has not enabled a zero dependence on food imports. Indeed today, Zambia, with Botswana, Lesotho and Swaziland have an import trade dependence in this sphere, mostly on RSA.

Second, agricultural output per head grew at a slower pace than did aggregate food output. Some countries (Lesotho, Mozambique and Zimbabwe) experienced a fall in this index during 1970–7. There is thus some evidence of stagnation in output per head as far as agricultural products are concerned.

Third, when food output per head is considered, the character of the problem is made a little clearer. The 1970–7 period witnessed much slower growth on this index than on aggregate food output alone. Again, certain economies were worse off in 1977 than in 1970; and some were no better placed than in 1966 (e.g. Lesotho, Zimbabwe and Mozambique).

It is also observable that RSA did not perform consistently well over 1966–77. This economy has a sizeable and fast-growing population (2.6 per cent per year), great rural poverty and malnutrition in the 'Bantustans' and a strong (non-African) export bias in food and non-food crops. Nonetheless, it is a major supplier of foodstuffs to southern African states. Even so, its long term capacity to act in this role is open to doubt, aside from the regime's possible greater future use of food as a political weapon (already once evidenced in the Lesotho case over the pricing of maize supplies in the 1970s following pressures exerted in an attempt to force recognition of Transkeian independence). More important, the governments of the region wish to be independent of RSA. They desire to secure self-sufficiency in food production. If that objective is to be quickly realized and sustained, then surplus producers must link with deficit states and a regional food policy must be developed. This might even have to embrace a re-evaluation of the role of regional/international trade in non-food crops which absorb a large volume of local resources, skills and finance.

Fourth, some measure of the current crisis concerning food deficits (in production and supply) can be found in country data on the supply of calories and proteins per head over 1961/3–72/4. Note that these data reflect net supply not simply domestic production. Only Lesotho (largely with food aid dependence), Swaziland, and Malawi, had a higher calories consumption per head at the end of the period. The other economies experienced a decline, albeit small in most cases.

Compared to regional and national dietary needs (see Table 2) there is also still much to be desired. Dietary energy supplies in Angola, Botswana, Mozambique, Swaziland, Tanzania and Zambia remained below FAO defined nutritional daily requirements in 1974. For the African population, Namibia and Zimbabwe would also be in that category. Moreover, these-states were low in relation to many others on the African continent. Hence the need to increase output, improve allocations patterns and ensure positive long term growth trends, assumes great importance.

Fifth, food problems could well be compounded in the future as a result of international migration movements. Greater displacement of labour from RSA will raise food demand in Botswana, Lesotho, Swaziland, Malawi, Zimbabwe and Mozambique. This will be a significant portion of total food demand in some countries, for example Lesotho, should current displacement processes be continued or accelerated. At the same time, these new conditions will bring smaller foreign exchange earnings and lower real domestic incomes to the rural household sectors of the region. The available household means of subsistence will thus be much diminished for a large segment of the population.

Finally, independence in Zimbabwe and shortly in Namibia may well be associated with greater displacement in production structures (say, over the period 1980–5) smaller regional export surpluses and higher import deficits, higher local food demands in these economies, and an indeterminate period of time until new production systems are installed and made effective. These prospects carry implications for all neighbouring states.

AGRICULTURAL COMMODITY COMPOSITION

Because of resource endowment, agricultural policy and commodity specialization not all countries are selfsufficient in crops and livestock products. This applies particularly to processed outputs which require agro-allied industrial capacity for their realization. For example, this appears to apply to Angola, Malawi, Mozambique, Tanzania, Zimbabwe and Zambia.

The production pattern indicates the potential for intraregional agricultural commodity specialization and exchange within defined boundary limits of selfsufficiency. In this respect each national economy faces a choice in some degree: either selfsufficiency is placed first and exchange is made secondary or else a measure of the former is specified and the balance is sought through bilateral/regional trade arrangements. Both courses involve risks.

In the former, costs may be prohibitive or very high in certain lines of production; trade opportunities may be temporarily foregone or permanently foreclosed; interregional food stability might be negatively affected and effective economic integration delayed or made an excessively prolonged exercise.

124

In the latter instance, risks arise from a new sort of dependence, the risks of reliability of supply and ability to deliver may increase; trading partners may be less willing to continue trade in the future; common natural disasters in the region, such as droughts, could affect all or unevenly prejudice smaller, weaker states.

Resolution of these issues involves a complex assessment requiring synchronized planning, timeconsuming negotiations, agreements on trade, regular revisions of supply/demand estimates, forward contracts, secured means of external finance, payments systems, quick and efficient marketing, a reliable regional transport network, and some basic political agreement. These are not elements to be hurried or patched together.

Certainly, the benefits of integration could be important both in the medium and long term. They could involve lower production costs, more rational use of economic resources, lesser dependence on RSA, stronger regionally linked policies, and eventually, higher standards of consumption. At the moment there exists little detailed assessment of the costs and benefits of schemes of this sort.

The regional production profile in the livestock sphere is similar in character to arable outputs (see Table 4). Here, too, the basis of a regional policy could also be worked at over time, albeit on the face of it all of the ten states can readily be selfsufficient or net exporters in meat and dairy products, although the majority are now net dairy product importers.

Beyond trade, new policies would also need to embrace shared technical assistance, training programmes, disease eradication measures, information exchange, conferences, a secretariat for the long term development of the industry, and research and advisory services.

The livestock industry's potential in the region and policies for its realization could also be examined and reviewed against ecological considerations, desertification questions (important for Botswana and Namibia), problems associated with smallholder herds (e.g. culling rates and offtake), joint abattoir facilities, and regional export policies to EEC and elsewhere in Africa. A not unimportant branch of this sector might be focussed on non-domesticated protein sources (and animals) as well as the managed use of bushmeat as a supplementary source of foodstuffs.

ECONOMICALLY ACTIVE POPULATION IN AGRICULTURE AND LABOUR FORCE GROWTH IN THE FUTURE

What are the dimensions of the problems to be dealt with in the future? Some indications can be derived from examination of data shown in Table 5. Here again the principal reference is to the migrant labour exporting economies of the region.

First, labour force growth rates are positive. They have been rising over the 1950s and 1960s for almost all economies. They were probably even higher in the 1970s. It is also important to note that in the 1965–70 period, the highest rate was recorded in RSA where unemployment is now measured

125

at around the two million level. This means that there will be pressures on RSA to diminish further its dependence on imported contract labour from neighbouring countries, thus displacing workers and increasing the permanent return flow to supplier countries. These economies will need to absorb even greater numbers locally, especially in domestic agriculture. Thus the pressures for the rapid development of viable rural sector alternatives are likely to grow.

Second, the need for higher labour absorption levels in agriculture will grow substantially even in the absence of an RSA decision against the continued employment of contract workers. This is so despite industrial and mineral expansion and growth in services employment. Future gross absorption requirements for the region are thus likely to be heavily biased towards agriculture. The problem will be further compounded by the fact that a smaller proportion of population will be active in agriculture but will need to provide food for a much greater total population.

Third, projections over 1975–90 show that absolute population numbers will expand rapidly. Even with declining labour force activity rates, as shown for most countries, the absolute growth in labour force will be an enormous challenge during the 1975–90 period. This applies whether only men are considered or whether aggregate data are used.

The implications of these figures are profound. Most households will be dependent on a livelihood derived from the rural sector. Food demand will expand with population growth, especially so if existing nutritional deficiencies are to be overcome. At the same time, resources will be scarce in the economic sense. Optimal use will thus have to be made of all existing productive capacity, and new capacity will need to be developed. In the planning of new largescale investments, co-ordinated regional policy and strategies might prove to be critical considerations.

AGRICULTURAL TRADE

The trade situation also influences the agrarian sectors. There are two prominent facets to this issue. On the one hand, intraregional trade is dominated by RSA, on the other, most economies are primary product exporters tied to world market conditions and trends.

The southern African countries are in a net deficit position with RSA. This applies to all economies except Tanzania and Angola which do not trade with RSA. Increasingly, agrarian exports from RSA to southern African economies have taken the form of basic foodstuffs such as maize, and imports needed for agricultural production (e.g. fertilizer).

Unfortunately, it is difficult to obtain reliable, up-to-date data on the composition of intraregional trade. However, it is clear from 1970–3 data (see Table 6) that the pattern of the past has been one of food and agricultural product export as well as food and agricultural product import. If this remains so today, as is likely, then there should be scope within this pattern for the agricultural sectors of the different economies to meet both the condition of reducing import/export dependence on RSA and diverting trade exchanges in some measure towards the group itself. Such initiatives currently sought as one aspect of the ECA's Preferential Trade Area (PTA) scheme, could also be designed to have positive employment implications as well as to contribute to regional food supply adequacy and stability.

At the same time, there still exist many obstacles to greater intraregional agricultural product trade: the inadequacy of transport links, tariff and non-tariff barriers, quantitative import restrictions, credit facility deficiencies (especially for small traders), the absence of satisfactory payments arrangements, prohibitive exchange control regulations, non-convertibility of many African currencies and dependence on the dollar, pound sterling and other external units of account. These sorts of difficulties could be partially dealt with through the PTA.

The second important aspect of agricultural trade relates to world market dependence. World terms of trade for developing countries, excluding petroleum exporters, have been moving in a negative direction over the 1970s, especially since 1973 (the overall index for 1976 = 87 against 1973 = 100).[4] The commodity terms of trade of selected agricultural products (considered against a basket of manufactures) show serious decline over 1973-6 for many of the region's key food export items, e.g. sugar, meat, wheat and maize.[5] Country terms of trade data are also strongly negative for the 1970-6 period in the case of most countries (e.g. Zimbabwe, Mozambique, Malawi, Tanzania).

A number of the southern African economies also suffer from other structural defects in trade patterns, such as relatively high commodity concentration ratios (in respect of exports), low net foreign exchange reserves in relation to import demands (e.g. Zambia), rising debt service ratios, large current account deficits as a proportion of GDP and export revenue instability.[6] Not all of these phenomena may be connected to agrarian export/import patterns; but their presence results in serious effects on long term agricultural sector planning and performance.

Most countries in the region must still import food. In the economies of Botswana, Lesotho and Swaziland, the cause relates in part to resource endowment and specialization patterns. In Mozambique and Angola the effects of the liberation war are still evident. There, reconstruction has not yet advanced to the point where it is possible to reject reliance on commercial imports or externally provided food assistance.[7] The issue is made more problematic by the growing refugee problem. A similar prospect now faces Zimbabwe and (later) Namibia for their initial periods of transition. While both Zambia and Tanzania are nearer selfsufficiency in staple foods, both are subject to severe droughts and have deficits in dairy products, vegetable, oil and wheat, etc. These developments could have serious regional implications. Indeed, unless southern African economies produce enough to meet local demand for essential agricultural products, foreign exchange and import requirements, there will develop a growing dependence on either world markets and/or RSA. Either option will tend to result in higher prices, deteriorating terms of trade and more serious politico-economic problems.

EMPLOYMENT, INCOME DISTRIBUTION AND POVERTY

Some data have already been given which indicate the size of the labour force in estate employment. Additional and important general points should also be made to make more complete this perspective on the agricultural sector in the region.

A. *Employment and Earnings Levels*

Stagnant or falling real average earnings over time characterize much of southern African estate agriculture. Thus in Zimbabwe average real agricultural labourers' earnings have been shown to be lower in 1974 than 1948.[8] This occurred during a period of rapid employment expansion to a level of 360,000 employees (around 39 per cent of the economy's labour force). No country in the southern African region shows any strong evidence of a sustained average real earnings growth over the 1960s and 1970s in respect of the bulk of their expanding estate labour force.

Second, there has existed a growth of wage labour in the smallholder sector of agriculture. This has resulted from the commercialization of the sector, the breakdown of the lineage economy, the introduction of export and cash crops, the growing incidence of rural stratification, and aid project and state policies in certain instances.

B. *Rural Income Concentration*

Another aspect relates to a concentration of rural income and wealth in the hands of a relatively small number of households.

In Botswana a 1976 Rural Income Distribution Survey found that 45 per cent of rural households had incomes below the austerely defined rural poverty datum line (1974 prices) relevant for their size and composition.[9] This proportion was 66 per cent in the case of freehold/estate farm employees. Poverty incidence recorded over the period was not significantly related to stagnant production or per head food output. The distribution of cattle (the principle rural movable asset) was much more skewed than the distribution of rural incomes. In fact, 5 per cent of households (or 10 per cent of cattle owning households) held 50 per cent of all cattle and 45 per cent of households held no cattle—this in a predominantly non-arable rural economy. The 1971 Census had reported this figure to be 41 per cent. Together with other evidence, these facts support the view that rural asset ownership has become more unequal over the last ten years. The same trend was visible in respect of overall and rural incomes which in 1974 recorded a Gini Coefficient of 0.57 in regard to the rural sector.[10]

In Malawi, a similar picture of acute poverty for smallholders and estate

128

households was identified for 1969. Then 9.3 per cent of smallholder households received no current cash incomes whilst a further 33.8 per cent obtained 45 per cent less than needed for meeting the income requirements of a household of two persons; yet average household size in this sector was 4.6 persons. Qualitative evidence was also found of a growing concentration in rural land ownership and usufruct, increasing numbers of landless persons, a concentration of incomes in those rural households with a capacity to market a surplus and increasing regional/district variations in income (as a result both of international project aid policy and impact and changing remittance patterns caused by the new situation affecting the volume/character and wage rates of the external contract labour supply to RSA and Zimbabwe).

In other migrant labour supplying economies (e.g. Lesotho, Swaziland and Mozambique), similar conditions and trends have been found.[11] These conditions have been compounded since 1974 by revised contract labour import policies adopted by RSA and by a declining foreign labour demand in pre-independent Zimbabwe since the 1960s. Both changes have reduced the overall inflows, concentrating incomes amongst migrants (as a result of wage stratification), and increasing the degree of inequality arising from the pattern of remittances. This in turn has added to other similar disequalizing pressures in the southern African countryside, as for example those which promote the interests of a small proportion of progressive farmers, lead to private land ownership of sizeable plots in or around lineage societies and result in an uneven allocation of investments and credits between areas and producers. The fact that the economies peripheral to RSA have had to absorb a large element of displaced labour from that country over the 1970s has added to the dimension of their rural poverty problems, since most of these workers have been rural based, often long term migrants.

In Tanzania, where relatively strong equity considerations have been part of policy formulation, the World Bank has argued that amongst smallholder households those in the rich regions on average achieved small increases in private real incomes over 1967–75.[12] By contrast, those in poor areas experienced significant declines. This indicates some worsening in the intrarural income distribution pattern, and by implication a rising incidence of poverty. However, this is not clear. Another study suggests real increases in rural incomes over 1967–78. The World Bank data may in large part reflect the high 1975 coffee prices and low 1975 cashew nut and food crop production, as the rich areas cash income was dominantly from coffee and the poor from cashew nut and food sales. The different 1978 results partly relate to lower coffee prices but also to radically higher food sales concentrated in middle and poor regions.

Another approach, based in part on an examination of nutritional data (Table 2), confirms a high incidence of acute rural poverty in large parts of southern Africa in the 1970s. These data, however, do not clearly identify the direction or intensity of trends. Rather, they point to chronic deficiencies

129

in the consumption of, and access to, food necessary for healthy subsistence. Complementary rural budget data confirm this broad picture (for Lesotho, Zimbabwe and RSA). Indeed, it would be surprising if recent southern African economic experience of lower growth rates in the 1970s, chronic balance of payments problems, in Zambia for example, and deteriorating primary commmodity prices (for instance, for sugar and other regionally important outputs like copper) permitted any improvement in conditions as they were found in the late 1960s. This is likely even assuming—as cannot be done—no worsening in the internal terms of trade and policy towards smallholders, marginal farmers, the landless, and estate employees.[13] Insofar as the latter have become increasingly preponderant in the wage-employment zones of southern central Africa (Malawi, Zambia, RSA, Zimbabwe and Namibia), there are strong reasons for accepting that there have been negative trends in average consumption levels. If crises areas are also taken into consideration—rural inhabitants in drought affected zones and in many recently wartorn economies (e.g. Mozambique, Zimbabwe and Namibia)—then the perspective on past trends in the 1970s looks far from encouraging. It must also be remembered that few southern African countries have effectively implemented income equalization-type policies. There are considerable structural biases still against the rural, especially non-modern, sectors and these biases have generally strengthened over the 1970s.

C. Development and Poverty Elimination: a Central Issue

These poverty issues need to be addressed in agrarian policy. Indeed, in many ways it is the central problem of the rural sector and development itself. Hence new regional strategies must be addressed in the light of their contribution to resolution of these issues. The evaluation of options, therefore, needs to embrace criteria related to poverty and distributional effects, the short and long term impact of new alternatives and a measure of the equitable allocation of costs and benefits between participating states.

SOME CONSTRAINTS AND POLICY ISSUES IN AGRICULTURAL DEVELOPMENT

A number of identifiable constraints to agricultural development exist in southern Africa. These vary in character and degree between countries. What follows here is an elaboration of the principal constraints based on both macro and sectoral perspectives. These are noted with reference to the agrarian structure, the use of productive capacity, the expansion or improvement of capacity, and the efficiency of the agrarian systems in operation in the various economies of the region.

Not all of these constraints can be dealt with by new or improved regional and/or international policies. But the latter policies could act directly or indirectly on some of these constraints in the short and long run. Others,

130

often the most critical ones, lie squarely in the realm of domestic economic policy and politics. Nonetheless, it is important to appreciate the overall context and difficulties facing the various economies if new policies are to be considered, formulated and eventually sanctioned for implementation.

THE MACRO-CONTEXT AND THE STRUCTURE OF AGRICULTURAL PRODUCTION

A. *Asset-Holding Patterns*

One of the most important macro-structural features relates to asset-holding patterns, especially in regard to land. In southern Africa private land coexists with state land and smallholders' plots (individually or communally grouped) under lineage forms of land allocation, usufruct and inheritance. In addition, various coöperative holding patterns are found. Over time the incidence of private holdings has risen. This has been especially true in minority ruled southern/central African economies where plantation sectors are large; but it has also happened in other market oriented economies such as Malawi and Botswana, partly under the influence of large scale and medium sized farming schemes. Meanwhile too, there appears to have been a concentraton in the access to usufruct rights and land in various parts. Recent communal holding and/or allocation trends in Mozambique, Angola and Tanzania have begun to alter the rate and pattern of land concentration, reversing the process in certain instances.

Trends of landholding inequality underpin income inequality and typically accentuate it. They have also been associated with the structural emergence of landlessness, tenancy and sharecropping—all these categories form sizeable elements of the rural poor. For these reasons land redistribution has a central role to play in correcting historical imbalances and reducing rural poverty. Such reforms might also be instrumental in increasing aggregate rural employment levels.

However, this still leaves unresolved strategic questions of the extent and scale of reforms, their timing and sequencing, the necessary ancillary policy support required, problems of control over allied technological changes, choice of poverty focus and selection of measures to ensure the sustainability of new ownership/usufruct patterns over time.

Regional/international policies cannot be easily directed towards land reform, but various forms of co-operation and assistance could be used to develop an acceptable approach to the issue, given sufficient political will to make necessary changes.

B. *Agricultural Reform*

At the same time land reform will not alone bring a transformation of rural production. Positive changes in the agrarian system are unlikely to result from alterations in the pattern of landholding. They need to be

131

accompanied by changes in the organization of production, incentive structures, technological applications and the overall development context. The changing alignment of these features may affect growth and efficiency, rates and forms of employment absorption, income distribution and the availability and allocation of investible surpluses.

For instance, the massive promotion of co-operatives may not necessarily alleviate these difficulties. Co-operatives only alter one element in the rural milieu and usually in favour of richer peasants or ranchers. Therefore, there seems no alternative to policy changes along a wide spectrum of elements in the agrarian economy, in order to obtain either improvement in performance or facilitate the transition from one inferior system to another adjudged to have greater potential capabilities in halting and reversing trends towards greater rural poverty. The special conditions of each economy also make it vital that economic strategy be perceived in country-specific terms. Indeed the prospects of naive replication are small and the risks high. Nonetheless, the crucial relation of the poverty problem of food supply and rural development is widely recognized. As the FAO Tenth Regional Conference for Africa reports: 'the problem of undernourishment calls for a broadbased attack on the poverty problem'.[14]

Under southern African conditions, resettlement to form village co-operative units involves large population movements and the potential short term disruption of production; but over time it could offer greater asset and income equality, lower cost in the provision of inputs and services and cheaper fixed costs to new land expansion. Under peaceful conditions (as in the Ujaama villagization process in Tanzania) the gains have been slow to emerge and have been partly dependent on incentive structures and central and local bureaucratic decisions about the degree of compulsion in villagization. Elsewhere, as in Mozambique, such villages (based on war-constructed aldeamentos) have partly emerged out of the aftermath of colonial war; hence immediate gains in comparison to the war period have been readily apparent. In both cases, however, long term returns will depend on the sustainability of the new systems of production. In neither case is a significant proportion of agricultural production (as opposed to other economic activity including small scale investment) actually communal in both application of labour and distribution of proceeds.

C. *State Policies on Investment, Subsidies and Prices*

State policy—at a macro-level—also plays a vital role. It can be so constructed as to favour, remain neutral towards or seriously disadvantage the rural sector. The resulting balance not only determines general incentives to producers in the sector but in its specific emphases affects the position of particular socio-economic groups within the rural economy.

Net transfers of resources out of agriculture can be compatible with poverty reduction provided non-agrarian accumulation does not rest upon the poorest of the rural sector. Similarly, transfers into agriculture need not necessarily benefit the poor, e.g. where high subsidies to capital or protectionism favour large scale producers who have few enforced obligations in respect of their employees (as has probably occurred in the plantation sector throughout southern Africa, and even more notably in respect to the pre-independent Zimbabwe's white farmer community).

The effects of equitable product pricing structures may also be offset by rural consumer pricing policy. This may be observed when account is taken of the particular configuration of expenditure patterns of the rural poor. Sizeable items of outlay in the latter's budget may be determined by usually inflexible administered prices, such as those for health, education and transport. Usually, the poor have little control over these price levels. Food prices, however, tend to fluctuate widely and more quickly than average prices. Only selfsubsistence producers find substantial isolation from this effect—and such groups now form a dwindling element of rural households in southern Africa. The distribution of gains and losses from high food prices has in most countries tended to favour better-off groups to the disadvantage of poorer wage earners, the landless and marginalized producers. State action to counter this involves more than a decision to exercise administrative fiat: it also requires greater control over the private sector, over price formulation policy and also over the transnational corporations supplying inputs or purchasing outputs.

The above mentioned macro-constraints which concern landholding, the organization of production, income inequality and state investment and price policies, play a major role in the agricultural sector. At the same time, more specific kinds of constraints can also be identified.

CONSTRAINTS ON THE USE AND ALLOCATION OF PRODUCTIVE CAPACITY

Land assets, technology, extension services and credit constitute important elements of productive capacity. In southern Africa, they are not always put to best use.

Certain economies have inadequate productive capcity; yet their existing capacity may not be fully or effectively utilized. Thus, for example, a land surplus situation is often found on estates in Zimbabwe, Namibia and Botswana, while there are adjacent areas of land scarcity.

In the field of technical services and research, resources are often orientated towards the requirements of largescale units, export crops or TNCs. Smallholders tend to benefit far less from systematic research programmes, e.g. in the field of technological transfer, hand tools and implements, information dissemination and so on. Not only do private organizations concentrate on supplying the needs of the non-smallholder sector but so, often, do state agencies, marketing boards and universities. A better organization of technological/research inputs and applications would go some way to dealing with existing development problems.

Extension services also tend to be allocated to better-off farmers. While the latter may be the ones likely to make best use of these resources in the short term, they are not the ones in most need of assistance. In general, too, it is probably correct to state that extension/farmer services could be much improved—in quantity, range of service, quality and frequency of contact and follow-up.

Credit continues to be allocated unevenly. Partly this arises from private sector allocation criteria—scarcity of loans, collateral needs and profitability. Similar patterns also apply to state credit institutions. In the case of state bodies using external funds it often relates to the tendency of the external funders to tie the credits to specific industrial or export crops. A better distribution could improve productivity in the lowest income households.

Misuse of land resources, the application of inappropriate technologies, an insufficiency of extension services and credit problems have acted in concert. They have also been important elements behind poor performance in agricultural (and especially food) production. Consequently, much of the region has become less self-sufficient—notably in essential foodstuffs; and problems of low yields and gradualist extension of new cultivated areas have thus remained.

THE EXPANSION AND IMPROVEMENT OF PRODUCTIVE CAPACITY

Perhaps only limited gains can be anticipated from changes in allocative patterns and from the minimization of unused capacity. All southern African economies could usefully benefit from expanded productive capacity. But this requires either broader level rationalization (perhaps on a regional level) or development assistance from external sources. Either mechanism might help reverse or ease certain of the existing constraints.

For example, skilled agricultural personnel are in short supply throughout the region. This covers administrators, technicians, veterinary services, machine operators and farm managers. Regional policy could help economize on these scarce resources; external assistance could supplement the available supply. It might also be used in expanding training programmes or in raising the quality of training given. In particular, more women need to receive agricultural training and have access to technical institutions. There is a dearth of qualified instructors who have an in-depth familiarity with local problems. Staff turnover levels in extension branches tend to be too high and have a serious negative effect on extension worker/farmer contacts and producer performance. Agricultural education and technical training in schools is still abysmal in relation to development needs.

New research facilities could be established on a regional basis. These could either be built around existing institutions, or they could take up new roles which have not been undertaken before. There is much sense in a co-ordinated regional approach on these issues—in the case of the livestock industry, in the field of grain production, and even in respect of export crops like tobacco, sugar and cotton.

External funds could be used to supplement credit programmes and expand them in new directions. New funding could even be applied regionally (in the case of a package of joint projects). The new allocations might be geared to smaller, more deprived households and be linked to other services and technical assistance.

Infrastructural problems hamper production. The result is higher input costs and more expensive marketing. New road systems, feeder roads, rail services and storage systems, as well as air links, could play a bigger part in regional food trade and agricultural output expansion. These developments need not necessarily be linked to international markets but might be orientated towards helping to keep domestic food prices lower by improving the volume and costs of supply, at the same time as providing more equitable opportunities for smaller producers.

Reconstruction problems have already had to be faced in Mozambique and Angola. This experience can be very important for Zimbabwe and (later) Namibia. It should be evaluated and specific difficulties identified.

The planning skills available to southern African countries are central to future development. Training and advice might be offered in these areas. Perhaps an interchange of data and information, as well as regular meetings between planners in the region, would be one way to facilitate improvements.

The knowledge base concerning soils, agro-ecological data and water systems (rainfall, dams, etc.) could be much improved in a similar manner. It is important in this connection that practical knowledge on these issues permeates to lower/district levels where it can be directly and adaptively applied. Measures should be taken to achieve this end. A better economic data base is needed, e.g. in the form of farm surveys, rural household income/expenditure surveys, censuses of agriculture.

The managerial constraint requires special attention. Too often southern African economies must depend on TNC expertise or expatriates. Local training needs to be developed at all levels. Specific training schemes might be directed towards large scale production and parastatal needs. Other schemes could complement the former by operating at the farm management level in the spheres of costing, budgeting and planning.

ALTERNATIVES AND PROPOSALS FOR THE FUTURE

Many development programmes and options are specific to particular economies or economy types.[15] There are however a large number of proposals with a regional dimension. In order to be brief and specific, a limited number of these are listed which relate to issues of such fundamental importance as the possible reduction in dependence on RSA, international assistance, agricultural sector reconstruction, technical assistance, personnel and training capacity, institutional needs and data/planning requirements. (The listing does not include any order of preference or recommendation.)

(a) The development of a Southern African Regional Food Plan, perhaps moulded around the Programme of the FAO Regional Food Plan for Africa. Initial objectives, in conjunction with the FAO's Food Security System, might be food security, storage and processing, e.g. intraregional loans of grain, as have been made by Tanzania to Mozambique, might be made more generally and automatically available. But beyond this, it could extend to the development of food production systems. The latter would need to embrace short, medium and long term programmes. Short term needs could focus on packages of improved production practices, better supporting services, the extension of mechanical power in agriculture, irrigation improvements, marine fishing development (in the context of control over foreign fleets) and the promotion of substitute foods (to help curb imports). Longer term needs would encompass investment in new irrigation capacities, eradication of human and livestock diseases (notably trypanosomiasis and onchocerciasis), more vigorous land and water conservation and infrastructural development. The ECA's Lusaka-based MULPOC is one institution, already in place, which might be utilized to undertake the preparatory and planning side of this task—in conjunction with FAO, other UN agencies and bilateral institutions. The International Centre for Research in Semi-arid Tropics (ICRISAT) could be requested to set up a regional centre.

(b) The establishment of an inventory of regional land resources, soil types and crop potentials—as a basis for regional investment policy and planning. This might be effected through the Inter-African Bureau for Soils.

(c) A Fund for regionally linked land settlement schemes and expansion in cultivated areas e.g. in border areas where agro-economic potential justifies large outlays for infrastructure and common services. This could be oriented towards both investment and input needs designed to expand permanent crop lands and develop irrigation schemes.

(d) Direct assistance to labour exporting countries in negotiations and policy formulation vis-à-vis contract labour supply to RSA—the aim being to co-ordinate and reduce dependence on this employment.

(e) A special investigation, on a comprehensive scale, of the possible contingency needs for regional agricultural development should relations between the regional states and RSA become strained if economic conditions in South Africa deteriorate in the next 5–10 years.

136

(f) Aid for measures needed to implement regional trade policy in agricultural (especially food) products—e.g. linked to the ECA's Preferential Trade Area scheme or to multicountry or regional production/trade agreements in respect to selected agricultural commodities. Aid could be channelled through the African Development Bank or the Arab Bank for Economic Development in Africa, as well as other established institutions, or through a new Regional Development Bank.

(g) A Regional Livestock Board with responsibility for co-ordination, research, planning and problem solving, with special responsibility for carrying capacity and anti-desertification research and information dissemination.

(h) Evaluation of reconstruction policies and experience in Mozambique and Angola with a view to lessons for Zimbabwe and (later) Namibia.

(i) A regional agricultural skills development programme suitably funded and staffed.

(j) A greater share of aid and finance for the agricultural sector from bilateral and multilateral institutions.

(k) Assistance in the planning and finance of land reform measures.

(l) A review of existing regional research and development capacity, especially that connected to agriculture, as well as future demands in this sphere in the medium and long term. This could serve as a basis for investment, planning, external assistance and co-ordinated reduction in current levels of dependence on RSA. It should cover all technical areas embracing agro-allied industries, institutional needs, and servicing requirements. Consideration could then be given to creating an institutional framework for regional specialization in meeting local research and development and technical needs (e.g. in the form of research, veterinary colleges, university faculties, etc.).

(m) An Agricultural Development Board, constituted of ministers and backed up by technical experts. It could meet regularly to co-ordinate and plan regional agrarian development. This could be based on agreed guidelines and terms of reference. It could attempt to resolve common problems and be used as an instrument for action on an international level vis-à-vis importers and other bodies.

(n) Examination of the position of the southern African countries in terms of current commodity agreements (e.g. the International Sugar Agreement) in order to promote the regional situation.

(o) Efforts designed to develop adequate data on the rural sectors of southern Africa. The data needs to be consistent with reality and planning needs and over time. The first form of consistency needed is national, but regional and international consistency—when not at the expense of national relevance, accuracy and applicability—is also desirable. This could take the form of greater co-ordination between national statistical offices and government departments. Standardization is needed not only in the form of annual accounts but also with regard to censuses taken from time to time. New data could also be gathered and finance provided for surveys. UN agencies such as ECA might also assist in this area. For example, data contained in the FAO's Regional Food Plan for Africa, which shows subregional figures based on agro-ecological and ECA-MULPOC country groupings, could be disaggregated and re-analysed on a newly defined regional basis for southern Africa itself.

(p) Investigations into regional fishing industry prospects and possible joint institutions on the west and east coasts of the continent.

(q) Investigations into regional forestry development schemes especially in border areas (e.g. Zimbabwe and Mozambique).

(r) Investigations into the character and performance of internal and external sources of finance for agricultural development in the region, with a view to devising measures to improve the use of current allocations and identify additional needs.

NOTES

1. See detailed comments in D. W. Blades, *Non-Monetary (Subsistence) Activities in the National Accounts of Developing Countries*, OECD Development Centre, Paris, 1975.
2. Data drawn from FAO, *The State of Food and Agriculture 1977*, Rome, 1978 (Annex Table 12).
3. *Ibid*, (Section 2–47).
4. *Ibid*, (Section 1–36).
5. IBRD, *Commodity Trade and Price Trends*, Washington, 1978.
6. On aspects of these issues see ECA, *Trade Promotion Among the Countries of Eastern and Southern Africa*, (ECA MULPOC/ LUSAKA, 27 October 1977).
7. For example, see data contained in UN Report of the Economic and Social Council, *Assistance to Mozambique*, (A/33/173), 1978; also SIDA, *Mozambique: Agricultural Sector Review*, Stockholm, 30 June 1978 (mimeo).
8. ILO, *Labour Conditions and Discrimination in Southern Rhodesia/Zimbabwe*, Geneva, 1977.
9. Republic of Botswana, *The Rural Income Distribution Survey of Botswana 1974/5*, CSO, Gaborone, 1976.

10. Republic of Botswana, *National Development Plan 1976-81*, Ministry of Finance and Development Planning, Gaborone, 1977.

11. See, for example, ILO, *Reducing Dependence: A Strategy for Productive Employment and Development in Swaziland*, JASPA, Addis Ababa, 1977; ILO, *Options for a Dependent Economy: Development, Employment and Equity Problems in Lesotho*, JASPA, Addis Ababa, 1978; Universidade Eduardo Mondlane, *The Mozambican Miner: A Study in the Export of Labour*, Maputo, 1977.

12. See, S. N. Acharya, Perspectives and Problems of Development in Low-Income, Sub-Saharan Africa, in *Two Studies of Development in Sub-Saharan Africa*, World Bank Staff Working Paper, No. 300, Washington, 1978. Alternative data from draft working paper by D. Ghai and R. Green prepared for ILO.

13. See, for Zambia, the study by F. J. Maimbo and J. Fry, An Investigation into the Change in the Terms of Trade Between Rural and Urban Sectors—Zambia, *African Social Research*, 12, 1971; and, for Tanzania, see, ILO, *Towards Self-Reliance: Development, Employment and Equity Issues in Tanzania*, JASPA Addis Ababa, 1978.

14. FAO, Regional Food Plan for Africa (ARC/78/5), Rome, July 1978.

15. See, for example 'First Steps Toward Economic Integration', SADCC Sectoral Paper (in this volume) and also SECID, Regional Overview of Development Concerns in the Agricultural Sectors of Southern Africa, Agency for International Development Colloquium on Development Issues and Opportunities for Co-operation in Southern Africa, Washington, 1979 (mimeo).

TABLE 1
Tractor use for selected countries in Southern Africa (1969/76)

	Total No. in Use		*Number of Tractors Per 1000 ha. of Arable Land and Land under Permanent Crops (1976)*
	1969-71	*1976*	
Botswana	78	92	0.1
Lesotho	410	1,000	2.5
Swaziland	1,211	1,950	9.7
Namibia	2,050	2,350	3.4
Zimbabwe	17,000	19,300	7.7
Mozambique	4,198	5,550	1.8
Malawi	843	1,000	0.4
Tanzania	5,593	7,400	1.2
TOTAL	31,383	38,642	2.3
RSA	155,042	188,000	12.9

Source: FAO, *Production Yearbook*, 1977

Note: For Angola and Zambia the figures in the last column were 5.2 and 0.8 respectively. As of 1976 Angola had 9,500 tractors whilst Zambia had 4,200 in use.

TABLE 2
Per caput dietary energy supplies in relation to nutritional requirements, selected developing countries and areas

	Average 1969–71	Average 1972–74	1970	1971	1972	1973	1974	Requirements
			Percent of requirements					Kilocalories per caput per day
AFRICA	92	91	92	92	91	90	91	2,340
Algeria	78	86	77	79	84	86	88	2,400
Angola	85	85	85	86	85	84	86	2,350
Benin	96	89	97	95	92	87	87	2,300
Botswana	91	87	90	94	89	87	85	2,320
Burundi	99	101	99	99	101	102	99	2,330
Cameroon	104	103	103	105	104	102	102	2,320
Central African Empire	96	103	97	99	102	104	102	2,260
Chad	88	74	89	83	76	72	75	2,380
Congo	99	102	97	101	106	103	98	2,220
Ethiopia	93	88	94	93	92	89	82	2,330
Gabon	97	97	95	97	97	96	98	2,340
Gambia	97	97	98	97	96	96	98	2,380
Ghana	99	100	99	99	100	99	101	2,300
Guinea	90	86	90	90	88	87	84	2,310
Ivory Coast	113	114	114	113	113	113	115	2,310
Kenya	97	92	98	99	93	92	91	2,320
Lesotho	96	97	95	97	90	99	100	2,280
Liberia	84	86	84	85	84	86	87	2,310
Madagascar	108	104	108	107	105	102	105	2,270
Malawi	101	104	103	104	104	105	103	2,320
Mali	88	75	88	88	75	74	75	2,350
Mauritania	86	81	87	85	79	82	82	2,310
Mauritius	105	107	106	108	109	105	108	2,270
Morocco	102	107	102	105	107	107	108	2,420
Mozambique	86	85	86	85	84	87	84	2,340
Niger	85	79	83	82	79	81	78	2,350
Nigeria	89	88	89	91	90	85	88	2,360
Rhodesia	100	104	96	102	103	99	108	2,390
Rwanda	94	91	96	95	91	91	90	2,320
Senegal	94	92	91	94	84	94	97	2,380
Sierra Leone	100	98	100	100	99	98	97	2,300
Somalia	81	83	80	83	86	84	79	2,310
Swaziland	89	91	90	94	93	92	89	2,320
Tanzania	85	84	88	83	82	85	86	2,320
Togo	94	94	94	96	95	92	96	2,300
Tunisia	93	99	93	96	99	98	102	2,390
Uganda	96	92	97	96	95	91	90	2,330

140

	Average 1969-71	Average	1970	1971	1972	1973	1974	Requirements
								Kilocalories per caput per day
			Percent of requirements					
Upper Volta	78	73	80	73	71	70	78	2,370
Zaire	91	83	92	87	82	83	85	2,220
Zambia	86	87	84	87	87	85	89	2,310

Source: FAO, *The State of Food and Agriculture* 1977, Rome, 1978.

TABLE 3
Cropping pattern in Southern Africa

	Angola	Bots	Les	Malaw	Mzqe	Nam	Swazi	Tan	Zam	Zimb
Wheat	X	X	X	X		X	X	X	X	X
Rice	X			X	X			X	X	X
Barley										X
Maize	X	X	X	X	X	X	X	X	X	X
Millet	X	X			X	X		X	X	X
Sorghum		X	X	X	X	X	X	X	X	X
Potatoes	X			X	X			X	X	X
Sweet Potatoes	X				X			X	X	X
Cassava	X			X	X			X		X
Pulses	X	X	X	X	X	X	X	X	X	X
Groundnuts	X	X		X	X			X	X	X
Oil Seeds	X	X		X	X			X	X	X
Cotton	X	X		X	X		X	X	X	X
Vegetables and Melon	X	X	X	X	X	X	X	X	X	X
Sugar Cane	X			X	X		X	X	X	X
Citrus	X			X	X		X	X	X	X
Bananas	X			X	X		X	X	X	X
Coffee	X			X	X			X	X	X
Cocoa	X									
Tea				X	X			X		X
Tobacco	X			X	X		X	X	X	X
Jute	X				X					
Sisal	X			X	X			X		

Source: FAO Production Yearbook 1977

X = grown in the country.

141

TABLE 4
Livestock pattern in Southern Africa (1977)

Livestock (000)	Angola	Botswana	Lesotho	Malawi	Mozambique	Namibia	Swaziland	Tanzania	Zambia	Zimbabwe	TOTAL
Horses, Asses, & Mules	53	49	113	–	20	111	17	160	2	105	630
Cattle	3,050	2,400	600	729	1,350	2,875	640	14,817	1,860	6,247	34,568
Sheep	210	450	1,680	89	95	5,085	37	3,000	50	818	11,514
Goats	920	1,100	920	763	350	2,026	280	4,700	292	2,167	13,518
Poultry	5,100	600	1,100	8,500	16,500	500	500	20,700	15,400	8,500	77,400

Source: FAO, *Production Yearbook*, 1977.

TABLE 5

Southern African economically active population: growth, allocation and projects, 1950–1990

	(30) Labour Force Annual Rates of Growth (%)				(31) Labour Force Allocation (thousands)						(32) Population Projections (total) Thousands			
	men		total		Agriculture		Industry		Services					
	1960/5	1965/70	1960/5	1965/70	1950	1970	1950	1970	1950	1970	1975	1980	1985	1990
Botswana	0.37	0.06	0.57	0.90	222	258	5	11	8	28	691	795	923	1,072
Lesotho	1.41	2.48	1.17	1.89	425	521	4	19	13	41	1,148	1,284	1,440	1,617
Swaziland	2.03	2.21	2.09	2.28	125	161	4	12	7	25	469	542	626	721
Namibia	2.54	2.61	2.61	2.67	109	146	17	55	33	62	883	1,024	1,192	1,390
Zimbabwe	3.31	3.30	3.29	3.27	732	1,198	101	252	165	425	6,272	7,460	8,895	10,616
Mozambique	1.80	1.97	1.78	1.95	2,125	2,484	109	430	218	467	9,223	10,476	11,962	13,697
Malawi	1.79	1.91	1.71	1.83	1,409	1,823	27	75	42	148	4,909	5,573	6,348	7,238
Tanzania	2.34	2.49	2.27	2.41	3,493	4,960	102	286	176	523	15,388	17,965	21,038	24,693
Zambia	2.48	2.61	2.37	2.48	882	1,215	62	146	121	307	5,004	5,872	6,933	8,213
Angola	1.60	1.76	1.63	1.79	848	995	114	221	178	345	6,394	7,276	8,343	9,607
Sub-total	n/a	n/a	n/a	n/a	10,370	13,761	545	1,507	961	2,371	50,381	58,267	67,700	78,864
South Africa	1.81	2.31	3.24	3.76	1,592	2,480	1,336	2,372	1,662	3,180	24,663	28,533	32,955	37,881
Total	n/a	n/a	n/a	n/a	11,962	16,241	1,881	3,879	2,623	5,551	75,044	86,800	100,655	116,745

Source: ILO, Labour Force Estimates and Projections 1950–2000, Geneva, 1977.

143

TABLE 5 continued

Southern African economically active population: growth, allocation and projects, 1950–1990

	(33) Labour Force Activity Rates					numbers				(34) Total Labour Force Growth			
						men		total		rates men		total	
	1970	1975	1980	1985	1990	1975	1990	1975	1990	1970/5	1985/90	1970/5	1985/90
Botswana	48.17	47.70	45.53	45.19	44.01	158	242	330	472	2.42	2.97	2.09	2.49
Lesotho	55.75	54.29	52.41	50.77	49.65	346	453	623	803	1.48	2.06	1.40	1.90
Swaziland	48.48	46.98	45.55	44.31	43.48	120	174	221	313	2.25	2.61	2.18	2.47
Namibia	34.33	33.20	31.98	31.06	30.25	226	326	293	420	2.30	2.59	2.19	2.58
Zimbabwe	35.32	34.10	32.82	31.75	30.81	1,507	2,322	2,139	3,277	2.73	3.05	2.67	3.02
Mozambique	41.06	39.55	37.74	36.06	34.69	2,723	3,585	3,648	4,751	1.61	2.01	1.53	1.94
Malawi	46.92	45.80	44.57	43.49	42.70	1,406	1,963	2,249	3,091	2.00	2.40	1.91	2.29
Tanzania	43.46	42.16	40.79	39.60	38.65	4,136	6,196	6,488	9,544	2.49	2.69	2.38	2.56
Zambia	38.85	37.61	36.29	34.99	33.87	1,270	1,912	1,882	2,782	2.55	2.71	2.44	2.59
Angola	27.54	26.99	26.35	25.70	24.66	1,571	2,165	1,726	2,420	1.92	2.10	2.02	2.23
Sub-Total	n/a	n/a	n/a	n/a	n/a	13,463	19,338	19,599	27,873	n/a	n/a	n/a	n/a
South Africa	37.36	37.08	38.53	35.36	35.19	6,035	8,486	9,145	13,332	2.28	2.43	2.63	2.73
Total	n/a	n/a	n/a	n/a	n/a	19,498	27,824	28,744	41,205	n/a	n/a	n/a	n/a

144

TABLE 6
Export/import composition in selected countries of
Southern Africa 1970–73

| Country | Merchandise Exports US$ millions Percentage | | | | | Merchandise Imports US$ millions Percentage | | | | |
	Value	Food	Other Agric.	Mineral	Mfg.	Value	Food	Fuel	Machinery	Other Mfg.
Botswana	–	–	–	–	–	–	–	–	–	–
Lesotho	5	27.1	52.1		20.8	34	29.5	5.7	11.5	53.3
Swaziland	–	–	–	–	–	–	–	–	–	–
Mozambique	175	57.2	23.0	10.3	9.5	327	21.6	8.4	35.2	34.8
Malawi	99	84.9	4.8	2.7	7.6	142	19.4	8.9	30.2	41.5
Zimbabwe[1]	499	41.1	1.6	25.3	32.0	417	21.8	4.9	31.7	41.6
South Africa	3528	30.1	11.3	28.2	30.4	5507	12.5	6.9	48.4	32.2

Source: World Bank, *World Tables 1976*, John Hopkins, Baltimore, 1976.

Notes: [1] In 1965 in the case of the proportions, 1973 for the value data.

Energy, Water and Mineral Resources

INTRODUCTION

Data available on energy, mineral and water resources in southern Africa are meagre, contradictory, unreliable and outdated. There is neither a statistical nor even a solid judgemental base on which to build policy options with any confidence except in the most general terms. Data use has therefore been minimized and the few statistics utilized in this paper must be taken with the utmost circumspection.

In the event, reliance had to be placed very heavily on the most recent editions available of UN statistical documents; annual or bi-annual national inventory materials for the continent (*African Contemporary Record, Africa South of the Sahara*, etc.); a selection of the better news magazines (e.g. *Africa Report*, the London *Economist, African Development*); and a miscellaneous collection of generally outdated journal articles. Dozens of books were investigated, but few were of substantive use. Permeating the information system was the intrinsic problem of bias in one direction or another.

The nature of the information problem is being emphasized, not as an excuse, but for two more positive reasons. One is that the reader must condition his/her interpretations of the discussion by an awareness of these deficiencies. Second, a priority activity of any proposed southern African co-operative institution should be an active and effective information centre. It could garner the real data base for the energy/water and other sectors. That base is largely comprised of surveys and feasibility studies done by consultants for international agencies, national governments and—in minerals—private firms. These primary and critical materials do not emerge into the public or the researcher's domain, nor do they very often enter in any meaningful sense into the knowledge of government decision takers or advisors.

BACKGROUND

GENERAL CHARACTER OF INTERSTATE CO-OPERATION

This is a policy paper. It deals with regional development options available in southern Africa to promote energy, mineral and water resource develop-

146

ment. The environment in which these policy developments must occur is first described briefly. That political economy and its dynamics condition and circumscribe the nature of such policy, yet, simultaneously, provide the challenge and prospects for its formulation and evolution. Individual sectors are then discussed.

Policy options for interstate development co-operation activities must be seen over time and in the light of:

(a) their political viability for each co-operating state and for the group as a whole;

(b) the volume, nature and interstate distribution of their political and economic benefits and costs;

(c) their political and economic priorities. That is, will the scarce human and financial resources expended provide net political and economic benefits greater than the use of those same resources in alternative (nationally oriented) ways?

THE REGION'S ECONOMY

Realistic interstate development policy making must face the region's basic facts of economic life:

(a) stark poverty; the bulk of the population lives at a precarious, insecure and inadequate level;

(b) utterly inadequate social, administrative and economic infrastructure;

(c) the virtually universal failure to develop the small farmer/small herder economy. There are some exceptions, e.g. in parts of Malawi and Tanzania;

(d) the dynamics of rural development tend toward worsening, not improving this base. These include erosion, deforestation, watershed debilitation, desertification, declining soil fertility, and cumulative impacts of recurrent droughts. Swollen urban unemployed populations are testimony to negative rural dynamics;

(e) distance: the region is far from world industrial centres, meaning higher transport costs for imports and exports. Within the region goods, and people, must travel enormous distances. Road and rail investment and variable costs per ton moved are extremely high. For the five landlocked nations, transit is dependent on the changing politics and economics of neighbours;

(f) dependence on a very narrow range of export commodities for foreign exchange. Earnings are thus highly sensitive to export volumes and prices;

147

(g) dependence upon a narrow range of markets which absorb the bulk of the exports;

(h) the historical dependence upon a reasonably narrow range of countries to supply imports, with the RSA a dominant source for five states and an important one for three;

(i) the dependence of governments upon highly restricted sources of revenue, typically taxes/duties on products of and, recently, equity participation in resource industries. Revenues like foreign exchange earnings are highly sensitive to export volumes and values;

(j) the general failure of the modern sector—mines, processing, plantations—to stimulate other elements in the economy. Backward and forward linkages, while gradually expanding, remain both meagre and fragile;

(k) sensitivity to petroleum prices and supplies. Despite surveying and exploratory drilling throughout the region, only Angola produces petroleum. Hydro and coalbased thermal power have significant prospects, but an assured supply of petroleum products will continue to be essential. Petroleum imports consume inordinate shares of foreign earnings;

(l) the dominating influence of transnational firms. Particularly through the mining and financing sectors TNCs influence the key production and foreign trade activities. Politically uncomfortable, their capital, technology, personnel and marketing resources are nonetheless still required.

POLITICAL ECONOMY DYNAMICS

Several basic dynamics influence the southern African political economy milieu. Their existence makes it important to avoid any rigid institutionalization as regional co-operation is introduced. There are numerous examples, in Africa and elsewhere of co-operative arrangements which were too rigid to be dynamically viable. These dynamics include:

A. The timing of Namibian independence;

B. The timing and nature of the political evolution of the Republic of South Africa;

C. The timing and nature of a range of evolving international forces as they affect the region, including:

(a) inflationary pressures, especially petroleum prices and availabilities;

(b) trends in the developed countries, and hence demands for the prices of the region's exports;

(c) the nature and availability of international credits, including bilateral and multilateral aid programmes, for governments and parastatals;

(d) the evolution of TNC strategies and capacities, particularly of those engaged in mineral and fossil fuel development;

(e) the nature and timing of production expansion in other parts of the world of the region's main exports; the evolution of comparative cost/price structures for the region's export production.

INTERSTATE POLICY REQUIREMENTS

These characteristics and dynamics suggest several requirements. One is that any multinational policy must be flexible. Internal and external political economic circumstances alter quickly and qualitatively. Multinational institutional machinery must be able to adjust to these alterations and do its best to predict them.

Second, regional policy must genuinely be accepted by each participating state. On many policy issues for which effective action is possible only by all or most regional states acting jointly, e.g. petroleum import policy, or the cartelization of a particular export mineral, genuine agreement of all to act in a specific way will by no means be easy to achieve. Yet short cuts dare not be tried if they will result in the introduction of policies that do not have, genuinely, the support of each member state.

In the light of this, a third feature becomes critical. Interstate co-operation policy must be developed and presented for consideration in packages. Any state can then trade off some costs for particular critical benefits from other measures.

Finally, the details of how and when the dependence on RSA will be reduced will be complex to decide and difficult to implement. There are clearly degrees of operational dependency and deficiencies in the ability of member states to finance greater independence.

Several states are so enmeshed with RSA investment, transport, market, customs, financial, employment and other systems that an abrupt divorce would spell economic suicide. Lesotho and Swaziland are in this category. This does not mean that such nations cannot seek diversification and greater balance, nor that regional co-operation is irrelevant; but that dependence reduction will be more limited and slower than they would wish.

At the opposite end of the spectrum are countries such as Tanzania, Angola and, almost to the same degree, Zambia plus (if it so wished) Malawi. Such nations either have little investment or trade connections, or have the resources to reduce dependence.

Mozambique has numerous ties, especially through RSA hydropower investments. Namibia is heavily entwined with the RSA, but has potential direct access to world markets and sources of supply and opportunities for co-operation with Angola and Botswana. Botswana has mining, transport and water development opportunities which can be oriented outwards instead of southward. Zimbabwe can now reorient away from RSA and has good transport links to regional neighbours; indeed prior to 1965 Southern Rhodesia was in many respects less dependent on RSA.

Permeating the region, however, is the dominance of RSA interests in the mining sector. Mining, petroleum supply, and transport are the most difficult areas of RSA dominance to minimize and therefore potentially the ones in which regional co-operation is critical.

OBJECTIVES OF MULTINATIONAL CO-ORDINATION

What are the common causes in southern Africa? What are the common enemies? Why seek co-ordinated policies? Any co-ordination policy not based on a cause common to the majority of those affected, and not directed against an enemy common to the majority, is going to fail.

REGIONAL COMMON CAUSES

What are the common causes or concerns in the region?

(a) the need to relieve the stark poverty and insecurity of the majority of peoples;

(b) a sense of helplessness with respect to the dominance and vagaries of the international economy;

(c) a sense of political frustration over the very narrow range of options which the states in fact enjoy and over the continued power of RSA, of the TNCs and of aid and financial agencies;

(d) a dearth of human and financial resources;

(e) the humiliating process of seeking and receiving external multilateral and bilateral aid which then often appears to serve the objectives of the donor more directly than those of the recipient;

(f) the psychologically uncomfortable awareness that the skilled expatriate remains central to the evolution and continuation of the more technologically sophisticated sectors;

(g) an awareness that, while southern African countries do differ from one another, no one country has the resources, population, or income[1] to make it critical on a global economic scale.

REGIONAL COMMON ENEMIES

The common enemies are the reasons for the common concerns. Regional co-operation policy therefore must be directed to overcoming them. The basic goals of economic growth and economic independence can be articulated as policy objectives including:

(a) diversification of economic activity within each country, to reduce vulnerability of fluctuations of particular export activities;

(b) given the smallness of the markets within any one country, policies are needed to promote production specializations in each country which rely upon markets in other regional countries;

(c) policies are needed which permit exporting states e.g. copper producers or cobalt producers, to combine, first among themselves, and then with other world producers, to exercise greater control over markets and prices;

(d) regionwide policies are needed to present a consistent front to trans-national corporations concerned with resource exploitation. This includes co-ordinated and similar policies in respect to equity partici-pation, taxation, law of contract and dispute settlement provisions; training and manpower development programmes, contributions to infrastructure, and similar issues. These would preclude playing off one country against another. There will be factors preventing complete policy identities, e.g. differences in exploitation/refining/processing costs due to resource quality differences and locations, but not of substantial co-ordination of approach.

(e) policies are needed which guarantee transportation routes and the smooth flow of traded commodities. These include existing and new routes;

(f) also needed are policies which promote greater regional utilization of each state's currently or could-be-developed resources. These include hydroelectric power, water, coal, natural gas (and possibly urea), iron, bauxite, petroleum and phosphates. Import substitution for many basic products is possible on a regional scale while unrealistic on a national scale. Once again trade-offs become critical, each state participating will need to gain export markets and production possibilities as well as im-port sources;

(g) policies are also needed to accelerate and rationalize survey, in-ventory, exploration and feasibility work required for assessing the region's resource base more fully. Specialized aid programmes could be mounted on a regional basis through regional institutions. Feasibility work on known interstate resources, particularly hydropower/irrigation resources and fertilizers could be accelerated.

Subsequent sections examine specific sectors and policy areas which could be subjects for interstate co-operation.

151

PETROLEUM, NATURAL GAS, PETROCHEMICALS, COAL, URANIUM

The purpose of this section is to discuss the region's mineral based energy resources. Uranium/thorium resources could have been grouped with non-energy minerals since they are unlikely to be used in the region before 2000. Geothermal and solar energy resources are not treated because information relevant to their use in the region is virtually nil. An effort is made to inventory each resource and to indicate its consumption. A final section suggests areas of possible policy co-ordination.

HYDROCARBON RESOURCES (PETROLEUM, NATURAL GAS)[2]

A. Reserves and Consumption

Angola produces 5–6 million tons of petroleum annually, and Zaire less than one million tons. Together they contribute some 2–2½ of Africa's total supply.[3] Angola is estimated to have some 180 million metric tons of oil reserves, and Zaire some 67 million. They are also thought to contain 42 and 1–2 billion m^3 respectively, of natural gas reserves. Mozambique also has proven natural gas reserves (estimated at the not insignificant figure of 85 billion m^3) as does Tanzania. Reserve estimates of both oil and natural gas are highly preliminary and subject to major amendment.[4]

Total energy consumption per head in the southern African region ranks among the world's lowest. Tables 1 and 2 provide data on energy consumption and petroleum dependence.

In the mid 1970s the impact of the petroleum and product prices was so severe that the UN agencies, (including the World Bank and the IMF) devised emergency programmes to assist the 'Most Seriously Affected' nations.

The per head energy use data are not indicative of the average person's use since 70–90 per cent of the energy is consumed by mines, processing and refining plants, other industry and transport. Of the balance, virtually all is consumed by urban, higher income groups. Table 2 emphasizes 1974 dependence on oil. Tanzania had some 96 per cent of total energy supply contributed by oil, Angola has a 91 per cent dependency.[5] Both could—and Tanzania has begun to—reduce this dependence by hydropower development. Malawi is 70 per cent dependent on oil, though once again the hydropower development now under way should lower this share. Mozambique and Zambia are about half dependent on oil (51 per cent, 45 per cent). The former has major natural gas and hydropower resources which can be developed; and Zambia in recent years has developed its hydropower and coal resources as energy substitution for petroleum. Since road, rail and air transport account for a third to over a half of national energy use, except in Zimbabwe, substitution is limited by the absence of modern coal burning transport equipment.

The Southern Africa Customs Union (RSA, Lesotho, Botswana,

152

Swaziland) shows a massive energy consumption, some five times the volume of all of the other nations combined. About 95 per cent of this would appear to be RSA's as oil consumption in Botswana, Lesotho and Swaziland is of the order of 500,000 tonnes. Oil consumption is a high percentage in the three countries with hydropower a secondary source in Swaziland and potentially in Lesotho, and coal a partial substitute in Botswana and potentially in Swaziland. Zimbabwe has a high total energy consumption, but it too is only 18 per cent based on oil (basically for air, road and increasingly—rail transport); ample hydropower is available, and a major thermal unit has been completed.

There are no comprehensive or precise data available on the share of oil used for electricity generation and for transport. The former has the potential of being replaced by coal thermal, geothermal, hydropower or, in due course perhaps, nuclear power. For the most part there is no replacement for the oil used for vehicles, pumps, lubricants etc. This need will rise as the economies grow so that substitution can be expected to contain, not radically reduce and still less eliminate, petroleum imports.

B. Oil and Gas Prospects

Table 3 provides 1977/8 information on the status of petroleum/natural gas development in the region. Only Angola is a current oil and gas producer. Petrofina (Belgian) discovered oil in 1955 near Luanda; these fields were gradually developed by Angolan/Portuguese and Texaco interests. Offshore oil development by the Gulf Oil Co. at the Cabinda enclave, in 1966, has provided the bulk of production. Offshore exploration and development in the subsequent decade has been undertaken by French, Portuguese, American and RSA interests; a new field off the mouth of the Congo River came on stream in 1972.[6]

Tanzania had significant onshore exploration over the 1950s and early 1960s with no results. Using new exploration techniques and offshore emphasis, the government and Agip revived activity in the late 1960s. As of the late 1970s Agip/Amoco drilling had located natural gas in the Rufiji River Delta. While the deposit is currently considered marginally too small for export development, the government is considering the gas as a feedstock for a basic chemicals manufacturing industry.[7] World Bank natural gas production projections give Tanzania a 1982 output of 11 billion cft and 15 billion cft in 1985.[8] Intensive drilling under government auspices has located shows of light oil and attempts are being made to prove an exploitable field. Mozambique has both onshore and offshore geologic possibilities, and has had exploratory drilling since the mid 1940s. Commercial gas deposits have been discovered at Ponde, to be moved by pipeline to the coast, and several other deposits have recognized potential. Oil exploration continues offshore, especially in the Zambezi delta. A gas pipeline to Zimbabwe and RSA is contemplated. Mozambique's refining capacity is also being expanded to permit exports to neighbours. The

153

natural gas resources could be the basis of a major chemical industry, including fertilizers.[9]

Hydrocarbon prospects in Zambia, Botswana, Swaziland, Malawi and Zimbabwe are generally viewed as bleak. Lesotho continues to foster oil exploration, however,[10] and there are good pointers in the Kalahari and Karroo basins—Namibia and Botswana respectively.[11] Though Zimbabwe has no known hydrocarbons, the extraction of gas and oil from coal has been rumoured for some time.

Offshore Namibia (south of the Angola fields) was the site of active exploration in the early 1970s. In 1975, however, the major interests pulled out. It is a moot point as to the role of the UN resolutions regarding resource exploitations in Namibia (declared illegal except by agreement with the UN Council for Namibia) in this departure. TNCs do not want to invest heavily without clear legal tenure, but geological prospects may also have appeared bleak. Exploration has continued, however, by the RSA Government's Southern Oil Exploration Corporation (SOEKER),[12] who appear to have located natural gas, possibly with significant condensate (oil).

C. Impact of World Hydrocarbon Price Increases

The 1973–4 quadrupling of crude oil prices contained all the elements of economic catastrophe. For southern African economies crude oil prices are still rising with 1980 likely to be almost double 1978. One extensive quotation summarises the issues:

> It is estimated that the cost of Africa's oil imports rose from about $500 million in 1973 to over $1,300 million in 1974.[a] With increasing consumption and the continued upward movement in prices since January 1977, this drain on currency reserves can only worsen. No African importer has escaped unscathed;[b] even those states which obtain their oil from non-Arab/African suppliers have been severely hit.
>
> Moreover, African countries face large balance-of-payment deficits, not only because of the increased cost of oil, but also as a result of the concomitant rise in the price of manufactured goods imported from the developed countries. These deficits can only be covered by foreign borrowing, and this in turn aggravates the already acute debt problem.[c] To make matters worse, the recession in Europe and the United States has reduced the demand for African raw materials, thereby decreasing their export value.[d] In addition, many countries have been plagued by prolonged drought and poor harvests, and this has necessitated the importation of food at high prices.[e]
>
> The fate of agriculture is inexorably dependent upon oil for a whole range of activities, from the running of tractors and water pumps to the production of fertilisers. Consequently, the higher charges for oil have increased the cost of agricultural exports at a time of falling world prices

and have simultaneously made foodstuffs more expensive on the domestic market. Some countries have attempted to soften the blow to consumers by subsidising essential commodities.

Thus, although no African state has experienced total catastrophe, the higher oil prices and attendant world inflation are continuing to threaten several already fragile economies. [13]

Table 4 provides other data on the ability of southern African economies to mobilize aid and thus afford the higher import bill. [14] It also shows debt service ratios which act as a constraint on new borrowing and the free use of foreign exchange receipts.

This was the approximate picture as of 1973 to early 1974 when oil prices escalated. Development aid has increased and normal debt service has been rising. Significant financial assistance has also flowed into these nations as a result of the oil crises. [15] Numerous international agencies began special programmes. OPEC nations' bilateral aid has also been important. [16]

Other multilateral aid included the United Nations Emergency Operation, and the International Monetary Fund's Oil Facility. The World Bank has used its Intermediate Financing Facility (Third Window), and the African Development Bank has a Fund. Many nations, including members of OPEC, and specifically Nigeria, raised their contributions to these agencies after 1975. [17] At least two southern African states have concluded petroleum supply agreements with Iraq which include credit provisions.

The regional and national development policy implications of higher oil prices must be divided into short and longer terms. Rates of economic growth have been severely prejudiced by the excessive demands on foreign exchange for petroleum imports, of petroleum based products (e.g. nitrogeneous fertilizers and other petrochemicals), and increased transport costs. All that most nations can do in the short term is keep borrowing on as concessionary terms as possible. The oil price problem unfortunately has coincided with droughts in many areas, and with a slump in world demand for many of the region's exports due to a sustained recession in the industrialized nations.

Over the medium term and in the longer term, alternative energy sources must be developed. Given the extremely high CIF petroleum prices, it is now economic to accelerate the development of known hydrocarbon resources which heretofore have been too expensive; and to put in train oil and gas exploration activities. The region may also have geothermal resources, and Mozambique has oil shales. [18]

In addition, it has become economic to examine alternatives for petroleum in electricity production, including coal, gas and oil from coal, hydroelectric and possibly nuclear power. At present, and probably for a long time, there will be no commercially viable substitute for petroleum products to run engines (transport, pumps, etc.), for lubricants, nor for petrochemicals, including nitrogeneous fertilizers.

Petrochemicals result from petroleum and natural gas refining, and from the processes of extraction of oil and gas from coal. Ammonia is the basic source of nitrogen in most fertilizer materials. It is 17 per cent hydrogen by weight. Hydrogen can be obtained from petroleum or natural gas, or by reacting steam with coke. Only Angola has the petroleum resources needed, and these seem committed to other uses. Angola has natural gas as well. There are methane gases in Lake Kivu but whether large scale extraction is practicable is not clear. Tanzania is considering the use of its offshore natural gas resources for chemical feedstock. Most promising of all may be the Mozambique gasfields where resource supply could undoubtedly support a regional nitrogenous fertilizer industry.

Since the region (and in particular Mozambique and Tanzania) has or could well have an abundance of reasonably cheap hydroelectric power, there is a strong possibility of pioneering large scale production of hydrogen feedstock (for ammonia) by electrolysis of water (water decomposition). One MW of electric capacity can produce about 600 metric tons of ammonia per year; only a small percentage of the region's (or Cabora Bassa's, or Stieglers Gorge's) hydroelectric capacity could provide the region with all of its nitrogen requirements.

It is important to note that the region contains all of the major ingredients for an integrated fertilizer industry. Phosphates are now being developed in Angola and in Zimbabwe. Zambia is pursuing phosphate discovery actively, and Malawi and Tanzania also have deposits (Ncheu). Sulphur is available in ample supply wherever copper is refined. Combined with the cheap hydroelectric power and Tanzania's potash (potassium salts), the region could organize a complete, integrated fertilizer industry,[19] an industry which would not be viable on the demand nor feasible on the production side for any single state.

COAL RESOURCES

Table 5 presents the most authoritative assessment available on the coal resources of the southern African nations under consideration. Data are for the early 1970s, and economically recoverable reserves and total known resources have been enlarged through subsequent proving out and exploration activities.

Economically recoverable coal reserves in Zambia have been estimated at 51 megatonnes, with perhaps three times that volume in total coal resources available. Coal and coke historically were imported from pre-independent Zimbabwe. With the development of Zambia's hydropower resources—Kafue, Kariba North Bank—and of its own coalmining sector, such imports have ceased. Coal has been exported to Malawi and Zaire from the Maamba Collieries. About one million tons are mined; most is pulverized for power plant and smelter use. Value approximates K 10–12 million annually.[20]

Given the availability of ample hydropower and level of reserves, effort should perhaps concentrate on the gasification of the poorer quality coals, and on the extraction of oils, since surplus electrical energy is available, and there are no known uranium/thorium resources.

Botswana has massive coal reserves. Exploration and development have been limited. There is every reason to think that economically recoverable reserves will increase—all the resources known to exist are viable and the 1979 estimates are over double those in the Table.

The 506 megatonnes of reserves shown in Table 5, all at the Morupule Field, is low grade non-coking coal, most of which is sold to the Power Corporation for generating power for the Selebi-Pikwe copper/nickel mining complex. Volume reached 200,000–250,000 tons annually but has dropped since the mine cut back. Increased volume is likely as Botswana plans to convert dieselpowered electric stations to coalfired. A second major coalfield exists at Mmombula, where over 400m tons have been proven. Anglo-American, BP and Shell are prospecting actively in other regions. Considerable impetus would be given to northern coal field development and exports to neighbours if the rail line to Zimbabwe were extended to the mines. Rail connections with Namibia[21] would allow access to European markets as terminal coal prices rise— perhaps in the late 1980s. Zimbabwe has a total known resource greater than that of any of the other southern African nations, some 6.6 billion tons. While only a quarter of this tonnage was thought to be economically viable in the early 1970s, a higher percentage should be by now. The Wankie mines have contributed not only to domestic requirements but also to exports. Between three and five million tons are mined annually, a figure which will doubtless rise with the completion of a major coalfired power plant. Because hydropower is plentiful (from an enhanced Kariba and other hydroprojects on the Zambezi) it is unlikely that more coal plants will be built.[22] However, while hydroprojects have markedly lower recurrent costs per kwh generated than coal plants, their initial investment costs per kwh are very much higher. The permanent employer impact, as distinct from construction employment, of coal thermal power generation is very much higher. With political stability, Zimbabwe must investigate thoroughly and expeditiously the extraction of petroleum and gas (for chemicals feedstocks) from its enormous coal resources. With the economies of large scale mining and coking, Zimbabwe could continue to export coke to neighbouring countries, including Zaire and Malawi.

Swaziland's coal reserves approximate those of Zimbabwe. Since exploration and proving out have been actively pursued, there are probably some two billion tons economic to mine. Given the phasing out of high grade iron ore reserves, coal has become Swaziland's most promising— indeed possibly the only major—mineral resource for longer term development. Though there are reserves of both bituminous and coking coal, many seams are faulted badly and are too deep for cheaper open pit mining. Anthracite has recently been proved and may provide the initial substantial export breakthrough. Some of the Mpaka mine's output has been exported to Kenya and Mozambique. As in Zambia and Botswana, coalmining can be a major employer of labour, especially relevant now that Swaziland is finding that more of its mine workers require employment at home as the number of jobs in RSA for Swazis declines.[23]

Other countries in the region with coal resources are Malawi and Tanzania.[24] Malawi's coal deposits are little known. There are deposits in northern Malawi, near Songwe, and at Chiromo in the south; the latter apparently are of no particular value at present.

Tanzania's coal deposits are uncertain as to exploitable quantity and quality. Quality problems and geological formations hamper exploitation of the Songwe-Kiwira coals in southern Tanzania. Two elements could make these resources viable on a scale larger than the present minor colliery and plans for a relatively small electric powerplant. One is the development of a cheap slurry pipeline for thermal or cokeable coal (or coke) for export. The other is the use of the coal in iron and steel manufacture. This latter is under active development at Liganga, not too far from the Ketewaka-Mchuchuma coal deposits. Iron ore composition is difficult, and may well only be economically viable if the vanadium can be extracted for sale,[25] and if regional or external markets for steel can be organized to allow a 500,000 tonne plant. There is limited interest in coal thermal power plants as hydropower development under construction (Kidatu Two/Three) is expected to meet demand through 1995–2000 and two river basin projects desired on other grounds, namely Steigler's Gorge and Rusumo Falls, are hampered by problems in developing power uses (perhaps iron and steel and nickel smelting respectively) for their dam components. If Steiglers Gorge and Rusumo cannot be financed by 1985 a reconsideration of capital cost and timing gains from coalbased thermal capacity may be needed.

URANIUM AND THORIUM

Several southern African nations have radioactive mineral resources. The information in Table 6 is rather incomplete. Angola seems to have a major radioactive mineral deposit. This is torbernite, a copper uranium phosphate found near Cuma on the Benguela Railway.[26] Zaire's uranium ore has been mined at Shinkolobwe, near Likasi, since 1915. There are other significant ores including uranium in the copper producing zones. Malawi's deposits of radioactive sands (thorium) at several places along Lake Nyasa's east shore have been under examination for nearly 25 years, mainly by the British atomic power authorities. There are also other deposits in the southern province. Many are under active exploration currently by Agip.

Not indicated in Table 6 are several other regional radioactive mineral resources. The most important is the Rossing uranium mine, near Swakopmund, in Namibia. It has a capacity of 120,000 tons of ore a year (5,000 tons of uranium oxide) reached in 1979. A major term contract

158

customer is British Nuclear Fuels. While official data on reserves are not available, Namibia's uranium resources are known to be large. A second mine, Langer Heinrich, of a size similar to Rossing, is under development, additional deposits have been partially proved and exploration is continuing.[27]

Mozambique has also tested deposits in Tete, and a government agency was established 20 years ago to pursue exploration. Zambia actually produced uranium from the Mindolo ore body of the Nkana copper mine as far back as 1957 but output was subsequently suspended. The copperbelt has meaningful deposits and exploration is active, most recently by Agip. Zimbabwe also has numerous and extensive deposits. They were such that 20 years ago the UK Atomic Energy Authority began mapping the entire country. The present status is unknown. Major uranium exploration programmes have been begun by German firms related to the coal and power industries in Botswana and Tanzania. The Tanzania prospects are believed—on the basis of a government aerial magnetic survey and initial Uranertz (Germany) exploration—to be highly promising.

POLICY CO-OPERATION AREAS

Given the paucity of hydrocarbon resources, it is difficult to suggest areas for interstate co-operation policies. A first step might be to inventory the region's known and probable hydrocarbon resources. This is difficult as the major private companies involved, and even government agencies, are loth to divulge information.

As detailed in the following section, each nation in the region should co-operate in the formulation of a regional electricity development plan. One ingredient in that plan would be the assessment of the region's dependence on hydrocarbons which would, with the inventory, enable a more effective conceptualization of regional requirements and substitution possibilities. In addition to production, refineries and pipelines are relevant. Systems could be developed and presented for external financing for the more rapid development of known oil and gas resources (Angola, Tanzania, Mozambique) and their optimal utilization over time in the region as a whole. Such planning and development should look ahead 20–30 years, and be closely integrated with the planning of other energy development sectors.

In the short term, high priority should be given to planning for the use of the Ndola and Maputo refineries—and, once recommissioned, the Zimbabwe refinery—to supply Botswana, Swaziland and, if possible, Lesotho in the event of oil sanctions against RSA. Transport problems are daunting for Lesotho. In each case a series of technical and contractual problems need to be arranged for well in advance if a switch is to be made before supplies run out when and if sanctions are imposed. Much the same applies to petrochemicals. Southern African nations may wish to co-operate on petrochemical development. Such co-operation could initially focus an integrated southern African fertilizer industry as suggested earlier. An interstate group would consider all fertilizer resources available, including natural gas, gas from coal, and the use of cheap hydropower for the extraction of hydrogen/ammonia from both coal and water. Co-operation on fertilizer, along with co-operation on electric power development, appears to be of the highest priority.

Coal development is less directly amenable to regional co-ordination. As a source of electric power its future use can be integrated with planning for regional electricity development. Second, certain types of coal are suitable for coking. While coke has many uses, a major one is as an ingredient in a regional iron and steel industry and its planning would be as part of that exercise (dealt with later in this paper). Third, interstate planning of coal exports and imports within the region may be useful. Coal is not an homogenous product. Deposits differ immensely in quality—carbon content, hardness, sulphur content, etc. Therefore there is room for an examination of future interstate trade dimensions. Equally, there is no reason why each nation would wish to develop its own coal resources to meet all its own requirements. In some states, coal may be the only viable resource, or one of a narrow range of development options. Under these circumstances the government will want to pursue its growth energetically. In other states, there are many development options so that a government must allocate scarce resources to those sectors where the net national gain is greatest. Zambia, Zimbabwe, Tanzania, Malawi, Mozambique and Angola have a very wide spectrum of options. They might find deferring investment in coal production nationally advantageous and choose to import coal/coke from states with fewer alternative resources if firm contractual and trade package arrangements could be developed.

HYDROELECTRIC POWER RESOURCES

CAPACITY AND USES

Table 7 provides reasonably recent data on installed and installable hydropower generation in the southern African region. Table 8 indicates actual power generated to 1973, and projected estimates for 1977 and 1980. Recorded data are not available to confirm the 1977 projection. Angola and Mozambique have the largest potential for hydropower development, though up to 1973 the two countries had installed and were using only tiny fractions of this potential, and even with Cabora Bassa Mozambique is using under a quarter of its potential. Zambia was generating in 1973 more hydropower than the eight other regional countries excluding pre-independent Zimbabwe. Output has increased in Zambia with Kariba North and Kafue commissioning and has grown up to 50-fold in Mozambique (now with the largest installed capacity in the region) with Cabora Bassa.

Among the larger nations, Zimbabwe has made the most use of its potential so far. By 1973, the 5,600 GWH generated was more than a quarter of its potential capacity. Despite significant potential, Botswana does not generate nor plan to generate hydropower. Swaziland will by 1982 have used its low cost hydro resources. Lesotho's hydropower development is conditional on a power or water sale agreement with RSA. Tanzania has a very large hydropower resource. To date these are largely undeveloped, although with the first stage of the Kidatu (Great Ruaha) project complete and subsequent stages under construction, output is rising rapidly. Malawi, on the other hand, with 400 GWH annual potential generation, was already using half of this potential in 1973.[28]

The potential for hydropower generation in Africa has long been seen as a major resource to support an increase in living standards.[29] Particular problems which must be anticipated are high rates of evaporation losses; major seasonal variations in rainfall, run-off rates and river flow; and the cyclical drought-prone pattern of rainfall in many areas.[30]

FACTORS GOVERNING INTERSTATE POLICY

A number of considerations govern the formulation of national and interstate hydropower development policy:

(a) Since major dam/hydropower projects are enormously expensive, their economics must be considered carefully. The real value of the foreign exchange, domestic funds, skilled labour and other scarce resources used must be assessed not only against the benefits which could accrue over time were those same resources put to other uses. Such projects need massive markets, and cannot be too far away as transmission losses can be high.

(b) Thus the planning, development and timing of such projects must be integrated with the phasing of power requirements, particularly those of mining/processing/refining chemicals and iron and steel. Too much generating capacity too soon, and too little too late, are very costly. The price of bad planning in southern Africa would be very high.

(c) Given the economic and financial pressures resulting from the escalation of petroleum prices it is urgent to develop alternatives to petroleum-fired thermal plants. Since electricity demands are growing rapidly, there is a presumption that net additions to generating capacity should be based on non-petroleum sources i.e. hydropower or coal.

(d) This felt urgency could result in nations pursuing the development of major hydroprojects to the exclusion of other alternatives, hydro or coal. The pace of growth of electrical power needs is critical in this context.

(e) First, there are many smaller hydroprojects possibilities, many of them 'run of the river'.[31] The consecutive development of each of these is more consistent with resources available: domestic funds, foreign exchange, debt repayment capability, construction/labour force capacities.

161

Smaller projects are, in general quicker and easier to plan and implement, and can meet incremental power needs on a phased basis.

(f) The region has extensive coal reserves. This resource should be examined carefully. Investment costs per kwh produced are lower, though recurrent costs are higher than hydro, but employment generated in both mining and transport is very much higher. The possibilities of gas and petroleum product extraction from coal have been developed and are in use elsewhere, notably in RSA.

(g) While many electrical power generation investments are strictly national concerns, including almost all plausible coalfired thermal operations, others have international implications and require multistate co-operation. For these projects, two or more states may be involved with the water resources since major river systems are often international boundaries. Further, portions of more than one country's market may be needed initially, or permanently, to absorb the power from a major project and make it economically sound.

(h) For the longer term the region should be moving towards an integrated grid. This is not a new concept. Included should be the nations of southern Africa covered by this conference, plus Zaire, which is already integrated with Zambia and given eastern Zaire mining development could profit from an expanded supply from a closer source than Inga (new Kinshasa). In this context of a grid all but the most minor projects cease to be national only and become units in a multinational system. The need for political stability and 'trust they neighbour' becomes very clear under these circumstances. [32]

(i) The major hydropower projects calling for multistate co-operation are complex, multipurpose schemes, with power generation as only one of a package of technical and economic possibilities and requirements, including irrigation and settlement, navigation, flood control, fisheries, recreation/tourism.

(j) There is need in these cases to plan the technical and financial development of these associated sectors. A significant volume of additional investment may be needed in other sectors to achieve the total benefits needed to justify the basic investment in the dam. Thus, total package planning becomes a matter of multistate planning, even though in some cases not all participating states will be concerned with all sectors.

INTERSTATE CO-OPERATION FOR HYDROPOWER DEVELOPMENT: SITES

The hydropower projects or sites whose developments will require interstate co-operation include the following six:

1. *The Ruvuma River bordered by Tanzania and Mozambique and rising partly in Malawi* (watershed in three countries). No detailed data are publicly available on the status of Ruvuma River development. Preliminary survey and identification of power, fisheries, navigation and irrigation possibilities have been undertaken. In 1977 a Mozambique-Tanzania Permanent Commission for Co-operation was established; discussions of joint river resource development occur through this Commission.[33]

2. *The Shire River, watershed in Malawi and Mozambique: joins Zambezi River in Mozambique.* While Malawi is relying heavily on Shire Valley hydropower developments, what Malawi does eventually will have clear implications for flood control and navigation projects on the lower reaches of the Zambezi. No joint planning of the interstate impact has taken place to date.[34]

3. *The Zambezi River System, shared by Zambia, Mozambique, Zimbabwe and Namibia.* With a watershed extending west into Angola and Namibia, the hydropower development possibilities on this system are immense. The Kariba dam system and the Cabora Bassa dam are already on the main river. The former has been developed by Zambia and Zimbabwe; the latter in Mozambique. A smaller Zambian station is located at Victoria Falls and Zambia's Kafue dam is on a tributary joining the main Zambezi south east of Lusaka. The former, now at 108 MW, will probably not be expanded as it would then hinder tourist use. Of the total 1,800 MW installed in Zambia, only 210 MW are thermal. The Kariba North Bank, Kafue, Victoria Falls and other smaller schemes account for the balance. Zambia now exports power to neighbours.[35] Zimbabwe, using Kariba South Bank, has ample electric power, particularly since Zambia completed the Kariba North Bank and no longer imports significant power. Zimbabwe is part of the Central African grid, linking Zambia, RSA and Mozambique.[36]

The Cabora Bassa project, one of the world's largest, is reasonably well documented. Completed in 1974 and designed for power export to Zimbabwe and the RSA it began exports in 1977. Power is now being used for mineral development in Mozambique, and potential exists for major mineral development through the availability of this power. The project includes large irrigation potential, and permits cheap river transportation from the sea to Tete Province (minerals, iron and steel) and into Zambia. Fisheries and tourism have increased potential, and critically needed flood control capacity on the Zambezi is improved. Downstream Boroma and Lupota gorges provide further hydropower potential. Further development of the Zambezi system must involve multistate deliberation to avoid surplus power capacity and to plan investments needed for optimal water management.[37]

163

4. *The Limpopo River: Mozambique, Zimbabwe and RSA.* Little analysis is available regarding current and prospective utlization of this middlesized river. Forming the boundary between Botswana and the RSA in its western reaches, and then between Zimbabwe and the RSA, it enters the Indian Ocean in Mozambique just north of Maputo. Its escarpment, and hydro and irrigation potential, are mainly in Mozambique. Several irrigation schemes are in place and others are under way, and the Massinger dam (on the Olifants River, an RSA tributary) for hydroelectric power, is under construction. Given the RSA's cumulative shortage of water resources, one can envision a conflict between RSA and Mozambican development plans.

5. *Molibamatso (Oxbow) Scheme, Eland River: Lesotho and RSA.* Negotiation on this power dam and irrigation scheme has been revived following a long period of suspension. Its basic purpose was to provide surplus water to RSA for irrigation, Lesothan power and irrigation use could not make it viable. Terms and prices have never been agreed and as the water would be diverted from the Orange River to meet RSA needs a conflict could arise with Namibia. Lesotho now plans to move ahead with a smaller hydro scheme near Bunthe.

6. *The Kunene River: Namibia and Angola.* This river has a complex of sites reasonably close to the Atlantic Ocean which could equal the Cabora Bassa with respect to hydropower potential, fisheries and flood control. The river is the boundary for some distance with Namibia and could provide massive quantities of irrigation water for that country. Designed to consist eventually of a dozen dams and power generation facilities, several of its first stages have been financed by the RSA Government which has spent up to US $100m (Matala and Gana dams—Ruacana Falls completed—Calueque dam incomplete). This full project has a potential of 1,000 kwh, Ruacana Falls—Calueque about a quarter of that. Angola could use the cheap power in the advancement of its mineral development, particularly for iron and steel production. Further development and co-operation await Namibian independence.[38]

As regards further projects, the Okavango is another interstate river with power potential in Angola and irrigation potential in Angola, Namibia and, most critically, Botswana. However, water rights agreements rather than joint projects seem to be the interstate requirement. The Kagera Basin scheme (power, irrigation, flood control, mining development) affects only Tanzania within the region but involves close co-operation with Rwanda, Burundi and—probably—Uganda outside it. Several rivers rise in RSA, transit Swaziland and flow into Mozambique. The immediate problem is that RSA proposes to divert up to 75 per cent of their flow to industrial, mining and irrigation uses before it crosses the border.

164

Policy can have three dimensions: national, multistate and regional. The first is national. Each nation's central planning organization (along with its Electricity Board, Power Commission, and other relevant agencies) should project as closely as possible alternative demands for and supplies of power over 5, 10, 20 and 50 year periods. Each current and possible future consuming sector and supplying source must be identified, and sets of assumptions generated regarding its future directions and rates of change. Initially, this would be a purely physical planning exercise, with economic, financial and institutional analysis coming later.

National supply sources such as coal, natural gas and strictly national hydropower sources need to be inventoried. Supplies from sources which should be managed in co-operation with other states (such as those listed above) must also be identified. Import possibilities must also be included, particularly energy imports from neighbours. When the numerous sectoral demands are combined with equally numerous supply projections by source, the nation can begin to see alternatives and to formulate the political, financial and other dimensions of long term policy. While elements of this exercise have been carried on in most southern African countries, work to date is too limited to support adequate strategic planning.

Dialogue with neighbours regarding development policy for a common hydropower resource e.g. the six major sites indicated in earlier sections, must be based on a firm awareness of where each particular project could fit into overall power development strategy of each country case. The phasing, size, and other basic elements of any common project development must be consistent with and supportive of the national plans of participating states. Because most multistate projects are also multipurpose, other sectors e.g. irrigation, transport, fisheries, flood control, must also have joint planning exercises integrated into national plans and programmes.

The regional perspective includes the term development of a southern African power grid. National and interstate plans should not be inconsistent with the eventual formation of a unified system. Therefore, such a system and its likely components should be roughly conceptualized quickly. Individual states would thus have general guidelines towards which to work.

This suggests that a Southern African Power Council should be established. The council could be a device through which technical assistance would be provided to participating states to assist with national energy planning exercises as well as handling regional perspective planning and co-ordination. As it would take time for it to be organized and functioning, initial steps towards its creation are urgent.

It is perhaps not too unrealistic to consider such an agency as becoming a vehicle through which electricity project funding occurs, a development bank for power. For this to happen the required expertise, initially mainly expatriate but as quickly as possible nationals from the states concerned, must be specialized and concentrated. No southern African country can by itself afford the full complement of personnel. A regional organization could reduce the still dominant influence of outside financial bodies and technical analysts over major investment decisions, choice of consultants and contractors etc.

NON-ENERGY MINERALS

BACKGROUND: THE SOUTHERN AFRICAN CONTRIBUTION

The purpose of this section is to sketch the southern African region's contribution to world output and reserves.[39] The global contribution is modest, though mineral output is the cornerstone of several economies.

Several nations in the region are among the top five developing country exporters (not necessarily producers) for specific minerals. Zambia is the developing world's largest copper exporter. Namibia is the fourth largest lead exporter among developing countries and in the top five for uranium oxide. Zambia ranks fifth in zinc. While modest industrial and total diamond producers, Namibia, Botswana, Angola, Lesotho and Tanzania account for over half of gemstone production. In addition, the region's nations contain important reserves. Zimbabwe is thought to have about one fifth of world chromium reserves. Zambia has 10 per cent of cobalt reserves (derived mainly from processing of copper) and 10 per cent of the world's copper reserves. However, of 27 leading minerals (by value of total output), only three (chromium, cobalt, copper) definitely, plus one (uranium oxide) probably, have major reserves in the southern African region. This limits the region's ability to improve its world market/price position.

Zaire and Zambia are dominant producers of cobalt—about 15 per cent Zaire and 10 per cent Zambia. Africa produces one fifth of the world's copper, Zambia one half of the African total. Namibia and Zimbabwe account for another tenth and Zaire a quarter.

Africa produces 80 per cent of the world's diamonds, and Zaire one third of the African total. Angola, Botswana and Namibia produce diamonds, each at about 1/6th of Zaire's level and Tanzania and Lesotho on a smaller scale. In gem diamonds, as noted, the regional states account for over half world output. In iron ore Angola and Swaziland have had meaningful exports. Namibia has substantial lead ore exports, and Zambia and Botswana modest ones.

Among the southern African countries only Angola has substantial phosphate deposits. Zimbabwe has a chrome mining sector, and one of the world's largest deposits of high grade chromite ore.[40]

THE IMPORTANCE OF MINERALS TO SOUTHERN AFRICAN ECONOMIES

The production, preliminary processing and transportation/handling of minerals is central to a majority of the southern African nations. Exceptions include Tanzania, Malawi, Lesotho and—except for transport—Mozambique. Less than one per cent of production in Tanzania and Malawi and 2-3 per cent in Lesotho is derived from minerals.

In Zambia mining and smelting contributes one quarter to one half of GDP (the percentage fluctuates widely with copper prices). The share has dropped together with the mining exports (nearly 100 per cent of all exports) because of price and production falls, not positive structural changes.[41] Much of the modern economy was developed to service the mining sector, thus direct and indirect mining income comprises the bulk of monetary GDP. Zimbabwe has only 6-8 per cent share of its GDP accounted for directly by mining. The share of minerals in export values is much higher—probably around 40 per cent.[42] Continuing war conditions have limited mining sector growth. In Swaziland mining is about 5-6 per cent of GDP, but iron ore and asbestos provide a fifth of total exports. Modest coal exports provide scope for expansion. Mining makes a significant contribution to GDP in Botswana, one sixth emanating directly from that sector. This share is rising with enhanced production. Minerals accounted for 58 per cent of export values in 1976. Namibia's mining sector is important and is estimated to account for over a third of GDP. Mineral products approximate 70 per cent of total export values with diamonds (36 per cent), uranium (14 per cent), copper (9 per cent) and lead, zinc, tin and other minerals (a combined 11 per cent) in 1977.

Angolan economic data are fragmentary and disturbed by continued insurgency. The mining contribution to GDP is high. Of the 31 bn escudo value of exports in 1974, crude oil exports were half, and diamonds and iron ore another 3.7 bn escudos. Minerals accounted for some 60 per cent of export values. There are indications that total mineral export values have since risen in real terms with oil increases offsetting other declines. Oil exports provide the government with three quarters of its revenue. Data from Mozambique are fragmentary and figures are sometimes incompatible. While there are no present meaningful mineral exports, there is major potential for coal, natural gas and nitrogenous fertilizers.[43]

In summary, the modern sector of the region is very heavily dependent on minerals for employment, government revenue, and foreign exchange. With limited exceptions, the region does not have strong supply shares on world markets or world mineral reserves. It is important to recognize some regional producers that are high cost (per unit of output) compared with competing regions, due to high capital and transportation (inputs and outputs) costs and an increasing need to mine more difficult, less pure and less accessible ore bodies. Investment for maintenance and for expansion and deepening has not been forthcoming in several states e.g. Zambia, Zimbabwe, Namibia (base metals) and Angola, due to the general slump in world mining since 1974, to the general investment insecurities perceived by large corporations and the effects of the prolonged Zimbabwean and

167

Namibian liberation struggles. Major capacity maintenance and new facility creation investment is urgently needed, especially now that Zimbabwe has achieved independence, and Namibia's will follow in the near future.

POLICY CO-OPERATION AREAS

Areas in which interstate policy co-operation may occur include transportation co-operation, covered in another Sectoral paper. In addition to road and rail co-operation on existing facilities, the improvement of capacity on and the upgrading of the existing systems, planning for, design of an investment in linear expansions of the road and rail network, including new lines and links with compatible technology, and further development of pipeline transportation appear appropriate. Transportation is particularly critical to mineral sector export performance, importation of supplies and equipment, the further integration of Botswana, Swaziland and Zimbabwe with export outlets in Namibia, Angola and Mozambique, and interstate trade in petroleum/mineral products, e.g. Tanzania-Zambia existing petroleum pipelines, and the proposed Zambia-Zaire and Angola-Zaire pipelines.

Other areas in which mineral development policy could be furthered co-operatively include policies in respect to exploration and development; acquisition and use of technology; multinational firms; greater integration of mineral processing and refining and metal fabrication within the region; the sector in stimulating industrial development planning of resource exploitation (including the phasing of reserve exhaustion); and achieving greater control over external markets and prices. For some of these a guideline for standard approaches to external financing agencies in the public or private sector could be developed.

A. *Exploration and Development*

There is a widespread lack of knowledge of total mineral resources available and of the share of those resources which could be economically recovered now or under defined conditions. While resource availability is a matter of fact, economic viability depends on the changing configuration of cost/price. Perhaps the least well explored nations are Angola, Zaire, Mozambique and Botswana, but others have enormous areas only superficially explored. There is also considerable data with major mining companies as yet not accessible to governments.

Opportunities exist for an appropriately staffed interstate unit to make an inventory of known resources. After a first inventory on a national basis, the governments could identify common, priority knowledge gaps. Co-operation could take the form of exploration concentrating on a specific mineral or minerals in each of the co-operating nations. It could also involve co-operation on overall exploration of contiguous land areas.

B. *Technology Improvements*

The region's mining sector features a wide disparity of production, handling and refining technologies. Techology in use at any one time spans the most ancient and rudimentary right through to highly sophisticated equipment and systems. The greater the profit margin, the longer more antiquated and high cost units can be used. In the light of the region's increasing cost/price pressures, and given ample hydropower potential for more efficient technology packages using more energy, it is important that the region's governments examine technology choice and develop strategies for technology improvement. Improvements can make exploration cheaper and more productive, mining less costly, and processing/refining not only more efficient, but also able to recover materials not heretofore recoverable. An interstate unit could organize this effort.

C. *Posture vis-à-vis Transnational Firms*

Major transnational firms historically have owned/operated this sector. Investment/production/export/pricing and other policies and planning have been their virtually exclusive prerogative. Recently, several governments have developed policies, programmes, and legal/institutional structures to participate more fully in decisions regarding investment, equity ownership, profit participation, indigenization of the labour force, borrowing and other financial matters. Zambia has the most experience in this area, but other nations have also been dealing more energetically with their mineral TNCs.[44]

There are several general issues. One is that such firms are more tractable when world prices are good, markets buoyant and profits high. The reverse is true when markets, prices and profits are poor or even negative. Second, only TNCs seem to have access to the technology, the volume of skilled technical manpower, and—less clearly—the equity finance required for the continuation and expansion of the sector, for some years to come. Third, once a government increases its managerial and financial participation, it simultaneously assumes a greater share of the economic risks and responsibilities. Fourth, the incidence of national government participation with multinationals is uneven. Therefore, fifth, the dominance of such corporations over national governments ranges from very powerful in several states to less so in others. It is now possible for TNCs to play off southern African nations against one another.

There is, therefore, room for consideration by southern African governments of a common front to the mining TNCs. It should be possible to work out minimum common national positions. The establishment of such minimums could probably improve the managerial and financial leverage of several governments. They could greatly limit the future playing off of one country against another. Particular attention should be paid to equity participation, taxation, training and development of citizens,

169

utilization of retained earnings (particularly shares for exploration and development, and upgrading of technology), and contributions to the sector's infrastructure requirements, especially transport.

D. *Linkages and the Integration of Processing/Refining/Fabricating within the Region*

Currently, almost all minerals leave their regional nation of production for processing and fabrication. Import and tariff regulations in the major industrialized importing nations inhibit the importation of highly processed or fabricated products. Many TNC mining firms are vertically integrated and manufacture intermediate and final products close to their main markets. Their contribution to national infrastructure costs is almost nil in the industrial nations, and they have access to large pools of skilled labour, for whom they need provide little or no infrastructure (e.g. housing). They are also close to the manufacturers and distributors of equipment and to servicing facilities. There they face few demands for government equity participation, indeed few government controls other than general taxation and environmental measures. The socio/political/economic world is both familiar and relatively stable.

From the point of view of the TNC, the prospect of shifting refining and fabricating to southern African states supplying raw materials has little or no appeal. This constitutes a formidable barrier to achieving further stages of mineral processing/manufacture. TNCs will only consider these possibilities either under the most favourable circumstances which a government can create and guarantee or when it has no other option except total withdrawal.

There are several elements: first the southern African region as a whole might very well provide a market large enough for certain intermediate and final products, though the market in any one nation does not. Secondly, the mining/processing sectors are estimated to require 50–70 per cent of their gross foreign exchange earnings for the importation of machinery and equipment, chemicals, explosives, fuel and other inputs. For the region as a whole, given the large total requirements of the sector, specialized plants could supply many of the items. In addition, taking a product further in its processing or fabrication, even though destined for external markets, need not necessarily take place in the mining state. Economies of scale and transportation could permit the raw or second stage material from several nations being transformed into intermediate or even final products in a single plant. Massive post-1973 increases in shipping rates increased the viability of weight reducing and per tonne value increasing processes.

The concept of interstate co-operation and co-ordination in the mineral sector is by no means new. Over the 1960s the ECA and UNIDO did studies along these lines. One was for the general integration of industries and markets for East and Central Africa. Other regional studies were for more narrowly defined subregions. A worldwide body of work exists on problems

170

and prospects of obtaining maximum economic impact (domestic backward and forward linkages) and from mineral extraction industries.[45] There is scope for a review of these issues for the region as a whole.

For several industries there is some urgency. In iron and steel, for example, the region could end with an enormous investment in excess capacity. Several states are at some stage planning iron and steel complexes, or expanding those that already exist. An interstate committee—or council or whatever—could first establish a research plan. A team of 6–8 technical and economic experts could provide a first survey of broad dimensions of these issues in six months' work. That would demarcate a range of initial prefeasibility activities. The experience of the East African Development Bank could be drawn upon.[46]

E. *Greater Control over Markets and Prices*

International cartelization is an attractive means for raw commodity producers to enhance their market position. Such cartels, to one degree or another, attempt to even out price fluctuations, create buffer stocks and improve average prices received over time. They can also be a medium for dissemination of information on technology and other fields of common interest.

In minerals, TNCs—not states—historically have attempted to form cartels. In recent years, however, developing country governments have become more directly involved in their mineral exporting sectors. Thus new style government cartels like CIPEC (copper), mixed company/state ones (e.g. uranium oxide) and old style private ones like the Central Selling Organization (diamonds) exist side by side.

Zambia and Zaire are founding members of CIPEC; other members are Chile, Peru and Indonesia. These countries produce some three quarters of all copper entering western international trade. CIPEC has not been notably successful. Several of the requirements for a successful cartel, including the need for the producers involved to have reasonably similar production costs and marketing arrangements have not to date been met. Scrap and recycling possibilities, threat of product substitution, and elasticity of demand for the product have posed further problems. CIPEC member nations differ markedly in socio/political objectives and in production costs. Because copper exports are vital to Zambia, Zaire and Chile it has been virtually impossible, politically and economically, to reduce production and stocks pile up making even enforced export limits appear paper tigers.

Mineral cartels for southern African governments must also overcome the resistance of major TNCs who dominate the industries and oppose any cartels not run by themselves. Speaking of Zambia's involvement in CIPEC with Zaire, Peru and Chile, one analyst writes:

The four nations confront a powerful set of multinational corporations

171

which, with extensive interlocking linkages . . . and farflung international interests spread throughout the developed as well as the developing world, enjoy much greater flexibility of action than any of the four countries' governments alone. Examination of their assets (see Moody's *Industrials and Financials*, New York, 1971) indicates that the companies have already begun to invest the compensation obtained for government participation in ownership from Zambia and other copper-producing countries to open new copper mines in other countries, ranging from neighbouring Botswana to the Australian trusteeship of New Guinea. They have also diversified their assets by purchasing shares in other giant corporations producing aluminium, copper's main competitor in developed country markets. Divided, the four copper-exporting countries can hope to exert little control over these giant firms' manipulation of world copper markets and prices . . . It is therefore sad to note that the infant organisation, CIPEC, which the Zambian Government did so much to promote in its initial efforts to achieve closer cooperation between the four producing nations, is apparently starved for want of government support (*The Times of Zambia*, 13 July 1972). [47]

A quick review of recent literature would tend to confirm the generally inhospitable environment facing further efforts to cartelize the region's minerals. [48] Cobalt is a byproduct of copper and nickel smelting, so its supply cannot be directly controlled.

Notwithstanding this, the governments of the southern African region could take a harder look both at their combined output and reserves and at marketing arrangements. While individually none appear large relative to TNCs or world production, the organization of regional groups, by mineral, could present more formidable bargaining fronts. [49]

TABLE 1

Energy Crisis: The 'Most Seriously Affected' Nations

COUNTRIES	Energy Cons./Capita, kg. coal equiv. (latest av. year)
MSA countries (1974 list)	
Lesotho	n.a.
Tanzania	119
Malagasy Republic	71
MSA countries added—1975	
Mozambique	178
Other Countries in Region	
Malawi	49
Zaire	77
Botswana	n.a.
Swaziland	n.a.
Zimbabwe	618
Angola	157
Zambia	458

Source: Compiled by K. A. Hammeeb from OECD, IBRD, IMF and UN sources published in 'The Oil Revolution and African Development', *African Affairs*, Vol. 75, 1976, pp. 356–8. Data extracted from larger tables.

TABLE 2

Oil in Energy Consumption, Southern Africa, 1974

(1)	(2)	(3)	(4)
	Millions of tons oil equivalent		
Country	Total Energy Consumption	Consumption of Oil	(3) as % of (2)
Angola	0.806	0.732	90.8
Malawi	0.188	0.131	69.7
Mauritius	0.158	0.154	97.5
Mozambique	0.868	0.442	50.9
Zimbabwe	3.339	0.552	16.5
Southern African Customs Union (a)	50.170	8.958	17.9
Tanzania	0.750	0.717	95.6
Zaire	1.246	0.637	51.1
Zambia	1.800	0.816	45.3

(a) includes RSA, Lesotho, Botswana and Swaziland

Source: UN, *World Energy Supplies, 1969–1974*, NY, 1976, and extracted from J. Baker, *op.cit.*, p. 204.

TABLE 3

Selected Southern African Nations Grouped by Income Classes and Prospects for Oil and Gas

Income Class[1]	Oil and Gas Prospect Groups[2]			
	Group A	Group B	Group C	Group D
Intermediate/Middle ($551–$1,135 per capita)	Angola		Namibia	Zambia
Lower Middle Income ($281–$550 per capita)			Mozambique	Botswana Swaziland Zimbabwe
Low Income ($280 or less per capita)	Zaire	Tanzania[3]	Madagascar	Lesotho Malawi

Notes:
[1] Income class based on World Bank national income and population estimates for 1976.
[2] *Group A:* current producers of oil/gas.
 Group B: non-OPEC nations currently non-producers but have proven reserves and could have commercial exploitation.
 Group C: non-OPEC countries conducting intensive exploratory activity and have favourable geological prospects for potential oil/gas discoveries.
 Group D: non-OPEC nations whose geological prospects for oil/gas at the present state of technical knowledge are not very favourable. In some countries exploration activity is still being carried on.
[3] Natural Gas only as of 1979; Group C for oil.

Source: World Bank, *Petroleum and Gas . . ., op.cit.*, pp. 1–2, Annex II.

TABLE 4

Southern African Nations: Selected Data on Population, Income, and Aid Receipts (data from 1969–1972).

Country	1971 per capita Income $	1971 population (millions)	Aid Receipts av. 1969–72 $ per capita	Aid Receipts av. 1969–72 as % of Total Imports	Debt Service 1972 as % of Exports
Lesotho*	100	0.941	n.a.	n.a.*	n.a.
Tanzania	110	13.249	4	13.8	8
Malagasy Republic	140	7.220	9	29.8	4
Mozambique	280	7.830	5	12.4	3
Malawi	90	4.550	8	28.4	8
Zaire	90	19.326	5	16.1	8
Botswana*	160	0.618	32	n.a.*	9
Swaziland*	190	0.433	25	n.a.*	13
Zimbabwe	320	5.500	—	—	3
Angola	370	5.572	6	7.8	1
Zambia	380	4.250	5	3.0	11

Source: Taken from larger table in K. A. Hammeed, *op. cit.*, pp. 356–7, and based on OECD, IBRD, IMF and UN statistics.

* Data for these nations integrated with those of RSA, as are Namibia's.

TABLE 5
Selected Southern African Countries: Reserves and Resources of Solid Fossil Fuels (in Megatonnes)

| Country | Reserves[1] | | Total[3] Resources |
	Economically Recoverable[2]	Total	
Middle Income			
Namibia	—	—	—
Zambia	51	74	154
Botswana	506	506	506
Zimbabwe	1,390	1,760	6,613
Swaziland	1,820	2,022	5,022
Low Income			
Malagasy	39	78	92
Malawi	—	—	38
Tanzania	180	309	370
Zaire	720	720	720

Source: World Energy Conference, Survey of Energy Resources, 1974, p. 61; and quoted in World Bank, *Energy and Petroleum* . . ., op. cit., p. 8 of Annex IV.

[1] Reserves are the fraction of resources that have been measured and assessed.

[2] Economically recoverable reserves are that fraction considered exploitable under present local economic conditions using existing available technology.

[3] Resources denotes total measured quantities that may be inferred to exist.

TABLE 6
Selected Southern African Countries: Uranium and Thorium Resources

| Country | Lower Cost Resources[3] | | | | Higher Cost Resources[4] |
| | Reasonably Assured Resources Energy Content | | | | Reasonably Assured and Additional Resources (tons) |
	Amount (tons)	Non-Breeders (Mill. Gwh.)	Breeders (Mill. Gwh.)	Resources (tons)	
Angola[1]	–	–	–	–	12,750
Malagasy[1]	–	–	–	–	560
Zaire[1]	1,780	0.43	26	1,700	–
Malawi[2]	–	n.a.	–	–	8,800

(Active prospecting and exploration in Botswana, Zambia, Tanzania)

Source: World Energy Conference and World Bank, *Energy and Petroleum* . . ., op. cit., p. 6 of Annex IV

[1] Uranium
[2] Thorium
[3] Less than $US 30/kg.
[4] More than $US 30/kg. denotes not reported

TABLE 7
Selected Southern African Countries: Hydro Resources—Installed and Installable Capacity

Country	Annual Potential Generation (GWH)
Middle Income	
Angola	48,320
Botswana	8,952
Mozambique	45,160
Zambia	15,336
Zimbabwe	20,000
Swaziland	2,800
Low Income	
Zaire	660,000
Lesotho	2,600
Malagasy Republic	320,000
Malawi	400
Tanzania	83,200

Source: World Energy Conference and World Bank, *Energy and Petroleum* . . ., op. cit., p. 2 of Annex IV.

TABLE 8

Selected Southern African Countries: Hydropower Generation, Selected Years to 1973, Anticipated for 1977 and 1980

Country	1955	1960	1965	1970	1971	1972	1973	1977	1980
Middle Income									
Angola	—	100	300	500	600	700	800	800	800
Botswana	—	—	—	—	—	—	—	—	—
Mozambique	—	100	200	300	200	300	200	11,000	11,000
Zambia	—	—	300	600	900	3,100	3,200	7,000	11,300
Zimbabwe	—	—	3,900	5,200	5,600	5,300	5,600	4,200	4,200
Swaziland	—	—	—	90	94	92	125	145	150
Low Income									
Zaire	1,300	2,400	2,600	3,200	3,400	3,300	3,800	5,400	6,600
Lesotho	—	—	—	—	—	—	—	—	—
Malagasy Republic	—	100	100	100	100	100	200	120	120
Malawi	—	—	—	100	100	200	200	330	470
Tanzania	100	100	200	300	300	300	300	580	820

Source: World Energy Conference and World Bank, Energy and Petroleum . . ., op. cit., pp. 3–5 of Annex IV and Swaziland Electricity Board.

NOTES

1. The countries in the World Bank's Lower Middle Income Group (per head income $281–550) are Angola, Botswana, Zimbabwe, Swaziland and Zambia. Those in the low income group ($280 or less) are Lesotho, Malawi, Mozambique and Tanzania. (See World Bank, *World Economic and Social Indicators*, Washington DC, July 1978, Sources and Notes, pp. 2–3 (Report No. 700/78/03). Low as these figures are because income distribution is everywhere unequal, these data naturally overstate markedly the level of income of 80–90 per cent of each nation's population.

2. Information on hydrocarbons has been garnered from a few main sources. The more important journals are *The Petroleum Economist*, the *Oil and Gas Journal*, and *World Oil*; others are *Africa, African Contemporary Record, African Development* and *Africa Research Bulletin* (Economic Financial and Technical Series). Also valuable were an article by Jonathan Baker 'Oil and African Development', *Journal of Modern African Studies*, 15, 2, 1977 pp. 175–212; an item called 'Oil—Impact of Energy Crisis on African Economies' by the Energy Unit of ECA's Natural Resources Division in *African Contemporary Review* (1974/5), pp. C185–9; and Vol 75 of 1976 of *African Affairs*— this contains several conference papers on 'Africa and the Oil Revolution'. Also relevant were several ECA documents. Though slightly dated, the first is entitled *Energy Development in the Countries of the East African Sub-Region* (prepared for the Conference on the Harmonization of Industrial Development Programmes in East Africa, Lusaka, 1965); Doc. No. E/CN.14/INR/104. The second is *The Sedimentary Basins in Africa and their Hydrocarbon Resources* (prepared for the Regional Conference on Petroleum Industry and Manpower Requirements in the Field of Hydrocarbons, Tripoli, 1974); Doc. No. E/CN.14/EP.47. Other papers for that Conference included an inventory of the petroleum industry during the 1960s. (E/CN.14/EP/48), and of the hydrocarbon processing/refining sector (E/CN.14/EP/49). Dated but of value is an ECA paper, *Energy in Zambia* prepared for a sub-regional meeting on energy in Central Africa, Brazzaville, January 1968 (E/CN.14/EP/32). Five recent World Bank Documents were also most useful: *Minerals and Energy in the Developing Countries*, May 1977 (Report No. 1588); *A Programme to Accelerate Petroleum Production in Developing Countries*, November 1978; *Petroleum and Gas in non-OPEC Developing Countries: 1976–1985*, April 1978 (World Bank Staff Working Paper No. 289 prepared by R. Vedalli); *Energy and Petroleum in non-OPEC Developing Countries 1974–8*), February 1976 (World Bank Staff Working Paper No. 229 prepared by A. Lambertini); and R. Bosson and B. Varon: *The Mining Industry and the Developing Countries*, NY, Oxford University Press (for the World Bank), 1977. The UN has also produced a useful recent report *Multilateral Development Assistance for the Exploration of Natural Resources*, October 1978—Report of the Secretary-General (No. A/33/256). A good number of recent UN

documents were examined. For a pertinent list, see Bosson and Varon, *op cit*, pp. 281–3.

3. Output has fluctuated markedly due to changing political factors, including the availability of expatriate technicians and the changing degrees of confidence felt by multinational firms.

4. The World Bank estimates Angola's present (1977–8) production capacity at about 175,000 b/d which could reach 200,000 b/d by 1980 and 250,000 b/d by 1985. Zaire is estimated by the Bank to produce some 25,000 b/d currently, which could rise to 50,000 b/d by 1980 and 100,000 b/d by 1985. See *World Bank, Petroleum and Gas . . . ., op cit*, p. 17 of Annex I.

5. Because of differing oil qualities, and the differing processing technologies in the numerous southern African nations' refineries, some nations such as Angola must export to refineries which can handle their petroleum and not to other countries and also, at present, must import petroleum for their own refineries which are not designed to handle domestic crude.

6. See the discussion in *Africa South of the Sahara, 1976/7*, p. 143. US Government restrictons on Gulf's participation were lifted in 1976 and production resumed.

7. See for example, note in *African Contemporary Record, 1975/6*, p. B338.

8. *World Bank, Petroleum and Gas . . . ., op cit*, p. 5.

9. For general (and limited) discussions see *Quarterly Economic Review of Angola, Mozambique, (Annual Supplement 1977)*, p. 22; *African Guide 1977*, p. 208; *African Development*, March 1974, and *Africa South of the Sahara*, (1976/7), p. 578.

10. See brief discussion in J. Baker, *op cit*, p. 183 *World Oil*, 179, 3 August 15, 1975, p. 142.

11. See ECA, *Sedimentary Basins . . .., op cit*, p. 46.

12. For brief discussion see *Africa South of the Sahara* (1976/7), p. 597 *African Development*, April 1975 (article by R. Manning); *African Contemporary Record* (1975/6), p. B562; and several issues of the *Petroleum Economist*—see particularly that of 15 August 1976, p. 56; and of January 1977, pp. 45–57 (article by John Wright entitled 'Prospects for New Oil Discoveries (Africa)').

13. From J. Baker, *op cit*, pp. 192.3. The footnotes contained in the quotation are the following:
p. 192
(a) *Africa* (London), No. 34, June 1974, p. 47.

(b) The terms 'Fourth World' and 'Most Seriously Affected' (M.S.A.) have recently been adopted to describe the less-developed countries which face severe difficulties, as a result of higher oil and food prices. Of the 45 countries so designated by the United Nations, the majority are African: namely: Benin, Burundi, Cameroon, Cape Verde, Central African Empire, Chad, Egypt, Ethiopia, Gambia, Ghana, Guinea,

Guinea-Bissau, Ivory Coast, Kenya, Lesotho, Malagasy, Mali, Mauritania, Mozambique, Niger, Senegal, Sierra Leone, Somalia, Sudan, Tanzania, Uganda and Upper Volta.

(c) Africa's external public debt increased from $9,200 million in 1967 to $28,500 million in 1974.

p. 193

(d) Surprisingly, some sectors, such as tourism, which were expected to suffer badly have not in fact done so. In Kenya, for example, tourism experienced a decline in 1973 (before the full impact of the higher oil prices was felt); but there have been signs of a recovery, indicated by a 3.5 per cent increase in the total number of tourists during the first eight months of 1974. See Barclays Bank Country Report: Kenya (London), 17 February 1975.

(e) Tanzania, for example, paid 20 times ($51.8 million) as much for cereal imports and three times as much ($66.5 million) for oil imports during January-July 1974 compared with the same period in the previous year. *Ibid*, Tanzania, 24 February 1975.

14. See also discussion in *Africa*, No. 77, January 1978, pp. 93-4.

15. The literature on these matters is rather extensive. See particularly J. Baker, *op cit*, pp. 193-9; the World Bank, *A Programme to Accelerate . . .*, and *Minerals and Energy . . .*, J. P. Lewis, 'Oil, Other Scarcities, and the Poor Countries', *World Politics*, 27, 1974/5, pp. 63-8; and K. A. Hammeed, *op cit*, and several issues of the *Petroleum Economist*— see particularly those of July 1974, 'Plans to Aid the Third World', pp. 247-50; and of June 1975, 'Meeting Africa's Oil Bill', pp. 222-3.

16. Over 1974/5 the following southern African nations received a total of $54 million in 25 year loans from the special Arab Fund for Africa: Botswana, Lesotho, Malagasy Republic, Malawi, Mauritius, Swaziland, Tanzania, Zaire, and Zambia. See E. Penrose, 'Africa and the Oil Revolution: an Introduction', *African Affairs*, 75, 1976, p. 282—data originally from *Middle East Economic Journal*.

17. There were some political difficulties in the IMF and the IBRD in acquiring more funds for these purposes. The most industrialized countries, historically the largest contributors, were in a state of anger and shock with all aspects of the price increase.

18. The United Nations Revolving Fund for Natural Resources Exploitation is considered (early 1979) as a source of finance for geothermal exploration and development (see UN, *Multilateral Development Assistance . . .*, *op cit* Annex, Para 90). The Fund already finances minerals exploitation. Oil shale and oil sand exploitation technology has been developed to the point, in the USA and Canada, where production costs are roughly equivalent to CIF values per barrel. The initial investment needed, however, is massive, and deposits must also be enormous. The Mozambique deposit has not yet been proven out.

19. The possibilities of a West African fertilizer sector, using constituent resources from many countries, has been studied for years by the ECA,

the IBRD, UNIDO etc. For recent material, see two items published by the International Fertilizer Development Centre, Florence, Alabama. (1) *West African Fertilizer Study, Vol. I—Regional Overview* (Technical Bulletin IFDC-T.3), February 1977, and (2) *The Potential for Regional Co-operation in Fertilizer—A Methodology Study* (Technical Bulletin IFDC.T.2), January 1976. It would not take long for the southern African region to launch a reasonably detailed survey of co-operative possibilities. Given international fertilizer prices, shortages of foreign exchange, and the need to maintain and increase agricultural output, this appears to be a priority activity.

20. See *Quarterly Economic Review of Zambia, Annual Supplement 1977*, p. 15 *Report on Zambia*, 1976, Lloyds Bank—Overseas Department, International Trade Promotion Section, London, 1976, p. 11; *Standard Chartered Review* various issues, including January 1977, p. 8, and December 1976, p. 8.

21. See *African Development*, January 1976, pp. 97 and 101; *Quarterly Economic Review for Southern Africa, Republic of South Africa, South West Africa, Botswana, Lesotho and Swaziland, Annual Supplement 1977*, pp. 41–3. This latter gives a proven resource volume of 4 billion tons, not the 5 billion shown in Table 5.

22. See *Quarterly Economic Review of Rhodeśia, Malawi, Annual Supplement 1977*, pp. 13–14; and *African Development*, February 1973, for earlier material. There are no data readily available on the capacity of the new thermal power plant nor its justification in the light of hydropower capacities.

23. Swaziland coal information sources are similar to those for Zambia and Botswana—notes 20 and 21 above.

24. Zaire may need to be considered in respect to certain southern African policy co-ordination activities. Its railway system is interlocked with those of Zambia, Angola and Tanzania and it may add an oil pipeline link to the Ndola (Zambia) refinery. Further the coal and hydro resources and power uses in eastern Zaire are sub-regionally logically linked to Zambia's.

25. Plans were announced for 500,000 tonnes iron and steel plant based on a different deposit in 1976, to cost (then) £150m. That particular project has now proven impracticable. The Liganga project would be a very low cost producer at 500,000 tonnes if the vanadium were to be commercially recoverable but a relatively high cost ore on a smaller scale or without the byproduct (which could be worth as much as the steel).

26. Supplementary data on minerals taken from numerous older geography textual materials. Particularly useful was G. H. T. Kimble, *Tropical Africa*, New York: The Twentieth Century Fund, 1960 (2 volumes). The comprehensive mineral discussion is Chapter 9 of Volume I.

27. For discussion, see the (London) *Economist*, 8 October 1977, pp. 97–8; and *African Development*, 1976, p. 679. The latter details the political

environment surrounding uranium development. See also *African Contemporary Record*, 1977–8.

28. These data are incomplete. Six potential hydroprojects in Malawi's Shire Valley have a capacity probably in excess of 1,000 GWH.

29. Basic information on Africa's hydro potential is garnered from numerous publications. See particularly E. Crouzet, *'La Caisse de l'energie: l'afrique et son potentiel hydro-electrique', Industries et travaux d'outremer*, December 1974, pp. 1044–51; ECA, *The Role of Energy in the Development of Human Settlement in Africa*, Addis Ababa, 1975 (Doc. No. E/CN.14/HUS/6) W. M. Warren and H. Rubin (eds) *Dams in Africa*, London: Cass 1968; J. Karst, 'L'afrique dans le cadre de la geographie mondiale et energie', *Industries et travaux d'outremer*, December 1974, pp. 105–63, and World Energy Conference, *Development of Conventional Energy Resources*, Istanbul, World Energy Conference, 1977 (Proceedings). Though dated, an ECA document inventories Africa's energy capacities and requirements—*Africa's Energy Requirements in the Decade 1970–1980* (Paper submitted to the Fourth Interregional Seminar on Development Planning: 'Development Prospects and Planning for the Coming Decade (with Special Reference to Africa)'), Addis Ababa, 1968 (Draft Doc. No. 68-237/150). Its projections appear to be fairly accurate.

30. These factors raise investment costs per kwh significantly, with large low-water/high-water ratios, the need for high storage/utilization ratios, etc. For some of these factors, see R. J. Harrison Church, 'A Geographical View', in Warren and Rubin (eds) *op cit*, pp. 1–12.

31. No comprehensive inventory of such possibilities exists. The basic literature points out the potential which, given topographic circumstances and nature of river flow, should be significant.

32. The grid is discussed in Keith Middlemas, *Cabora Bassa: Engineering and Politics in Southern Africa*, London: Weidenfeld and Nicolson, 1975. Originally the main projects were to be Kunene (Angola), thermal projects (Wankie) in Rhodesia, the Kafue and Kariba complexes, units on the Shire River (Malawi), the Oxbow project in Lesotho, and the hydrothermal system of the RSA including SWA.

33. Tanzania has several national river systems whose development for hydropower may preceed the Ruvuma's. These include the Pangani Basin, and particularly the Steigler's Gorge site on the Great Ruana-Rufiji system, currently considered as a power source for southern Tanzanian heavy industrial development. See *African Development*, December 1971, p. T.27 (article entitled 'Mining Prospects Appear Limited').

34. Malawi has developed two major sites on the Shire for power (and irrigation) at Nkula and Tedzani, in stages. International financing was available for dams and for transmission systems to urban areas. Their further development, plus four other possible sites, might also make feasible the processing of Malawi's bauxite. Contrary to the estimate shown in Table 7 the Shire can probably produce 1,000 MW. Malawi

may also have 150 MW further potential on Bua River (central region) and South Rukuru Rivers (northern region). See *Malawi Economic Survey*, August 1971, p. M.15; the *Standard Chartered Review*, March 1977, p. 9 and May 1977, p. 8; and *Africa South of the Sahara*, 1976/7, p. 518.

35. For Zambian power information, see *Standard Chartered Review*, March 1977, p. 11; *Africa South of the Sahara,* 1976/7, p. 1010 and 1024, and *African Development*, Ctober 1971, October 1973 and October 1974, and World Bank Appraisal Reports; *Zambia: Kafue Hydroelectric Project*, May 1973 (Report No. 86a-ZA); *Kariba North Project*, June 1974, (Report No. 1–1380a-ZA).

36. On Zimbabwe's power sector, see *Quarterly Economic Review of Rhodesia, Malawi, Annual Supplement, 1977,* pp. 13–14; see also recurrent reviews in *African Development*.

37. For background see Middlemas, *Cabora Bassa . . .*, *op cit*, W. A. Hance 'Cabora Bassa Hydro Project', *African Report*, May 1970, pp. 20–1; *Quarterly Economic Review of Angola, Mozambique, Annual Supplement 1977* pp. 22–3; Lloyds Bank Ltd, Overseas Department, International Trade Promotion Section; *Mozambique*, London 1975, pp. 12–13; and *Africa South of the Sahara 1976/7*, p. 579.

38. For details on the Kunene project see, for example, *Africa South of the Sahara 1976/7*, p. 144.

39. There is a considerable body of material on mineral sectors of developing countries. UN family items include: Geology and Mining Division (Resources and Transport Section), *Mineral Resources Development with Particular Reference to Developing Countries*, 1970; Resources and Transport Division, *Small Scale Mining in the Developing Countries*, 1972; UNIDO *Non-Ferrous Metals: A Survey of their Production and Potential in the Developing Countries*, New York 1972; UN Advisory Committee on the Application of Science and Technology to Development, *Natural Resources of Developing Countries—Investigation Development and Rational Utilisation*, 1970; *Multilateral Developing . . .*, *op cit*, see also World Bank, *Minerals and Energy . . .*, *op. cit.*, Bosson and Varon, *The Mining Industry . . .*, *op cit*, B. Baron and K. Takeuchi, 'Developing Countries and non-fuel Minerals', *Foreign Affairs*, 52, 3 April 1974, pp. 497–510; A. R. Berger (ed), *Geo-scientists and the Third World: A Collective Critique of Existing Programme*, Ottawa: Geological Survey of Canada, 1975 (Paper 1974–5) and *Africa South of the Sahara 1976/7*, pp. 1129–38 (Minerals Section). A detailed study of transportation sector requirements in central, east central and southern Africa conducted by Stanford Research Institute for USAID with the participation of a dozen countries: *Middle Africa Transportation Survey*, included detailed projections for demand of transport from the minerals sector. *Supporting Document No. 3* of the *Survey* contains the most complete generally available inventory and analysis of the region's minerals, and

their projected development (tonnages, locations, investment costs, as well as transport requirements).

0. Different sources give varying estimates. In addition to the references above, see US Bureau of Mines publications; *U.N. Statistical Yearbooks*, annual trade and commodity material produced by the IMF and the World Bank. Further estimates are found in R. Prain, 'Metals and Africa: Economic Power in an International Setting', *African Affairs*, 77, 307, April 1978, pp. 236–46.

1. Over 1966–76 Zambia's share of the world copper market dropped from 12–13 per cent to 8–9 per cent. Zambia still mines over 70 per cent of its copper underground which is more expensive than open pit mining. Rising labour, equipment, and other input costs have meant that for half of the 1970s there was no profit in the copper sector. Unit costs are also rising due to skilled labour shortages and the need to mine less easily accessible ores. Rail transportation system difficulties have exacerbated export problems. The lack of surplus over much of the 1970s has limited existing investment and net additions to capacity. At low prices, the mines consume the bulk of the foreign exchange earned leaving little available for other development purposes. Government covered revenues have also fallen, severely constraining public spending. For earlier relationships between the copper sector, foreign exchange earnings and government budgets, see Charles Harvey, 'The Control of Inflation in a Very Open Economy: Zambia 1964–9', *Eastern Africa Economic Review*, 3, 1, 1971, pp. 41–6.

2. Data can be deceptive. For example, chromite ore is processed to ferrochrome, and its export value classified under manufactured products. Zimbabwe (after RSA) is the western world's second largest chromite producer.

3. Semi analytical articles are reasonably plentiful for most of the anglophone nations. See in particular *Standard Chartered Review, African Development, Africa, The Economist, Africa Guide*, and the *Quarterly Economic Review of Southern Africa* by the Economist Intelligence Unit.

4. There are several studies of Zambia's efforts to assume greater control over its mining sector. Besides the historical record available in regular journals and magazines, see Anthony Martin, *Minding Their Own Business*, London: Hutchinson 1972; Mark Bostock and Charles Harvey, *Economic Independence and Zambian Copper*, New York: Praeger, 1972; Muna Ndulo, *The Requirement of Domestic Participation in New Mining Ventures in Zambia*, African Social Research, June 1978, pp. 399–427; and *Corporate Power in an African State: The Political Impact of Multinational Mining Companies in Zambia*, Berkeley: University of California Press, 1975. For the role of government in manufacturing, see Percy Selwyn, *Industries in the Southern African Periphery (A Study of Industrial Development in Botswana, Lesotho and Swaziland)*, London: Croom Helm, 1975 (for the Institute of Development Studies, University of Sussex).

45. See, for example ECA, *Industrial Co-ordination in East Africa: A Quantified Approach to First Approximation* (paper for the Conference on Harmonization of Industrial Development Programmes in East Africa, Lusaka, 1965), Addis Ababa, 1965 (Doc. No. E/CN. 14/INR/102). East Africa included 12 countries. This document paid particular attention to metals and engineering industries; ECA and the Cairo Centre for Industrial Development, *Industrialisation, Economic Co-operation and Transport—Hypothesis of Work in the Region of the Great African Lakes*, (paper prepared for Symposium on Industrial Development in Africa, Cairo, 1966) Addis Ababa, 1966 (Doc. No. E/CN. 14/AS/IV/7); ECA *Development of the Steel Industry in East and Central Africa*, Addis Ababa, 1967 (Doc. No. E/Cn.14/INR/87); ECA *Note by the Secretariat on some Aspects of the Financing of Multinational Projects* (prepared for East and Central African States Sectoral Meeting on Industry and Energy), Addis Ababa, 1969 (Draft Doc. No. M69-2762); and ECA *A Programme to Accelerate Foreign Investment and Technical Assistance for the Implementation of Industrial Projects*, Addis Ababa, 1970 (Draft Doc. No. M70-1328). This was followed by a supplement (M70-1560) providing a work plan for an East African Investment Centre. The problem of using a resource extraction industry to stimulate the industrial sector has been addressed in different ways. See, for example, B. V. Bechdolt, A. E. Scaperlanda and E. C. Perry, *Non-replenishable Natural Resources and Industrialisation Strategies in Developing Economies*, Vienna, UNIDO, 1974 (Doc. No. ID/CCNF. 3/B.6)—paper prepared for the Second General Conference of UNIDO, Lima 1975; and Intergovernmental Council of Copper Exporting Countries, *Copper as a Factor of Industrial Development, Ibid* (Doc. No. ID/CONF. 3/B.13). See also C. A. Gibson, 'The Mining Industry as an Exporter', Rhodesian Journal of Economics, 6, 4 December 1972, pp. 72–81 and M. T. Nziramasanga, 'Domestic Plan', *Eastern Africa Economic Review*, 6, 2 December 1974, pp. 1–17.

46. If EADB's Kampala archives remain in existence, they contain an excellent library of relevant materials. The EADB organized detailed studies of several industries with the objective of East African industrial integration. The East African Community's Secretariat in Arusha also developed more detailed feasibility studies on several basic industries including iron and steel and fertilizers, which could be inter-state priorities in the southern African region.

47. Ann Seidman, 'Ending Dependence on Copper in Zambia?', *African Social Research*, 15 June 1973, pp. 381–6 (Review article of Bostock and Harvey (eds), *Economic Independence . . ., op cit*) includes a discussion of Zambia's industrial integration possibilities with Tanzania.

48. A standard on cartels is R. F. Mikesell, 'More Third World Cartels Ahead?', *Challenge*, November/December, 1974 pp. 24–30. A presentation by Sir Ronald Prain, based on TNC experience and outlook is cited at (40) above.

49. This is especially true in two areas:

(a) Company or mixed cartels (diamonds and uranium oxide) which succeed admirably so far as consumer price boosting goes, cannot be replaced by state cartels, and therefore present problems of barganing for better shares of the achieved cartel surplus (as Botswana and Tanzania have done to some effect in diamonds);

(b) Interposing single channel stateowned export sellers, (e.g. Zambia's Memaco for copper) between the producers and the industrial economy buyers to limit transfer pricing and related devices which lower export receipts in TNC controlled transaction chains. .

Employment and Skills

INTRODUCTION

Six of the countries in southern Africa, Tanzania, Malawi, Zambia, Botswana, Lesotho and Swaziland, have been independent for well over a decade. Over that period each of their governments has initiated profound social and economic change. Economic structures are now much more diversified, and the real value of production has been greatly increased; more of the incomes from this production flow increasingly to citizen rather than metropolitan interests; progress has been made toward citizening the labour force; major increases in social services provision, particularly of education and health, have been made. Many more adjustments will take place, but in each of these states the economy and polity are set on a course which promotes change within an established network.

The other countries within the region are rather different. For Mozambique and Angola independence from Portugal has been won very recently. The wars in each of these countries disrupted industrial and agricultural production, causing major resource problems and, in particular, brought scarcities of food, foreign exchange and investible resources. Acute shortages of skilled workers have been exacerbated by the departure of most of the Portuguese settlers. Decisions have been taken by these governments to bring about needed changes in patterns of ownership, production and distribution. But the structural changes which these entail are still very much under way, with solutions to some of the key strategy questions facing each nation still being sought.

In the remaining two countries considered in this paper, Zimbabwe and Namibia—such changes are yet to begin. The illegal minority governments of these countries, ruling in Zimbabwe until March 1980 and in Namibia today, have acted in the context of discriminatory economic, social and political structures which systematically and pervasively benefit mainly the tiny white minority. The transition to legitimate majority rule will witness fundamental shifts in production and employment relations which will probably be no less profound than those in Mozambique and Angola. In some ways, however, the problems will be even more extreme. The scale of the likely exodus of whites will create exceptionally acute shortages of local skills, and the problems of maintaining output whilst tackling the pressing problems of social and economic reconstruction will be extremely severe.

The fact that these ten countries are at such different stages in the transitional process implies that within the region a very wide range of employment problems—different in scale and often in kind—are to be found. This paper attempts to indicate the nature of this diversity, but also to point to common themes and problems which all of these countries face. The paper is in three sections. The first indicates the problems of, and priorities for, domestic labour utilization in the region, including an analysis of the issue of migrant labour. The second examines the critical problem of skilled labour shortages. The final section indicates a range of initiatives at both the regional and international levels which seem to be required if these problems are to be tackled effectively.

THE PRESENT PATTERN OF LABOUR UTILIZATION

DEVELOPMENT POLICY AND DOMESTIC EMPLOYMENT

The ten southern African countries have a combined population of over 55 million people and a combined national product of over US $8 billions per year (approximately $150 per head) in 1976/7 (Basic Data Table 6). About one eighth of the labour force in these countries is in receipt of regular wages or salaries from formal employment. The $3\frac{1}{2}$ million formal jobs in the region include one quarter of a million which are currently held by Europeans, and a further half million held by Africans working outside their own country.

There are, however, very considerable differences between countries within the region. At present, Zimbabwe and Namibia account for half of the economic output, one third of the formal jobs, and contain almost two thirds of the European workers in the region. Reflecting such differences of economic power, the flows of migrant workers have been away from the majority-ruled countries in the region, towards the Republic of South Africa and pre-independence Zimbabwe. Although most countries in the former group are net providers of migrant labour, Malawi, Botswana, Lesotho and Mozambique are the source of more than 85 per cent of these foreign labour flows. In addition, the proportion of the labour force within the majority-ruled states with regular domestic employment varies from about 5 per cent or 6 per cent in Lesotho and Tanzania, to about 25 per cent in Swaziland. This compares with about 30 per cent in Zimbabwe and over 40 per cent in Namibia. The remainder of the population (between 20 and 25 million workers in these ten countries) are dependent upon informal and subsistence agricultural activities of various kinds, in environments with vastly different soil fertility, rainfall and infrastructural endowments.

Common to all countries, however is the fact that the increase in the number of regular wage and salaried employment opportunities in the domestic formal sector has not been able to keep pace with the growth of the domestic labour force. Nor can it do so within the foreseeable future—with the possible exception of Namibia after transition to legitimate majority rule, where an annual growth of formal employment of about 7 per cent would be required. Even in Botswana, which achieved real economic growth rates of over 20 per cent per year between 1969 and 1974, formal job creation only absorbed between half and two thirds of the increment to the labour force over those years. In other countries, where growth has been much lower, labour absorption has been correspondingly less.

As a result, the absolute size of the rural labour force outside formal wage employment has been growing rapidly, probably by about four or five million people over the past decade. Thus of critical importance to all countries in the region are policies aimed at improving labour use and incomes from informal and subsistence sector activities. In the majority-ruled countries of the region, two broad approaches can be discerned:

1. Tanzania, Mozambique, Angola. These countries have embarked upon a development path which involves a replacement of capitalist/colonial employment patterns and relations by a socialist organization of production. Although the detailed approaches differ, the broad elements of each strategy has included the nationalization of existing large enterprises in the formal sector, and the development of state corporations to form the main vehicles for new investment initiatives in the productive sectors. The introduction of sharply progressive taxation to cover all forms of privately controlled wealth and income, in order to reduce income inequalities over time, has been a feature of Tanzanian policy. While recognizing the importance of sustained formal sector output growth in order to produce growing revenues, exports and investible funds, a distinguishing characteristic of the policies adopted by those three countries is the emphasis given to the rural sector. Measures to stimulate rural production, especially of food, and the provision of rural services within a co-operative ownership/endeavour framework are of central importance to their strategies.

In the case of Tanzania, under the *ujamaa* villagization programme, the government has established villages in the hope that over time more and more productive activity will be based upon co-operative labour. Initially people were encouraged to move their homes to form larger communities for which basic services could more easily be provided. The services were in some cases used as an incentive to procure the move of families and for them to embark upon communal production.

Broadly similar intentions are apparent in Angola and Mozambique. Both countries have had to cope with the enormous problems of social and economic reconstruction in the aftermath of war, which has caused disruption of agricultural and industrial production. Shortages of foreign exchange became acute as a result of the fall in export revenues—

191

exacerbated in the case of Mozambique by a dramatic reduction in recruitment of its labourers by the RSA mines. In both countries, therefore, there has been an urgent need to restore earlier production levels, consistent with moving towards a socialist transformation of society. A number of large enterprises in all sectors, including those abandoned by departing Portuguese owners, have come under state control. In agriculture, state farms have been established, and it is the intention in both countries to broaden already initiated systems of co-operative production in the rural areas.

The combined populations of these three countries is 35 million i.e. two thirds of the population of the region as a whole. Over 90 per cent of these people are dependent upon agriculture for their livelihood. Their per head incomes are lower than any other countries in the region with the exception of Malawi. There is no doubt, then, about the size of the challenge to be faced in the rural sector, nor about the wisdom of giving the creation of work opportunities in this sector the highest priority for the focus of development policy.

Judging by the experience of Tanzania, the emphasis upon equity and selfreliance implicit in this approach to development is consistent with a continued growth in total national production, except when there are major setbacks due to drought or flood conditions. Nevertheless, the skills needed in order to sustain such a development strategy are considerable, even though the skill mix required is often different from that for strategies which put primary emphasis upon capital-intensive development in the formal sector. The challenge of organizing, of training and of providing credit, extension, marketing and bookkeeping services to a highly dispersed rural population requires the deployment of many thousands of people skilled in these tasks. Tanzania's leaders would be the first to say how difficult this is. In Mozambique and Angola, faced with the recent disruptions to formal sector output, the exodus of the Portuguese and the return of many migrant workers from abroad, the employment problems of the next few years will be extreme.

2. Zambia, Botswana, Lesotho, Swaziland, Malawi. These countries have been tending to concentrate upon modern sector growth and diversification (mining in the case of the first two, estate agriculture and associated processing in the case of the last two) in order to enhance the public resources available for future rural development. Most have welcomed and provided considerable incentives to attract foreign investment, although there are substantial differences in the degree of state participation in production (strong participation in Zambia, weak in Malawi and Swaziland). An approach which gave considerable emphasis to maximizing government revenues was made inevitable in the 1960s by the heavy dependence of the Governments of Botswana, Lesotho, Swaziland and Malawi upon Britain for recurrent revenue support. The

re-negotiation of the Customs Union Agreement with RSA in 1969 to some extent replaced the dependence of the first three countries upon Britain by an increased dependence upon RSA, but in the cases of Swaziland and Botswana, the subsequent growth and diversification of their economies has decreased their earlier vulnerability to disruptions of revenues from any single source.

With increased economic strength has come an ability to tackle some of the pressing problems of rural poverty, and an awareness that modern sector development alone would leave these problems untouched. Mining is highly capital intensive, and for all its pre-eminence in Zambian total income (25 per cent of GDP, 98 per cent of exports), it accounts for only 16 per cent of that country's formal employment. The Botswana Government, too, appreciates that while minerals will provide a large and growing proportion of national income it is a poor generator of employment. Even Swaziland, with its small population, its diversified estates and processing sectors, its proximity to RSA markets and buoyant tourist industry, has so far absorbed no more than one quarter of its domestic labour force in formal employment. Each of these countries, then, recognizes that work opportunities for the majority of the people will have to be provided by means other than formal sector growth.

The approaches taken towards rural development in these countries do not follow the collectivist/socialist pattern of Tanzania, Mozambique and Angola. In general, in these countries, rural development efforts are focussed upon improving agricultural productivity through the provision of extension services, inputs and guaranteed prices for farmers, and through the provision of more general rural infrastructure, i.e. roads, water, education and health services. In some cases (Malawi, Swaziland) designated rural development areas become the target for special government efforts, ensuring a package of investments related to increasing the output of a particular range of products. In others, efforts are made to stimulate small scale manufacturing and services based upon a rural market (Botswana Brigades, Botswana Enterprise Development Units, Malawi Young Pioneers, Swaziland Enterprise Development Corporation). In most cases these efforts are occurring within the context of traditional tenure and production patterns, although in Botswana a land reform is currently taking place which will commercialize some of the grazing land in existing tribal areas. This is intended to have positive effects upon conservation of the range and upon output, but it also runs a danger of displacing labour and strengthening the position of the large cattle owners at some cost to smaller farmers.

One of the unintended effects of development policy in this group of countries, an effect which is increasingly recognized by the governments concerned, is that the national distribution of income has tended to become worse over time: the richer groups have been increasing their incomes faster than the poor (less so in Lesotho, and perhaps Malawi, than elsewhere). Formal sector development has tended to benefit disproportionately a small proportion of nationals and—often significantly so—the international interests supplying the capital on commercial terms.

In the absence of effective incomes policies, local elites have replaced the outgoing expatriate colonial and post-colonial groups. There has been little change in the overall distribution of net earnings. These new groups now have strong vested interests in preserving the status quo, thereby making significant shifts in the focus of development policy very difficult to achieve. These trends have been exacerbated by the fact that the balance of investment has been weighted heavily towards the urban centres, and rates of urbanization have been very high. Botswana where, since independence, over three quarters of public investment has been directed to the towns, has had the highest urbanization rates in Africa. New formal job opportunities have thus occurred mainly in the urban centres. Because wages have been much higher than returns from alternative rural employment, thereby accelerating rural urban migration, urban unemployment has emerged as a major problem in Swaziland, Botswana and Zambia.

Meanwhile, even though widely spread development is an important explicitly stated aim of each government, the proportion of public expenditure going to productive rural investment remains small. Urban facilities, once established, tend to have growing, rather than constant or declining, needs for financial servicing and upgrading. Since the urban dwellers are usually amongst the most educated, articulate and powerful members of the community, governments find it very difficult to avoid responding to their demands.

There are, of course, many things that can be done to increase the rate of labour absorption per unit of capital used by the formal sector. Three of the governments in the region (Zambia, Swaziland, Botswana), have recently commissioned reports from international agencies on employment policies. These have highlighted the need for change and adjustment in policies relating to, inter alia, capital subsidies, domestic industry protection, licensing requirements, tendering procedures and wages and incomes. Each has also shown, explicitly or implicitly, that the most critical question for labour use in all these countries is how to increase the amount and the proportion of total national investment flowing to the rural areas. This obviously raises profound technical and administrative issues, but the critical constraint is often found in the existing balance of social and political pressures. It takes a great amount of courage and commitment for a government to reduce or even to hold constant the real level of urban investment over successive years. Yet for rapid increases in the incomes of the majority of the people to be achieved, this is precisely what is required.

THE SCALE OF MIGRATION AND FUTURE TRENDS

Over half a million Africans from the other countries in the region at

194

present hold jobs in RSA or Zimbabwe, and one in six of all formally employed Africans in the region as a whole (excluding RSA) are migrant workers. Basic Data Table 6 provides estimates for the scale of this migration for each country. It can be seen that the countries most severely affected by the migrant labour system are Lesotho and Botswana, where one third and one fifth of the labour force respectively are working abroad at any time—mainly in the Republic of South Africa. In addition, Swaziland, Mozambique, Malawi and Zambia are also significant net suppliers of labour.

Most discussions of the problem of migrant labour in southern Africa focus upon those working in the RSA gold and coal mines affiliated to the South African Chamber of Mines. The reasons for this are first that these comprise the largest single group of employers recruiting foreign labour and second that regular and fairly accurate statistics have been kept over the years by the South African Mine Labour Organizations (Witwatersrand Native Labour Association—now TEBA—and the Native Recruitment Corporation) on the annual flow of recruits by country of origin. Recent data from this source are summarized in Table 1. It is important to realize, however, that there are other RSA recruiting organizations which are operating officially in the independent states, and that many other workers cross national borders, legally or illegally, to find work in RSA and Zimbabwe on a regular basis. Comparison of the estimates given in Table 1 and Basic Data Table 6 suggests that the South African Chamber of Mines recruitment statistics cover only about half of all the estimated non-citizen migrants working in RSA and only about one third of those in RSA and Zimbabwe combined. Even though they are partial, however, it is worth considering the data shown in Table 1, as they provide important insights upon current and likely future trends.

It is well known that the pattern of recruitment of labour by the RSA mining sector has changed substantially during the past few years. Three factors have been mainly responsible. First, following an air crash at Francistown in April 1974, when 74 Malawian miners returning home were killed, President Banda suspended all further recruitment of Malawians for the mines. Second, in 1976, recruitment of workers from Mozambique was dramatically reduced following the expiry of the earlier recruitment agreement between the Portuguese and the RSA Government. Third, mine wages began to increase rapidly from 1973 onwards, in part fuelled by labour shortages generated by the two factors mentioned above, which allowed a largely compensatory increase in recruitment of labour from within the Republic of South Africa, and from Botswana, Lesotho and Swaziland. In addition, an agreement to recruit up to 20,000 labourers per year was negotiated with the illegal UDI regime in Zimbabwe in December 1974. The net result of all these changes is that—at least for the mines represented by the data in Table 1—mine labour from RSA itself has increased from one fifth to over one half of the mine labour force; recruits from Mozambique

195

and Malawi have been reduced from one half to scarcely more than 10 per cent of the labour force; finally there was until 1977 some increase in recruitment from Botswana, Lesotho and Swaziland and new supplies came from Zimbabwe, then Southern Rhodesia.

Historically, the presence of a large non-citizen African migrant labour force has acted in the interests of the white, and against the interests of the black, community in RSA. It has depressed wages and increased unemployment outside the mining sector, and has created even less favourable circumstances in which to make effective demands for improved wages and working conditions in the mines themselves. Wilson (1972) has shown that the real wages for blacks in the mining sector were probably lower in the mid 1960s than at the beginning of the century. The ruthless exploitation of the advantages presented by a regional labour force has allowed the employers in RSA to profit greatly over the last 80 years.

Nevertheless, the policy of increasing the proportion of RSA blacks employed on the mines has come about not only as a contingency response to the recent political development in the supplier states, but also as part of a deliberate strategy by the employers to reduce dependence upon foreign workers. The present supplier states are seen in RSA as increasingly unpredictable sources of labour, particularly as the armed struggle for liberation moves steadily south and will focus finally and within the not too distant future upon the Republic of South Africa itself. An increasing dependence upon labour from the homelands is seen as a safer policy, and one which will bring few additional costs to the mines. As the transition to so-called independence for these regions is made, the South African Government will no doubt use the same arguments to absolve itself from all responsibility for the support of the dependents of workers from the homelands as are used in the context of foreign workers today.

To this end, the existing trend towards an increased recruitment of black South Africans will probably continue, as will increased mechanization, together with a policy of encouraging a stable workforce by reducing the recruitment of novices from supplier states. Latest indications are that the mines have cut back recruitment of labour from Botswana, Lesotho and Swaziland by about 20 per cent during 1978/9. This trend is likely to continue over the next few years. Sudden termination is unlikely because it will take the labour market in RSA some time to adjust, and new technologies can be introduced only slowly. The net result will probably be a lower level of foreign recruitment from a range of different supply sources, with the RSA Government attempting to continue exploiting different attitudes and policies of the sending states to their own advantage.

The likely future for migrant labour working other than for Chamber of Mines employers is less clear. Such recruitment is not centrally organized, and is more responsive to local labour market conditions in the areas close to the employers concerned. Estate farmers for example, will probably continue to recruit seasonal agricultural labour from Botswana for as long as the Botswana authorities and the RSA regulations will permit it. On balance, however, a downward trend of recruitment can be expected as the South African Government increases the pressure on employers to hire local labour in the face of rising levels of domestic unemployment. A recession prompted by the introduction of economic sanctions on RSA would accelerate these trends.

From the point of view of the supplier states, the pros and cons of the migrant labour system are fairly clear. The benefits are confined to income effects—income for (mainly) the poorer households, foreign exchange to strengthen the balance of payments, and additional government revenues from fees charged to the recruiters and the employers. Weighed against this are the increased dependency upon RSA for the nations and the individuals concerned, the production lost because of the absence of males of working age, and the enormous social costs of family separation together with the personal humiliation associated with life under apartheid in the prisonlike conditions of the mining compounds. Both from the perspectives of the sending states, which need to reduce dependence upon RSA, and of the South African blacks, it is clear that a lengthy continuation of the existing system is undesirable. But the difficulties of terminating these arrangements vary considerably amongst the supplier countries.

The problem of reabsorption of migrant labourers must be tackled as part of the domestic employment creation strategies of each of the majority-ruled countries in the region. The most intractable case will be that of Lesotho. As shown in Basic Data Table 6, one third of the Basutho labour force works in RSA—half of whom are engaged by employers associated with the Chamber of Mines. Employment of Basutho in the Republic of South Africa is over six times total formal employment in Lesotho. Even over the long term, it is difficult to see how this proportion of a growing labour force can be productively reabsorbed in the domestic economy except at high cost. Tourism can certainly be further developed, but this provides few jobs. Manufacturing industries would probably need extensive and extended subsidy, and the prospects for absorption of large numbers of workers in agriculture are not good in view of Lesotho's poor soils. At present, over 40 per cent of national income comes from the earnings of migrant labourers in RSA. Termination of the system, without compensatory financial transfers from other sources, would pauperize the great majority of Basotho households.

The problems of reabsorption are more manageable in the case of Botswana, although here too the extent of present dependence upon migrant labour is such that its sudden termination would bring high costs: allowing for illegal migrancy, one fifth of the citizen labour force works abroad, remittances comprise one fifth of household income for the poorest decile (tenth) of the rural population (Colclough and Fallon, 1979), and employment in RSA is a tenth greater than formal employment in Botswana. On the other hand, migrancy is not generally a permanent occupation, as it is for many Basutho, and the obstacles to rapidly increasing domestic labour use are much less formidable. Batswana tend to use the migrant labour system as a means of building up enough capital to buy cattle and to start farming. A range of solutions could be tried, but analysis shows that the most important priorities are to provide the poorer families with access to draught-power, and to increase substantially the resources for both production and research in arable agriculture (Colclough and McCarthy, 1979; Lipton, 1978). Policy initiatives are also needed in other sectors, some of which are now under consideration by the Botswana Government.

In the other supplier states, the problems of terminating migrant labour flows to RSA are less serious. Swaziland, with about 8 per cent of its labour force employed in RSA, and with a much higher proportion of its domestic workers engaged in formal sector jobs (25 per cent compared to 17 per cent in Botswana, or about three times as many as work in the Republic), is less critically dependent upon work in RSA than either Botswana or Lesotho. Moreover, it can be seen from Table 1 that Mozambique and Malawi have already coped with severance from the migrant labour system for the majority of people who were formerly involved. In both cases this must have caused severe difficulties for thousands of families over the last few years—although no information is available to suggest how and with what success the migrants concerned have been reabsorbed in the domestic rural sector.

In fact, Mozambique and Malawi now have many more of their workers in Zimbabwe than in RSA. About 200,000 people, mainly from these countries, but also including significant numbers of Zambians, and a few thousand Batswana, now hold jobs in Zimbabwe (Basic Data Table 6). Many of these workers have become semi-permanent residents, and have severed links with their homes to much greater extent than usually happens with those working in RSA where the system prevents it. Here too, however, it would be unwise to count upon such work opportunities being available indefinitely. The Government of Zimbabwe is now faced with urgent problems of social and economic reconstruction and structural change, of rising unemployment amongst its citizens, of absorbing many tens of thousands of returning refugees, and probably also the 50,000 or so Zimbabweans currently working in RSA. Inevitably it cannot give any over-riding priority to the protection of jobs held by non-citizen Africans. Domestic employment policy in Mozambique, Malawi and Zambia must therefore face the repatriation of most of their citizens working in Zimbabwe—possibly many of them within the next two years.

Nevertheless, except in Lesotho and to a lesser extent in Botswana, the problem of reabsorption of migrants is manageable, albeit difficult and costly, for the majority-ruled countries of southern Africa—particularly when compared with the much bigger problem of under-utilization of domestic labour, and with the rapid annual growth of the domestic labour force. The rural sector in each country will have to absorb most of these additional workers. To this end, long term national policies for agricultural and rural development must be devised which aim to provide production work opportunities for the people who are displaced from abroad, and for those who are without adequate work at home. Meanwhile the strategy in the supplier states should be to maximize the domestic benefits from the migrant labour system for as long as it continues to operate, and to prepare contingency arrangements which would reduce the costs of a sudden reduction or termination of the present opportunities facing migrant workers. Desirable actions at the regional and international levels which would further these aims are discussed in the final section of this paper.

PROBLEMS IN THE SKILLED LABOUR MARKET

HISTORICAL BACKGROUND

In all countries in the region, modern production structures were established during the colonial period without adequate supporting mechanisms to create the required skills among the indigenous population.

This occurred by design rather than by neglect. The gross inadequacy of educational services to Africans was part of the apparatus of domination and subjugation of the local populations—a means of preventing Africans and Europeans competing on equal terms in the labour market. In Zimbabwe for as long as it was under white rule and in Namibia to this day, the colonists have reinforced these policies with complex job reservation and other mechanisms in order to divide whites and blacks into non-competing groups. Outside RSA itself, these labour policies took their most extreme form in these two territories, but their elements were present in varying degrees throughout the region prior to the independence of the countries concerned.

As a result of this state of affairs, post primary education and training prior to independence covered only a tiny proportion of the population. Although mission secondary schools often provided education of a high standard, this rarely went beyond a basic three year post primary cycle. The number of Africans who had managed to gain higher education was derisorily small. In Zambia there were fewer than one hundred African graduates in 1964. In Botswana, Lesotho and Swaziland the numbers were much less even than that. Ironically only Zimbabwe, because of the length and violence of its transition, has come to independence with large numbers of African graduates. The total may indeed be as high as six thousand.

Even more problematic from an employment point of view was the virtual non-existence of technical education. It is true that the gaps in the technical fields often relate back to an inadequate mathematics grounding at primary level—even today numeracy, throughout the region, remains more elusive amongst the population than literacy. But even technical

199

studies, the opportunities for pursuing these within their own countries were almost non-existent, particularly in comparison with the needs. In Zimbabwe and Zambia (though not in Namibia) where the mining and manufacturing sectors were developed early, some training in technical skills became established. But this was limited to comparatively low levels, leading to occupations where settler interests were not threatened. In jobs where there was a strong white involvement, the response to labour shortages was usually to import more labour from abroad, rather than to provide the training infrastructure which would have been needed to secure African advancement.

The result was that in the six countries which achieved their independence during the 1960s, European workers occupied between 10 per cent and 15 per cent of all jobs in the formal sector at independence. At the higher levels of the occupational structure there were hardly any Africans, and the small number of citizens who had succeeded in attaining advanced qualifications were usually working in the schools and primary teacher training colleges, rather than in government or the directly productive sectors. As a consequence of this systemic neglect, the manpower problems facing the newly independent states were awesome—similar in quantitative terms, though not in speed of transition required, to those facing Zimbabwe, Mozambique and Angola today and, to an even greater extent, to those which will face Namibia in the near future.

THE POLICY RESPONSE AND THE EMERGENCE OF NEW PROBLEMS

The main policy response to the acute manpower shortages facing Tanzania, Malawi, Zambia, Botswana, Lesotho and Swaziland has been a massive increase in the provision of formal schooling. Over the first decade of independence, secondary school enrolments doubled in Tanzania and tripled in Swaziland; in Zambia they increase fivefold, and in Botswana their growth was more than sixfold. Universities were established in all these states, and here too enrolments have increased very rapidly. Educational policy has thus been dominated by the concern to expand the fledgling systems inherited from colonial days. Important attempts have been made to secure qualitative improvements at primary level by the provision of better equipment and trained teachers and by the reduction of rates of attrition and of class size. In Tanzania the reforms have gone much further. Inevitably, however, in all countries the major emphasis in terms of the allocation of both financial and administrative resources has been placed upon the post primary system.

In part as a result of this emphasis, progress has been made in localizing the labour force in all these countries: in every case, non-citizen workers now comprise less than one tenth of formal employment (Basic Data Table 6). Of even greater importance is that the influence wielded by foreign workers has been much reduced. They are now concentrated in technical and supportive professional jobs, and no longer occupy the highest decision-making posts in government. On balance, however, the high initial expectations of national policy makers have been disappointed. Although the proportional importance of expatriates has fallen, in absolute terms there are now twice as many non-citizen workers in Botswana as there were in 1966; there are more also in Swaziland and Lesotho, and Zambia, with 33,000 expatriate employees, now has about the same number as were employed at independence. Only in Tanzania has really dramatic progress with localization been achieved, with scarcely more than 1 per cent of all formal jobs now being held by non-citizens.

This differential progress with localization is primarily a reflection of differences in economic structure. The very rapid modern sector growth in Botswana, and to a lesser extent in Swaziland, has outstripped the capacity of even a greatly expanded formal education system to supply qualified recruits. In Zambia, on the other hand, the dominance and technical complexity of copper mining largely accounts for the continued presence of so many non-citizen workers: this sector accounts for over one third of all non-citizens employed in Zambia, and the number of expatriate mining personnel has actually increased by about 50 per cent since independence.

There is also, however, growing evidence that the different relative emphases which have been given to the expansion of schools, universities and other forms of post secondary education and training have not always promoted localization goals. Each of these countries has now had at least one manpower plan since independence, but in most cases these plans have strongly emphasized the role of the schools in forming required skills, and perhaps underplayed the crucial importance of various forms of formal and non-formal training. Three of these plans (Zambia 1966, Botswana 1973 and Swaziland 1978) attempted to quantify the need for training, based upon survey evidence, but only in the last was caution expressed about the desirability of further secondary school expansion, and significant importance given in the recommendations to means of promoting employment-linked training schemes for the formal sector. As a result, present trends suggest that post primary school leaver unemployment will become a general problem fairly soon. In some countries this has already happened: unemployment of 'O' level school leavers emerged in Zambia in the early 1970s, and in Swaziland it had begun to appear in 1978. This relatively new phenomenon (in southern Africa) of rising levels of educated unemployment coexisting with a continued dependence upon the skills of non-citizens, is likely to become more widespread over the next few years.

Governments are attempting to tackle this problem in various ways.

First, there is an increased concern to ensure that the future focus of educational expenditures is upon providing a sound basic education for all (including, especially in the case of Tanzania, greater emphasis on adult education for those who never had access to primary school), rather than allowing an increasing proportion of resources to be pre-empted by

201

providing an expensive higher education for a small minority.

Second, there are moves towards making schooling more suitable for the needs of the majority of children. Such policies include attempts to localize curricula, the introduction of mother tongues as media of instruction, introducing productive work and pre-vocational training into the syllabus, challenging the examination-oriented rote learning approaches of existing systems, and introducing alternative means of assessment and selection, both for promotion within education and from education to jobs. The Tanzanian policies of education for selfreliance have incorporated such reforms during the last ten years. A recent comprehensive review of the Zambian education system included these and other measures amongst its proposals. The policies of Botswana and Swaziland are also moving in these directions.

Third, increased emphasis is being placed upon other institutional mechanisms in order to promote localization. Whilst selective expansion of university departments, particularly in science-based disciplines, is still needed throughout the region, many of the most critical skills can best be acquired outside the formal school through university structure. In particular, the prime requisite is to ensure more structured job experience for new educated recruits, and more clearly organized learning on the job, supported by release or sandwich arrangements for the acquisition of a wide range of technical skills. Such training is the main way by which localization of the formal sector labour force can be speeded up. Training levies and other incentives schemes need to be introduced by more states as a means of increasing the amount of training undertaken by private employers. In particular, the training function must be seen as a prime responsibility for those expatriates now working in technical jobs. Although some further expansion of facilities for university and technical training is desirable, in general in these countries the institutional facilities to provide the required skills already exist. The major problem is in making them function effectively, and in ensuring that training, employment and incentive structures reflect the changing priorities on a year-to-year basis.

Mozambique and Angola are at a much earlier stage in dealing with all of these problems. Their policies in education are closer to those of Tanzania than to those of other countries in the group: emphasis is put upon basic literacy, and therefore upon primary and adult education; education is strongly integrated with work, both during and after completion of each stage of schooling; strong emphasis is placed upon worker education, and the government organizes many small training courses for worker upgrading. Quantitatively, these countries face a localization problem which is greater than that of Zambia. No statistical information is yet available to allow precise magnitudes to be assessed, and the establishment of such data will presumably be an early priority for the two governments concerned.

Zimbabwe today and Namibia tomorrow face special problems. Both of these countries have relatively well developed production structures, making them, relative to the distribution of populations, the richest nations in the southern African region outside the RSA itself. However, owing to the racialist policies which have been pursued in education and training, the maintenance of these production levels is at present highly dependent upon the skills held by white settlers and expatriates.

Transition to independence in each of these countries brings/will bring radical changes in production relations, particularly in agriculture, mining and manufacturing, with land reforms and increased state participation in production; radical shifts in the nature and patterns of provision of services, particularly in health and education; probable sharp changes in the distribution of net earnings from work, with large average reductions at the top end of the profile. One consequence of these changes will be a major exodus of whites, particularly of those in the more skilled or senior positions.

In many ways this is highly desirable. In Namibia, a large proportion of the whites have RSA nationality, and their continuation, particularly in government service, would in any case be inappropriate. More generally, the ingrained colonial attitudes held by many such persons, including those with long settler histories, will not be helpful under new arrangements. As a result, however, major gaps will be created amongst the most skilled and experienced sections of the labour force.

In aggregate terms, this could mean the loss of between 11 per cent and 15 per cent of the formally employed labour force in both cases. But between 70 per cent and 80 per cent of the skilled labour force is likely to be lost, i.e. more than 25,000 skilled persons from Namibia, and as many as 80,000 to 100,000 in the case of Zimbabwe. By and large, these skills will have to be replaced. The structural changes in production, ownership and distribution likely to be introduced will undoubtedly change the skill mix, particularly in agriculture, education, health and government. But in spite of these changes in the composition of skills required, the overall aggregate need for educated and trained persons is unlikely to be much reduced. Indeed, in Namibia at least it is more likely to be increased. Thus, under most conceivable scenarios for the first years of independence in Zimbabwe and Namibia, there will be major problems of qualitative, quantitative and structural readjustment in the manpower field.

The strategy adopted in order to tackle these problems will have to comprise a number of different elements.

First there will be a need to identify those Africans—and there are tens of thousands—who have acquired skills by informal means outside the school or university system, and who are suitable for rapid upgrading to skilled jobs in the formal sector. This will involve designing specific short term courses for upgrade training in a wide range of clerical, artisan and technical fields. Essentially, a flexible system of adult education, training and testing centres is needed, in order to identify existing and potential skills, to organize the basic training required, and to link into other, more structured training institutions which provide longer term instruction for the acquisition of priority skills.

Second, infrastructure required for the execution of medium and long term economic and structural change. These decisions will need to be based upon a careful analysis of the transitional and projected employment structure, in turn based upon economic and political priorities, and detailed staffing analogues from other independent African states.

Third, a framework for regional co-operation in training for a range of high priority but expensive-to-acquire skills needs to be established.

Fourth, technical co-operation with other countries, to secure the temporary provision of skilled workers, will inevitably be needed during the transitional and immediate post independence phase. The dimensions, sources and nature of this programme need careful thought, as does a framework to facilitate a rapid reduction of dependence upon such outside sources of skills over a short period of time.

The initiatives which appear to be required at the regional and international levels are indicated in the next and final section of this paper.

REGIONAL AND INTERNATIONAL INITIATIVES

MIGRANT LABOUR

The analysis in this paper has shown that RSA remains critically dependent upon migrant labour from surrounding states, but that this dependence is gradually being reduced. For various strategic and economic reasons however, migration is likely to continue, though at a lower level, in the future. Early termination of labour flows is likely only in the event of a deterioration of RSA's economic position as a result of international economic sanctions or of the armed struggle moving into RSA itself. In this situation, a range of actions at the regional and international levels are desirable.

A. *Regional Initiatives*

The supplier states have an interest in co-ordinating their policies on migrant labour with a view to maximizing the flow of benefits over the short and medium term. To this end, meetings were held during 1978 in Lusaka to discuss matters of common concern. Negotiations with the mines for improving working and living conditions will obviously be more effective if all supplier states speak with a common voice. There is also much to be gained from reviewing alternative national policies for the reabsorption of returning migrants in the event of rapid changes of political or economic circumstances in the Republic of South Africa.

One of the most obvious areas of common interest is the fees collected from labour recruiters. Apart from the small charges made for recruitment licences, attestation fees are currently levied by the supplier states on a per

204

head basis. These vary between R5 per labourer recruited in Swaziland and R15 per labourer in Lesotho. The evidence suggests that if all supplier states were to adopt the same level of attestation fees for mine work, the level of charges could be raised very substantially without significantly reducing the flow of recruits in the short term. These are obviously very strong moral and economic arguments in favour of such a move: attestation fees of even R100 per man recruited would increase African labour costs in the mines by less than 10 per cent, far less than could be reasonably demanded as compensation by the supplier states for the loss of tax revenues on value added in RSA by their own nationals.

B. *International Co-operation*

There are other initiatives which require both regional and international co-operation. Swaziland and Botswana, but more especially Lesotho, would require substantial additional aid in the event of a sudden contraction of employment opportunities in RSA, in order to avoid huge income losses to the poorer families. the scale of transfers would be at least of the order of $5 million, $20 million and $100 million per year respectively, if full compensation were to be provided. In the cases of Swaziland and Botswana, as was argued earlier in this paper, domestic employment policies can be designed which are capable of absorbing repatriated migrant labourers within the medium term. The case of Lesotho is rather different, in that large amounts of aid will be needed over the long term if that country's present dependence upon employment in RSA is to be removed.

In this connection, an urgent study of employment possibilities in Lesotho is required. This should focus upon identifying public projects which are capable both of absorbing large amounts of unskilled labour, and of providing the capital to sustain and employ a growing labour force. The costs of such a programme will be large. But short term investments of this magnitude will be less costly and more beneficial over the long run than undertaking to continue the scale of recurrent support, which would otherwise be required, into the indefinite future.

In the case of Lesotho especially, there is good reason to seek international support for poor peasant oriented rural development and formal employment creation related to skills acquired in RSA now. Migrant levels have begun to fall and the reabsorption problem is already confronting many households. To delay further the building up of international support until a crisis emerges will guarantee that the support will be too little and too late. International support relations, like other institutions, take time to establish, get working smoothly and expand.

TRAINING AND TECHNICAL CO-OPERATION

A. *The Requirements*

The most urgent skilled manpower problems to be faced in southern Africa over the next few years are those generated by the transition to legitimate majority rule in Zimbabwe and shortly Namibia. These countries at present account for over half of all the whites employed in the region, the majority of whom will have to be replaced within the first decade of independence and possibly much sooner. This is not to underestimate the profound manpower problems at present faced by Mozambique and Angola: here almost one million Portuguese residents (including workers and dependents) have left since 1975, and have been replaced by much smaller number of other non-citizens, mainly from Cuba, Latin American and eastern Europe. Substantial shortages of skills remain. However, large numbers of the Portuguese workers were unskilled or semi-skilled, which is not in general true of the whites working in Zimbabwe and Namibia. Moreover, because industrial structures in these countries are more developed relative to the skill level of their African populations, transitional problems will be more acute than those which have been faced by other countries in the region.

Recent estimates show that whites in Zimbabwe and Namibia dominate the professional and technical occupations (UN Institute of Namibia 1978; Colclough and Murray 1979). The most acute shortages, in the event of a European exodus, are likely to occur in the engineering, geological, medical, veterinary, dentistry, accounting, legal and architectural professions. There will also be a more general shortage of workers in science-based occupations, including science teachers, and of technicians, artisan foremen, and skilled craftsmen at all levels of the production hierarchy. The number of Africans who have acquired such skills domestically through formal training are very few. Although between six and eight thousand Zimbabweans have received scholarships for training abroad since 1966, the numbers trained in the above fields are still far less than will be required. Namibia is in a much worse position, with no more than about three hundred graduates from post secondary courses abroad.

Although the magnitude of the training requirements are greater in Zimbabwe and Namibia than elsewhere, the skill priorities themselves are not significantly different from those of the other countries in the region. In all of these occupations, which mainly require specialized training at post secondary levels, shortages are widespread.

B. *Regional Co-operation*

Each country has developed—or will shortly do so—an infrastructure sufficient to meet its needs for workers with general educational qualifications, including the basic university disciplines which lead to jobs in government adminstration, management and the teaching profession. Nevertheless, regional co-operation in the development of more specialized education and training courses along the following lines is highly desirable:

(a) In some occupations and countries, the immediate requirements for citizenization purposes are very large, relative to long term needs of growth and replacement. This is true for civil, electrical and mechanical engineers, geologists, other mining skills and related technicians in Zambia, Zimbabwe, Namibia and, to a lesser extent, Botswana. An appropriate strategy here might be to expand the school of mines at the University of Zambia, and the faculty of engineering at the University of Zimbabwe, to admit more nationals and also students from these other states. During the first few years significant numbers of Batswana and Namibians would study elsewhere in Africa or in the UK. Over the medium term, however, more of the increased capacity in Lusaka and Salisbury could be taken up by other non-nationals, as the immediate localization problem diminished in these two countries.

(b) National faculties of medicine, dentistry, forestry and veterinary science are too expensive to justify in view of likely student numbers in Botswana, Lesotho, Swaziland and Namibia. Economies of scale in these disciplines are very high. Their provision should be tackled on a multi-national basis, taking account of the needs of all the states in the region.

(c) The needs of other graduate specialisms will in some cases be small. Degree courses in architecture, surveying, town and regional planning should be established. the structure of these courses should take more account of local needs and resources than courses available in western universities. But limited enrolments will require that these be introduced on a regional, rather than a national basis. In addition, undergraduate courses in non-priority disciplines e.g. some European languages, religious studies, psychology, together with most postgraduate degree courses, should not be represented in more than two or three of the national universities during the early years.

(d) With regard to sub-degree programmes, the possibility of making firm long term arrangements amongst English speaking countries in the region should also be explored. Railway training is an urgent priority for Zimbabwe, Botswana and Namibia. In view of the strong possibility of additional railway links among these three countries, some co-operative approach to training and staffing is desirable. Facilities are already well developed at the railway training school in Bulawayo. These could be expanded, or alternatively a new centre could be built up as part of a new maintenance and servicing centre which will almost certainly be required in Botswana and/or Namibia.

(e) As regards other skills, Swaziland would be an appropriate centre for forestry training, Namibia for fisheries; Botswana and Swaziland, in the context of expansion of the Institute of Development Management, for planning, finance, taxation and customs administration. Training for these latter skills, which are still scarce throughout the region, could also be developed at a number of centres, including the Institute of Finance

Management in Dar es Salaam, on the basis of particular national strengths, facilities and specialisms.

(f) The training of science, engineering, and medical technicians is such a large and urgent priority that most countries will wish to establish their own facilities. Botswana, Lesotho, Swaziland and Namibia may wish to explore the possibility of using facilities in other countries in the region on grounds of cost effectiveness, but even in these countries, national programmes would in most cases be viable. In general, also, it would seem sensible to integrate this tertiary level training in one national institution. The Malawian polytechnic concept appears particularly relevant and applicable to other countries. The danger is always that the unit costs of training will be pulled up by association with unversity departments; but with strong leadership and clear commitment this need not necessarily be the case.

This proposal for regional co-operation in tertiary level training does not envisage the creation of new joint universities or colleges. Recent experience with the University of Botswana, Lesotho and Swaziland demonstrates the inevitability of tension arising from a commitment to use national funds to build up jointly owned facilities in other countries.

It remains true, however, that unless students from one country are able to be trained in another, many tertiary level courses which are needed in the region will not be viable. If regional training initiatives are to succeed, the capital costs will need to be met from external sources, as part of a technical co-operation programme financed by the international community. This would be separate from and in addition to monies received by individual countries through existing bilateral and multilateral channels. For some countries, also, provision of recurrent costs will be important because of foreign exchange constraints. Certainly, for the host state to be willing, over the long or even medium term, to provide a substantial number of places for citizens of other regional states, it must receive the full recurrent costs either from the sending states or through international co-operation. Such financial guarantees would facilitate the negotiation of medium term agreements between different countries in the region with regard to sharing the costs of particular tertiary level courses in a fashion which would be advantageous to all partners.

TEMPORARY EXPATRIATE MANPOWER

Zimbabwe and Namibia combined could need the temporary assistance of up to 75,000 skilled expatriates during the immediate post-independence period (Green's figure of 15,000–17,500 for Namibia, together with Colclough's estimate of about 60 per cent of the level of white employment in pre-independence Zimbabwe). In both cases, holding post-independence requirements down to these levels would represent and require a very sharp, significant and rapid step towards citizenization of the labour force. But, relative to the size of the national populations, this still implies a need for very large programmes of technical co-operation.

If one third of these recruits were financed through technical co-operation arrangements, the costs to the international community, at current rates, would be around £300 million per year. In recruiting these persons full use should be made of friendly governments and agencies. If the destabilizing presence of unsuitable expatriates is to be avoided, it is important that a high proportion of these foreign personnel are interviewed and selected by Zimbabweans and Namibians themselves. To aid this process, strong recruitment-vetting offices could usefully be established by the two governments. One aim is likely to be the recruitment of technical co-operation personnel from other friendly Third World countries with skilled labour surpluses in some fields. Some countries in the region have already initiated technical co-operation agreements with Nigeria and discussions have also taken place with India. The opportunity to extend and strengthen such trends could usefully be taken in Zimbabwe and Namibia.

INSTITUTIONAL NEEDS AND DATA REQUIREMENTS

In order to facilitate and co-ordinate technical co-operation in training amongst independent states in southern Africa, a small regional technical co-operation planning unit would be useful. The tasks of this unit would include the following:

A. Preparation of medium/long term indicative plans, based upon manpower and employment perspectives for each country, for areas of training where regional co-operation would be to the advantage of all partners. These plans could identify subject and programme areas not addressed under existing national programmes, required national enrolments, existing institutions which could be expanded to meet such needs, and new institutions required.

B. Identification of specific project proposals for multi-country and regional co-operation in training, for approval by national representatives.

C. Preparation of project documents, in collaboration with national planning offices, for financing by a southern African development co-operation fund or its equivalent.

This regional planning unit might be responsible to, and provide the secretariat for a regional council for technical co-operation, comprising senior officers from Education or Planning Ministries in each country. This council, meeting perhaps bi-annually, could have authority to approve or modify both the perspective plans drawn up by the regional planning team, and the specific project proposals identified in the context of this planning framework.

To enable the work of such a regional planning unit to reflect national needs it would be necessary for close contact with national planning teams to be maintained. National units would provide the regional team with documentation, statistics, projections and suggestions, based upon national priorities. The regional personnel would concentrate on regional and co-ordination aspects of data requirements, project preparation and aspects of manpower and educational planning. The national units would in no sense be subordinate to the regional planning team. While interests would overlap, primary functions would be different, and responsibilities would be complementary.

Any particular national government would retain the right to implement any expansion or new initiative in education and training that it wishes, but it would also have the choice of placing the project in a regional context, by submitting it to the regional team and ultimately the council, for evaluation in the light of the needs of all the countries concerned.

Although initially the above work programme would be the main priority for such a regional planning unit, there are other important areas of work to which it could also make a major contribution. The data which it would help to generate and analyse would provide an important input to the design of national and regional employment strategies. Equally, its work would be of obvious importance to the issue of migrant labour. Staff of the unit could provide the secretariat for meetings among supplier states. Analysis of policy options facing these states, both as regards migrant labourers in RSA, and movement of workers among themselves, could also be usefully undertaken by the regional team.

With regard to data, one of the most urgent priorities will be the strengthening and updating of statistics on manpower and employment—particularly for Zimbabwe, Namibia, Mozambique and Angola.* The main reason why detailed quantitative estimates for training and technical co-operation needs have not been included in this paper is that the data available for these countries are of very variable quality and relevance. Moreover, even in the independent English speaking states, only Botswana, Swaziland and Tanzania have reliable information which is sufficiently recent and comprehensive to enable such estimates to be made. The generation of such data, which does not require a great commitment of resources, would obviously remain a national responsibility. The regional planning unit could, however, provide a considerable service to national units by advising on how best to update these national statistics in a way

*Mozambique and Angola may wish to have a more limited role in the technical co-operation framework owing to the constraints imposed by language differences. There would however, be very strong arguments in favour of their being represented both in the planning unit and the council, to enable the large areas of mutual interest between the Portuguese speaking and English speaking countries to be exploited wherever possible.

which allows easy comparison between countries, and provides a proper framework for decision making at the regional level.

TABLE 1
African Workers employed on mines affiliated to the South African Chamber of Mines,[1] by Country of Origin, 1970–77 (thousands)

Year	South Africa	Lesotho	Botswana	Swaziland	Mozambique	Other[2]	TOTAL
1970	96.9	71.1	16.3	5.4	113.3	98.2	401.2
1971	86.5	68.7	16.0	4.8	102.4	107.8	386.2
1972	87.2	78.5	17.5	4.3	97.7	129.2	414.3
1973	86.2	87.2	16.8	4.5	99.4	128.0	422.2
1974	90.1	78.3	14.7	5.5	101.8	73.1	363.5
1975	121.8	85.5	16.6	7.2	118.0	15.5	364.7
1976	174.6	88.3	25.9	12.0	68.4	22.0	391.2
1977	217.1	100.0	24.8	11.8	38.2	28.7	420.5

Notes
[1] Affiliated mines include all large gold mines, the coal mines of the Transvaal, and a few others. These data cover slightly more than half of total African employment in mining in South Africa. Data are for December each year except for 1976 and 1977 when they refer to July and April, respectively.
[2] Until 1975 this group were mainly from Malawi. After that date, they mainly comprise recruits from Southern Rhodesia.

SOURCE DOCUMENTS

Colclough, C. and P. Fallon, 'Rural Poverty in Botswana', 1979; Ghai, D. and S. Radwan, *Rural Poverty and Agrarian Policies in Africa*, ILO, Geneva, (forthcoming).

Colclough, C. and McCarthy, *The Political Economy of Botswana: A Study of Growth and Distribution*, Oxford, 1979.

Commonwealth Secretariat, *Immediate Manpower and Training Needs of an Independent Zimbabwe*, by C. Colclough and R. Murray, London, (mimeo), 1979.

Steen, R. H., *Manpower Estimates and Development Implications for Namibia*. UN Institute for Namibia—Lusaka, 1978.

Malawi Government, *Manpower Survey*, Zomba, 1971.

Patriotic Front, *Zimbabwe Manpower Study*, Vols. 2 and 3, IUEF, Geneva (mimeo), 1978.

Republic of Botswana, *Manpower and Employment in Botswana*, report by C. Colclough, Gaborone, 1973.

Republic of Botswana, *Employment and Labour Use in Botswana*, report by M. Lipton, Gaborone, 1978.

Republic of Zambia, *Manpower Report*, Lusaka, 1966.

211

Swaziland Government, *Skills for the Future: Education and Manpower Perspectives in Swaziland*, C. Colclough and P. Wingfield-Digby, Mbabane, 1978.

UNESCO, *Higher Education and the Labour Market in Zambia*, B. Sanyal, *et al*, I.I.E.P., Paris, 1976.

United Nations Institute for Namibia, *Toward Manpower Development for Namibia*, report by R. Green, Lusaka (mimeo), 1978.

United Republic of Tanzania, *Annual Manpower Report to the President*, Dar es Salaam, (mimeo), 1974.

Wilson, F., *Labour in the South African Gold Mines, 1911–1969*, Cambridge, 1972.

Trade Patterns: Past, Present, Future

INTRODUCTION

This paper will outline trade patterns in an historical perspective as a means of appreciating the modalities of and the potential for increasing the scale and changing the content of intraregional trade in the future. The overriding purpose lies in establishing the potential of regional trade as a means of:

1. Reducing economic dependence on outside forces—especially the Republic of South Africa—that are hostile to economic and political independence of the countries of the region;

2. Enhancing overall economic strength and collective selfreliance within the region.

The existing pattern of trade will be studied in historical perspective to show how the present patterns have been created. It is important to trace the historical determinants to understand the way in which existing patterns operate and therefore how they can be harnessed and altered for new purposes. The conditions under which intraregional trade can be harnessed for the benefit of the countries of the region, and what trade patterns would emerge, would then be easy to work out. Furthermore, we shall explore future regional trade potentials by examining to what extent import demand could be met by existing export supplies and potentials within the region.

We end by presenting briefly some of the institutional arrangements that intraregional trade can take, thrashing out the minimum principles that can underly such co-operation if the results are to be positive all round. In this regard we shall rely on existing theoretical thinking and, of course, on the wealth of recent experience with regional trading arrangements within and outside the region. The region is defined to include Angola, Botswana, Lesotho, Malawi, Mozambique, Swaziland, Tanzania, Zambia, Zimbabwe and the still occupied Namibia.

213

EVOLUTION OF EXISTING TRADE PATTERNS

PRE-COLONIAL ECONOMY AND TRADE

In pre-colonial central and southern Africa, the predominant mode of production was generally characterized by the village community which guaranteed usufruct to the major means of production (land), co-operative land tilling, harvesting and in some cases co-operative livestock rearing. There was a total absence of wage labour. Emphasis on co-operation differed from area to area, but these African economies were generally oriented towards selfsufficiency in agricultural produce, limited lines of manufacture and meat supplies. The major lines of industry were characterized by iron, copper and gold mining, washing and smelting, tobacco growing and curing, cotton growing and weaving, pottery and the making of tools, hoes and other agricultural implements. [1]

Innovation and technology were closely connected with the requirements of solving immediate production problems in agriculture and industry, with the pace of technology introduction and absorption geared to the resource base and to the ability of the village community to digest the new techniques without dismembering itself.

Within the region trade was generally conducted around agricultural food products, salts, meat, iron implements and tools, and pots. Extraregional trade of the area with the Muslims and later with the Portuguese mainly involved the exchange of gold, copper and ivory for imports of cloth, beads, porcelain and—much later—armaments. [2] European colonialism destroyed the existing production, social and trading system and forcibly reoriented African labour and production to European capitalist interests.

COLONIAL PATTERNS OF TRADE AND INTRA-TRADE

In economic terms the main driving force for the scramble and subsequent colonization of central southern African countries was the quest on the part of European capitalism for extracting economic surplus in the form of specific commodities. Extracted surplus took the form of expatriation of agricultural and mineral raw material supplies, tropical spices and food-stuffs. Returns from direct investment and portfolio capital in the colonies were made possible by commodity production and exportation. Markets for Europe's manufacturing industries were also created by the foreign exchange generated by exports.

For Africa this meant a drastic restructuring of domestic agriculture, mining, manufacturing, internal and external trade and the redeployment of the labour force. Local efforts in innovation and technology were blocked and the capital-intensive regime of mature capitalism was substituted in some sectors, though in others profitability dictated labour-intensive methods. Low wages were applied to both sectors via open or covert forced labour regimes. In short the local economies were transformed and functioned as specialized production and market dependencies of the metropolitan economies. External trade came to assume a disproportionate place in the economy of the region: it was the main avenue for surplus extraction. In many ways it became internal trade for the European capitalists. The principle of international exchange lost all meaning. An eminent British economist of the period, John Stuart Mill, in referring to the principles that came to underlie the new trade in a correspondingly colonized region stated:

> The West Indies . . . are a place where England finds it convenient to carry on the production of sugar, coffee, and a few other tropical commodities. All the capital employed is English; almost all that industry is carried out for English uses . . . The trade with the West Indies is, therefore, hardly to be considered as external trade, but resembles the traffic between town and country, and is amenable to the principles of home trade.[3]

Mill could have added that the labour used was not English, but African, Indian and Chinese and that the capital had been accumulated partly from expropriated surplus from other colonies. But one thing which does stand out is that production was done for English requirements and that the commodity transfers did not cost England anything except for part of the capital. For the West Indies and even more so for the countries of the southern African region, colonial trade harnessed surplus for European capitalist development while simultaneously creating underdeveloped, dependent, peripheral capitalist structures in the colonies.

In evaluating the colonial trade pattern in the region, the purposes for which trade was conducted and the form that trade—including trade among the colonies—took, are inseparable. Intracolony trade was not conducted for African purposes nor for their benefit. Even trade in food consumed by Africans was seen as a direct input into export commodity production. Because the African had been commandeered to labour for foreign interests, he needed energy to produce.

Intracolonial trade, (e.g. among the three colonies of the then Federation of Rhodesia and Nyasaland, among the then East African Common Services Organization colonial economies or between Mozambique and Angola under Portuguese rule) served primarily metropolitan interests and secondarily local settler colonial interests located in the subcentres of Kenya and pre-independence Zimbabwe. RSA trade links with the southern African territories were of the same pattern. For post-independence external and regional trade to be beneficial and meaningful the colonial mode of production i.e. metropolitan ownership relations, and the content of production and technology used, would need to be reformed and redirected. It would appear that the scale and content of intratrade can contribute to overall regional economic strength only as part of an overall programme of disengagement and selfreliance at the national level. Otherwise the gains

215

from regional trade would just leak away externally as they did under colonial rule. Production and control of surplus canot be treated separately.

In the paragraphs immediately following we shall briefly outline the pattern of colonial trade with the metropolitan economies and the pattern of intratrade at the periphery mainly on experience with the now defunct Federation for illustrative purposes.

In terms of the framework above, colony-to-metropolis trade consisted mostly of unprocessed mineral and agricultural products. The type of products shipped differed according to the extent to which the metropolitan powers' requirements of a particular product could be supplied to the colony, which in turn depended on resource endowments and climatic and soil conditions at the periphery.

Mineral supplies are quite diverse with iron ore, coal and asbestos coming mainly from Zimbabwe and Swaziland; copper from Zambia, Namibia, Botswana and Zimbabwe, chrome from Zimbabwe; diamonds from Angola, Namibia, Botswana, Lesotho and Tanzania; gold from Zimbabwe; nickel from Botswana and Zimbabwe; oil from Angola; and uranium and lithium were supplied by Namibia and Zimbabwe respectively.

Agricultural and fishery produce also had diversified sources. Fish and fishery products came mainly from Angola, Namibia and Mozambique; wood pulp from Swaziland; tobacco from Zimbabwe and Malawi; cotton and sisal mainly from Tanzania, Mozambique, Angola and Zimbabwe (cotton); wool and mohair from Lesotho and Namibia; tea from Tanzania, Malawi and Mozambique; coffee from Angola and Tanzania; beef from Botswana, Zimbabwe and Namibia; and finally sugar from Swaziland, Mozambique and Zimbabwe.

These resource flows from the colonies required metropolitan capital investment in mines, ranches and plantations in addition to investment in transportation and other infrastructure. These flows also required a constellation of other services to buttress these activities including primary processing in cases of bulk commodities; hence the setting up of enclaves of European economies around areas of extractive activities and also the creation of so-called native reserves, homelands etc., as labour reserves.

The colonial export enclaves developed into secondary centres of commercial and servicing activities. In time these developed manufacturing and repair industries to meet the needs of the major extractive activities. There was growth of intracolonial trade in local foodstuffs to supply the growing centres of population and in some lines of manufactures by the local subsidiaries of metropolitan corporations and by settler firms. European settler communities were powerful representatives of metropolitan interests but had special economic interests of their own and, in the case of central Africa, were able to secure political autonomy from the colonial power and to conduct a sort of sub imperialism of their own on pre-independent Zambia and Malawi under the overall aegis of Britain. RSA, of course, was the archetype of the settler controlled sub imperial power.

With pre-independence settler-ruled Zimbabwe at the helm, the Federation was formed in 1953. It was able to mount a serious programme of increasing regional trade by pooling together cheap labour from Malawi (see Table 1) foreign exchange receipts from Zambia and a large market for Zimbabwean manufacturing subsidiaries of RSA, American and British based corporations. Zambian copper foreign exchange receipts came under the Federal Government and were available to Zimbabwe-based firms to expand their scales of operation to supply the Federal market. Malawi labour was harnessed to grow agricultural raw materials at home and—as migrants—to provide workers for mining and for the new manufacturing industry. In addition, processed food and coal was provided from Zimbabwe to Zambia to power and service the mining industry—further underdeveloping Malawi and Zambia.

This pattern of intratrade has not only undermined Zambia's present food producing capacity and increased its dependence, but has also marginalized Zimbabwean society by integrating it fully into the peripheral capitalist system whose driving force in terms of setting consumption patterns/tastes, product design and technology was based on external interests. As Table 1 shows, the pattern of labour flows were such that by 1969, 34 per cent of all adult African employees in wage employment were foreign; in agriculture the foreign African percentage was 53 per cent and it was 50 per cent in mining—the largest numbers coming from Malawi and Mozambique in that order.

An idea of the intracolonial trade pattern can be obtained by reference to Table 2 which lists totals of Zimbabwean domestic merchandise exports (last row) to all its trading partners in 1965. The top rows of the table list exports of selected manufactured articles from Zimbabwe to all regional partners, RSA and to the outside world. A total of $131.3 million in exports went to the region—i.e. about 33 per cent out of a total of $398.9m. Of the $131.3m going to the region, about 55 per cent consisted of manufactured products (excluding foodstuffs, beverages and manufactured tobacco). Zambia received the lion's share followed by Malawi, Botswana and Mozambique. The process of integrating the other countries of the region into the sub-system controlled through pre-independence Zimbabwe was reversed after the beginning of the rebellion by the reduction of economic links due to the imposition of sanctions.

Other trade flows of the region involved export receipts of Swaziland and Namibia who were major net foreign exchange earners for the rand area centred on RSA. They provided captive export markets for RSA and therefore almost their total foreign receipts were effectively available to the economy of the Republic. Migrant labour from Lesotho, Malawi, Mozambique, Botswana and Swaziland was critical to mining operations and farming in RSA. Further north, pre-independence Tanzania and Uganda provided a market for Kenya-based subsidiaries of foreign and settler manufacturing companies while their raw materials deliveries to the metropolitan were shipped mainly through Kenya providing a base for its large commercial, financial and transport sectors.

The historical genesis of colonial trade patterns with the metropolis and within the region, shows how mode of production, material resources, labour supply, pattern and content of production, technology and demand are linked in determining the resultant intra- and extraregional pattern of trade. This linkage provides an historical context for analysing post-independence patterns.

POST INDEPENDENCE TRADE PATTERNS

OVERALL TRADE SITUATION

Upon independence the countries of the region pursued policies which have had some impact on the pattern of extra- and intraregional trade. In independent countries of the region, there has been questioning of the colonial peripheral capitalist mode of production, some changes in resource availabilities and relatively small changes in the ratio of direct intra- to extraregional trade. It is hard to notice much change in the technology policy pursued or, in a majority of the economies, in the pattern and content of production.

At the level of overall trade flows the percentage of intraregional to total trade has averaged 2 per cent to 3 per cent. Mozambique and Malawi are notably above average for both 1974–5 and 1976–7. (See Tables 3 and 4.)

Total level of intraregional trade declined slightly from $52m in the 1974–5 to $49.9m in 1976–7. The two leading regional exporters, Mozambique and Zambia, lost ground in the Angolan market in the case of Mozambique and in the Malawian and Tanzania markets in the case of Zambia. Botswana increased its regional exports, especially to Zambia.

Among the five main regional importers, three, viz. Zambia, Tanzania and Mozambique, significantly increased their purchases, although Tanzania's intraregional imports fell somewhat as a share of its total import bill. The other two, Malawi and Angola, significantly reduced both the relative and absolute level of their intraregional imports. The increases included Zambian imports from Botswana, Swaziland and Tanzania—consisting mainly of meat, citrus fruits and pulses from the first two and cigarettes, cotton, coffee and tea from Tanzania. The Tanzanian-Mozambican tie has been particularly strong with Mozambique supplying cement in exchange for maize and other foodstuffs.

The annual trade protocol within the Mozambique/Tanzania Co-operation Agreement is an example of production oriented trade development outside any standard common market or preferential area arrangements. Mozambique's goals have to date been to restore industrial production in existing plants much of whose market departed with the settlers—e.g. cement, refrigerators. While Tanzania has sought to achieve outlets for products in which it had a relatively strong output base e.g. textiles, maize, tyres and tubes, each has sought to fill gaps in availability by exports allowing fuller use of capacity. The annual targets are set in terms of particular goods with monetary (and sometimes quantitative) goals set for each category. Over 1976–9 trade grew rapidly—from about $4 million in the first year to $17.5 million in the last.

In the region as a whole dependence on external forces continues. The capitalist mode of production has been questioned fundamentally in Angola, Mozambique, and Tanzania. Even though foreign capitalist enterprises still operate, the dominant mode of production and more important, the trend, is towards socialist production relations. In Zambia and Swaziland, the state has made major strides in reclaiming local resources and participating in production. In Swaziland reliance on the peripheral capitalist mode has recently been augmented by a systematic strategy of state participation in large enterprises on a joint venture basis.

In resource terms there has been an expansion of known reserves of some minerals—phosphates, iron ore and coal in Tanzania, iron ore in Mozambique, diamonds, copper and nickel in Botswana, oil in Angola, uranium and copper in Namibia.

Technology policies are the weakest link. There appears to be insufficient attention paid to this element of the production system. To the extent that policies on foreign technology absorption and adaptation or policies on the development of an indigenous technological capability exist, they lack overall consistency and co-ordination from sector to sector. Tanzania appears to be aware of the issues. It actively participated in international forums dealing with technology and development issues. National action is by no means negligible but to date lacks both coherence and major impact.

In several economies the makeup of production has not changed very much. There have been greater efforts to alter production and trade patterns in states rejecting the traditional peripheral capitalist mode of production. In Tanzania, for instance, the structure of production has changed significantly in favour of manufacturing. The share of manufacturing and processing rose from below 4 per cent at independence to above 10 per cent in 1977.[4] Production composition has shifted radically with intermediate goods (chemical rubber products, metal manufactures) the largest component by 1976.

It is still common to find large tracts of the most fertile lands used as export crop plantations. Industry often still means little more than initial processing of minerals and crops prior to export. There continue to be very limited organic links between products produced for export and the content of domestic manufacturing and consumption.[5]

To compound the problem even where agricultural research institutes exist, their research is usually geared to exports and industrial input crops, not staple food crops. The region still suffers from food shortages. By subsidizing grain production (partly to benefit their European farmers, partly to keep labour costs down and partly to increase export earnings) the settler regimes in pre-independence Zimbabwe and in RSA have compounded the problems faced by several of the states in seeking domestic staple food selfsufficiency.

The region is still very dependent on imports of wide ranges of manufactured consumer and capital goods even though the area produces all the raw mineral ores for metalworking and machine-building industries. The last section of this paper will explore methods and approaches to pooling production and trade efforts at the regional level to fill this gap.

The labour front is characterized by continued export of migrant workers to RSA. Severe conflicts arise between domestic foreign exchange needs and job creation capacity on the one hand and the dependency reinforcement/structural deformation and social disintegration effects of migration on the other. In some states farm labour export to RSA coexists with domestic food deficits and food imports from RSA. For instance potatoes and citrus fruits imported by Botswana from RSA are known to be cultivated by Botswana migrant labourers. In a study of comparable migration from labour reserves within RSA, Houghton and Walton found migration responsible for much of rural blight and stagnation:

> In many cases land is not ploughed for the simple reason that there is no one to do the ploughing. [6]

Mozambique and Malawi have reduced migrant labour exports to the mines and farms of RSA from average levels above 100,000 and 130,000 respectively in the early 1970s to about one fifth those levels in 1978. Lesotho, Botswana and Swaziland in contrast have not as yet formulated or begun to implement a strategy of disengagement. [7] An earlier study on the underdevelopmental and spread effects of a labour exporting strategy concluded:

> Labour-exporting, if it could be regarded as a 'growth pole' at all, does transmit growth, not to the peripheral economy, but to the labour-importing centre. . . . Our analysis has shown that the poverty at the periphery is not merely independently juxtaposed with the prosperity at the centre of the subsystem (RSA), but these are interconnected in a mutually supportive manner. [8]

It is therefore clear that one area of immediate action in strengthening domestic economic muscle and reducing RSA hegemony in the region lies in early review and action on labour exports.

PATTERN OF IMPORT DEMAND

In recent years the general content of agricultural production in most regional economies has not fundamentally departed from the colonial pattern. The export syndrome centred on agricultural export crops accompanied by a general neglect of food crops still demobilizes agricultural

220

policy in many countries. (Table 5 illustrates this situation). For a region richly endowed in agricultural resources an unnecessary percentage of foreign exchange receipts is still devoted to imports of basic food staples.

The picture is changing, especially in Angola, Mozambique, Zambia and Tanzania. In the former two, strenuous efforts are being made to reorient production and forge a link between resources availability, the content of production and demand for basic wage goods among the people. Continuous military attacks by the settler regimes of pre-independence Zimbabwe and of RSA combined with flood conditions have slowed the pace of progress, as has the collapse of former settler production units which has cut both foreign exchange available for agricultural transformation and, to a lesser extent, commercial food production for urban markets. Tanzania over 1975–8 virtually eliminated its staple food deficits, and became a net regional exporter of maize and certain staple foods. However, bad weather in 1978–80 plus storage problems caused a food deficit in 1980. It is also the case that Tanzania has yet to achieve self-sufficiency in dairy products, vegetable oil and wheat. In Zambia, strenuous efforts are being made to augment domestic food output but the actual outturn fluctuates between food deficits and surpluses. Collection, storage, marketing and stocks management as well as production and price setting still appear to require further attention.

The situation in Botswana and Swaziland is rather different. Swaziland—despite attempts to encourage local production—is increasingly dependent on RSA for maize even in years of good weather. It is totally dependent in respect to wheat, flour and vegetable oil and largely so for dairy products and urban vegetable and fruit supply. In Botswana there has been an over-emphasis on the livestock industry whose output is geared mainly to beef exports to RSA and to the Common Market in Europe. RSA-subsidized production combined with the absence of an active domestic strategy has resulted in growing imports of maize, wheat, dairy products, vegetable oil, fruits and vegetables. Organization of marketing, pricing policy and availability of inputs, including extension services, are more serious constraints than the—admittedly serious—ecological obstacles.

The manufactured goods import pattern is predictable considering the low capacity of several of the manufacturing sectors to go beyond the simple pre-export processing stage. Productive capacity gaps are compounded and perpetuated by a general lack of integrated policies on industry, mining, agriculture, technology and domestic demand. The historic patterns tend to reproduce themselves in the absence of clear and forceful action programmes to alter them.

Selected manufactured articles listed account for the bulk of imports, with capital goods—mainly machinery and transport equipment—leading the list (see Table 6). Iron and steel products and other metal manufactures, textiles, manufactured fertilizer, other chemical products and petroleum products come next. The areas of greatest progress in selfsufficiency are furniture, shoes and footwear, soaps and dyes. Another area of progress has been in petroleum refining in Tanzania, Angola, Mozambique and Zambia, albeit only in Angola is this based on domestic (or for that matter regional) crude oil.

The dominant sources of imports are the traditional colonial powers and the regional sub imperial states. Since 1965 there has been a sharp shift of sources of supply away from Zimbabwe, but the RSA share in regional imports has remained high. However, in part this is a statistical illusion as many pre-independence Zimbabwean exports were shipped via RSA and stated to be of RSA origin.

There has been a structural shift in Tanzanian imports with industrial diversification and increasing selfsufficiency, especially in shoes, textiles, furniture, dyes and soaps. RSA and Zimbabwe trade was never large and ceased in respect of the RSA at Tanzania's independence and with pre-independence Zimbabwe at the outbreak of the rebellion. Angola and Mozambique recently experienced two types of shift: a horizontal shift from metropolitan Portugal to other sources of procurement and a scale shift in imports of luxury consumer goods with the departure of substantial numbers of Portuguese settlers. With the independence of Zimbabwe, there are now wide opportunities to diversify sources away from RSA to an independent regional state.

FINANCING OF IMPORT DEMAND

The financing of the above levels of imports has largely continued to be met by exports of raw or minimally processed mineral and agricultural products. One of the disadvantages of this mode of import financing lies in the fact that the terms of trade have generally shifted over time against producers of raw materials, which means that regional exporters have had to increase volumes of exports just to finance the same basket of imported manufactures. The majority of the countries of the region have experienced consistently worsening terms of trade since 1970. The only exceptional years were 1973 and 1977 when boom conditions in coffee and tea dominated results. Zambia was an exception as copper prices peaked in 1974 and then remained depressed until 1979.[9] As a result export earnings have become increasingly less adequate to cover even minimum import requirements for most of the region's economies. The partial exceptions, Botswana and Swaziland, have enjoyed very rapid expansion of primary exports from very low base levels. The future of these bursts of export growth is open to doubt.

Imports have also been financed by aid flows. The growth of aid flows to the southern African region has been in contrast to stagnant real levels globally, but for some states they have been grossly inadequate and their future expansion is uncertain. In the region only Tanzania and Botswana have benefitted in any meaningful way from partial debt relief measures negotiated within the UNCTAD framework in March 1978.[10]

222

There has also been a resort to borrowing on the Eurocurrency markets by several of the countries. Between 1971 and the middle of 1978 the total level of borrowings were: Zambia $335m, Malawi $55.3m, Botswana $45m and Swaziland $3.0m.[11] Substantial additional Swaziland borrowing has since taken place or is in process.

Imports were also financed to a minor extent by the export of manufactured goods. However—excluding raw metal—most manufactured goods exports have been either to RSA or to regional states, not to industrial capitalist economies. Exports of manufactures offer good long run opportunities if they could be effected. In practice, manufactured and processed exports of developing countries face a number of obstacles in the markets of developed capitalist countries—markets from which the countries of the region have obtained the major share of import supplies to date. A brief outline of these obstacles may help in understanding the workings of that system, so as to indicate the economic importance of a redirection of policy in ways that enhance regional economic strength and overall collective selfreliance.

Developed capitalist countries usually set higher nominal tariff rates on processed or semiprocessed products than on raw materials from developing countries. This policy provides even higher effective protection for metropolitan raw material processing industries and therefore severe obstacles to processing exports in developing countries. Second, freight costs set by metropolitan carriers are roughly related to value per tonne. Therefore, they are generally higher for processed or manufactured than for raw material exports and in general increase with the degree of processing for exports.[12] Moreover, under the Generalized System of Preferences (GSP) of the United States, the EEC and Japan some of the major items of current export interest to the southern African region, namely textiles, footwear, leather and products, are excluded. (Table 7 illustrates the pattern of tariff and freight rate discrimination for the United States).

Third, the large metropolitan-based companies which dominate production and trade in most raw materials frequently restrict imports of processed goods to metropolitan and other developing country markets by restrictive business practices such as cartel forming (involving price fixing, price discrimination and joint marketing arrangements through their subsidiaries in different countries). Corporate headquarters often use their powers to fix input prices and output prices to subsidiaries worldwide to effect the movement of profits etc., from one country to another.[13] To thwart these procedures host countries in the region could set up local competitors. But to be effective, these competitors would have to participate fully in all phases of the processing and marketing cycle including international marketing.

One of the problems the local competitor would face is the investment cost of building production complexes for each phase of processing, especially in view of the fact that minimum size plants are generally very

223

large (and even bigger if the plants are to benefit from economies of scale) and costly to build. That is especially true in mineral processing where an optimum capacity copper smelting plant i.e. of 100,000 tons per year, was estimated in 1975 to cost $600m, exclusive of infrastructural costs. A corresponding nickel smelting plant of 25–30,000 tons per year was estimated at $480m. Agricultural processing plants cost much less. For instance, a 20,000 tonne sisal twine plant was estimated to cost about $9m. [14]

This section has outlined the current trade patterns of the region, focussing on the content and sources imports. It has traced the modalities of import financing from agricultural and mineral export receipts to external assistance and borrowing. Finally, it has noted ways by which the production of processed and manufactured goods for both export and domestic use are constrained by various protectionist policies at the centre and by various considerations of investment costs and the obstructing hand of transnational corporations. This presentation of the way in which existing trade patterns operate and their constraints should provide a starting point from which to explore conditions and situations under which increased intraregional trade could benefit the participating economies, as well as how and to what extent the future content of demand could be met by production within the region.

COLLECTIVE SELFRELIANCE AND SATISFYING FUTURE REGIONAL IMPORT DEMAND

SCOPE OF INCREASING INTRAREGIONAL TRADE

With a total surface area of 5,709 million square miles, a 1977 mid-year population of 52.8 million inhabitants, an area richly endowed with agriculture, fishery and mineral resources, and an average GDP per head of about $315, the southern African region has great potentials for intraregional production specialization and exchange (see Table 8). Total imports of goods for the region in 1977 stood at about $4 billion when adjusted for Namibia's trade with the Republic of South Africa. [15]

By the end of the next decade imports of goods could conceivably rise by over $3.5 billion in real constant price terms; that assumes an average annual growth rate of GDP of around 5 per cent and an average import-elasticity of demand of 1.0. That would imply an average annual growth of income of 2.5 per cent per head and a population growth of 2.5 per cent.

To achieve those rates would require high growth of raw or semi-processed mineral and agricultural commodity exports if the pattern and content of production in manufacturing remains static—and if obstacles for manufactured exports to the metropolitan market persist or intensify. Such raw material exports would guarantee the continuation of existing patterns in resource use and product content which perpetuate and reinforce dependence on generally hostile external forces.

Increased intraregional trade could reduce external dependence and enhance overall collective selfreliance by providing much of the food and raw material requirements and a substantial share of manufactured goods needs, thereby reducing the share of imports from outside the region and especially from RSA. Second, increased intraregional trade, if backed up by appropriate machinery, would widen the market and make possible economies of scale in production with lower unit costs while simultaneously altering the structure of production to meet regional demand. Third, increased intratrade would open up new possibilities of specialization in production and marketing, inducing economic factors to diversify away from primary export orientation to world manufacturing. Fourth, increased intratrade can lead to increased contacts which create the climate for collaboration across frontiers—collaboration that permits a pooling of resources in ways which make possible the undertaking of production projects that would otherwise be beyond the financial or technical capability of one or several units. The prohibitive cost of optimum size processing and manufacturing plants, especially in the mineral processing, metal manufacturing and capital goods sectors, could be justified within a framework of regional co-ordination of production and trade but not on a national market basis.

In general, specialization could be both inter-industry and intra-industry. Inter-industry specialization could exist if countries of the region agree to provide preferential markets for the products of industries located in one or more specified economies in the region and to give these industries other appropriate support. In agriculture, patterns of production and trade could be formalized through negotiated agreements on medium term import demand and export supply guarantees and pricing formulas. (See Table 9 for the existing patterns of industry production and trade. A ✓ signifies agricultural products, fisheries; while potential future patterns are marked with an * sign). In the case of Botswana, for instance, the table shows that while live animals and meat are produced in Botswana, they are currently exported to RSA, Zambia and outside the region, but that these products might, either with existing or expanded capacity, find additional markets in meat deficit economies such as Angola. Although dairy products are not currently exported in significant amounts, Zambia has a potential production and export capacity which could be directed to supplying, amongst others, Malawi and Mozambique.

Intra-industry specialization refers to a situation in which a single final product is produced from components and parts produced by firms located in different parts of the region. This form of specialization is more common in manufacturing. Intra-industry specialization can take the form of specialization in processes and is applicable in mining, smelting and metal products fabrication. Copper matter from Botswana could be sent to Zambia for refining and basic fabrication and then to Zimbabwe for making electrical machinery or to Tanzania for making utensils, cutlery and

225

tools for regional and export markets. Specialization in processes has great potentials in rationally ordered regional trading arrangements. It requires co-ordination of production units through joint ownership or through a medium to long term set of contractual arrangements. (See Table 10 for actual and potential mineral products.)

In general, industrial collaboration agreements provide a promising modality for mutually beneficial co-operative relationships. This could take various forms: co-production of a single product directly or indirectly by pulling together components of a final product; joint ventures; licensing and subcontracting agreements, and joint tendering and marketing of products. These forms could be combined. For instance, Tanzania and Mozambique agreed to build jointly a highway and bridge to link the two countries at the Ruvuma River. The agreement has elements of a co-product and could also include joint tendering if external contractors are required.

CONDITIONS OF STRENGTHENING INTRA-TRADE

Certain prerequisites can be identified for intra-trade to be meaningful in increasing overall collective selfreliance and reducing dependence on external forces. One of the first prerequisites is to reestablish the dynamic link (destroyed during the colonial period) between the mode of production, human and natural resources, pattern and content of production, and basic wage goods, basic services and investment components of demand.

Policies which leave the peripheral capitalist mode of production in the regulatory hands of transnational corporations—e.g. so called free trade areas and laissez-faire common markets—can hardly lead to reduction of overall dependence even if they do increase regional trade. Further, they are likely to maximize inequality in division of gains thus creating contradictions which erode, rather than build, regional co-ordination.

Second, there appears to be a need to retain the link between demand and the consumption requirements of the broad masses. Food and mass market manufactured goods based on regional raw materials are logical candidates for regional production and trade co-ordination on technical and production cost as well as dependence reduction grounds.

Third, a unified and consistent technology policy needs to be developed for each country with harmonization and co-operation at the regional level as essential ingredients. The science policy thus developed should be applicable at sectoral level and should lead to the formulation of a science and technology plan as an integral component of national and regional development planning. The policy areas should include types of technology transferred, reductions of the costs of technology transfer, adoption and adaptation, and the development of a domestic technological capability. National and regional centres and institutions for the transfer, adaptation and development of technology need to be set up and strengthened so that the link between resources and the content of production is dynamically advanced.[16]

226

The initial framework for increasing regional trade should be flexible. The case for detailed, limited programmes and agreements is easy to establish as partners need to see clearly and to balance accurately their gains and costs: otherwise disappointed hopes will lead to a stagnation or reversal of the regional dynamic.

A similar danger applies to approaches which stress openness and free trade with limited state participation. Transnational corporations could come in freely and locate in the centres which are seemingly more advanced or more integrated wth the external forces from which the states of the region are striving to disengage. Location in such centres, having more technologically developed infrastructure, would exacerbate the already uneven and unequal process of growth and the reproduction of deformed social structures not only between countries, but also within the country in which these centres are located.

Finally, while in the short term trade expansion can be built up on existing output capacities, in the long run it cannot be separated from the levels and patterns of producing expansion. Trade is not an end in itself but a means to increasing production and employment possibilities and reducing production and consumption costs. Therefore, medium term regional and subregional trade expansion cannot be separated from co-ordination of selected production capacity decisions.

TOWARDS A PRODUCTION-CENTRED APPROACH TO TRADE

The original work on free trade areas (no tariffs within the region), customs unions (common external tariff) and economic unions (common economic policies) was done within the neo-classical free trade theory model.[17] Regional free trade areas were perceived as second best alternatives to global free trade. The case for them was that diversity of resources (different natural comparative advantage) and economies of scale in a larger economic area (leading to acquired comparative advantage through specialization) would lower costs and increase output.

In the short term, benefits would come from competition and concentration of output in the most efficient firms: the implications include output cutbacks and closures in less efficient units. Over the long term, benefits would come from economies of scale and of specialization in new production units.

A distinction is drawn in the basic classical customs union model between trade creation (among member economies) and trade diversion (away from outside economies). The former is endorsed and the latter criticized on standard global allocational efficiency grounds.

Several problems arise in applied analysis as well as application:

A. There is no automatic mechanism to ensure equal, equitable or even positive gains for each member. Therefore, either fiscal transfers (as in

227

SACU), regional development banking (as in the former East African Community), or/and industrial allocation (as in the Andean Pact and Association of South East Asian Nations) tend to be needed to buy the weaker partners' acceptance of higher cost imports from the stronger.

B. The allocational efficiency losses on trade diversion are basically costs to outsiders unless one assumes full employment in the regional economies. Therefore, a 'some production is better than no production' approach tends to be adopted especially in respect to manufacturing, usually with an infant economy plus economies of scale justification.

C. Trade diversion is a slightly unreal concept if the regional economies face export ceilings which are either de facto (e.g. limits to exploitable resources or/and total inability to break through to manufactured exports) or de jure (e.g. EEC quotas on Botswana beef, Central Selling Organization quotas on Botswana diamonds—both negotiated but neither totally flexible nor open to unilateral amendment by Botswana). In that case imports from outside the region are basically constrained by the export ceiling and all intraregional trade can be viewed as trade creation.[18]

D. Trade does not automatically flow from absence of customs barriers, e.g. Botswana/Angola trade is blocked by lack of transport links even more effectively than by SACU. Therefore, to function, an economic co-ordination programme may need to include areas of policy well beyond common market creation.

Most orthodox economic integration literature and most efforts toward Third World regional schemes have taken these points on board to a greater or lesser degree.[19] However, the record suggests that even these modifications may not be sufficient, or that the theory is largely irrelevant to the actual purposes, processes and problems of Third World economic co-ordination.

SACU[20] is a common market plus a fiscal redistribution mechanism. Because the RSA is larger, more technologically advanced, characterized by powerful private cartels and in full command of the all terms and conditions such as what rebates are allowable on what items, there is little doubt that SACU diverts both imports (from outside the union area) and production. For instance Botswana, Lesotho, Swaziland and Namibia produce less, import more—and import from RSA rather than from lowest cost sources. The offset is a large fiscal transfer, which in the short run more than offsets the losses from production and higher cost imports. However, it tends to limit consideration of—and raise the cost of shifting to—alternative policies to protect Botswana rather than RSA production.

The former East African Community was in form a Common Market, plus joint services, plus a regional development bank, plus an interim intra-regional preference (Transfer Tax) scheme.[21] In practice it was intended to include a production co-ordination (industrial allocation) side but this failed to come into being before the Amin coup halted progress. The loss of momentum, very bad management of the joint railway enterprise, arguments about trade and gains division and the shock of the 1974–7 balance of payments crisis greatly weakened EAC. Attempts either to return it to a pure laissez-faire model, or to transform it into a system based on the co-ordination of production, failed and it collapsed in 1977.[22]

The Economic Community of West African States (ECOWAS)[23] has the most elaborate provisions of any traditional economic community ever floated. Fiscal transfers, regional bank, joint projects, agricultural co-ordinations, functional and technical co-operation—and whatever else might arise—an ECOWAS article can be found to cover it. In fact the key goals are a preferential area to free trade area to customs union sequence plus a large regional bank/aid agency.

All articles and timetables are very vague and ECOWAS has experienced great difficulties in actually beginning operations in any serious way, either on trade preferences or on regional financial transfers.[24]

TOWARD A DIFFERENT MODEL

Much of the criticism of the standard customs union model flows from general critiques of neo-classical, free trade development models. It is, in fact, not readily incorporated in the Vinerian mould except in a purely formal sense because it posits a transition away from purely north/south axes of exchange/control and, in the case of some writers, a transition toward socialism. Initially much of this critique was cast in fairly standard customs union terms[25] that over time has become less typical.[26]

Five main themes have emerged:

1. Economic co-ordination as a means to economic liberation (or in milder variants 'room to manoeuvre') by extending the range of practicable economic activities, broadening the range of relevant partners, reducing the leverage of degree of dependence on any one external partner (TNC or State).[27]

2. Primacy of active, new[28] production oriented over passive, new trade facilitating measures (e.g. industrial co-ordination, multinational ventures, financial institutions among Third World states seen as ultimately more critical than tariff preferences or clearing arrangements).

3. The importance of using regionalism to co-ordinate policies vis-à-vis foreign firms, in order to shift the balance of power and the pattern of bargaining in favour of the states and against the TNCs (as in OPEC and the Andean Pact).[29]

4. Doubts about the positive contribution of free trade, because it may create more losses and frictions than gainers and co-ordination

229

advances[30] and thus violate the principle of the primacy of prompt, perceived gains for each participant.[31]

5. The necessity of examining, operating and analysing co-ordination as an ongoing political economic process with multiple actors, not a comparative static technical economic exercise carried out by neo-academic analysts or consultants.[32]

The logic of this critique has not been fully explored—let alone agreed. There is no presently functioning African regional exercise built on it. Bilaterally the Mozambique/Tanzania arrangements probably qualify but are still quite explicitly interim, experimental and somewhat limited in scope and time horizon so far as present trade protocol operations are concerned.

However, several implications do emerge:

A. The appropriate strategy and tactics for any particular co-ordination scheme (bilateral, regional or sectoral e.g. Botswana/Namibia, southern Africa, independent African diamond producing states) cannot be deduced directly from pure theory; they must also be built up from state needs, constraints, goals and resources.

B. It cannot be automatically assumed that trade is the key or the initial sector for co-ordination.

C. Common interests perceived as pursued more effectively together than separately, leading to visible and adequate gains, are critical to viability and stability. Neo-classical gains are usually rather beside the point even when they exist and can be computed.

NOTES

1. See among others Palmer and Parsons (eds.) *The Roots of Rural Poverty in Central and Southern Africa* (Heinemann, 1977); Karl Marx, *Pre-Capitalist Economic Formations*, New York: International Publishers, 1965 version, pp. 67–92; George Dalton, 'Tribal and Peasant Societies', *Quarterly Journal of Economics* (LXXVI), and Kimambo and Temu, *A History of Tanzania*, Nairobi: East African Publishing House, 1970.

2. Phimister, 'Alluvian Gold Mining and Trade in Nineteenth Century South Central Africa', *Journal of African History*, Vol. 15, 1974 and Gray and Birmingham (eds.) *Pre-Colonial African Trade*, London: Oxford University Press, 1970.

3. Cited by John H. Williams, 'The Theory of International Trade Reconsidered', *Economic Journal*, Vol. 39 (June 1929) and reprinted in American Economic Association, *Readings in the Theory of International Trade*, H. Ellis and L. A. Metzler (eds.) Philadelphia: Blakiston Co, 1979.

4. Government of Tanzania, *Economic Survey*, 1976/7.

5. For a study of the role of dynamic linkages in the process of transition between social systems, see the most up-to-date work of Clive Thomas, *Dependence and Transformation*, New York, Monthly Review Press, 1974.

6. H. Houghton and E. Walton, *The Economy of a Native Reserve*, Pietermaritzberg: Shuter and Shoter, 1952, pp. 112–14.

7. See G. Walker and W. Lovelace, 'Labour Migration in Southern Africa and Possible Supplier State Alternatives', Washington DC: Pacific Consultants, 1978 (mimeo). See also 'Employment and Skills', SADCC Sectoral Paper, in this volume.

8. K. Moyana, 'The Political Economy of the Migrant Labour System: Implications for Agricultural Growth and Rural Development in Southern Africa', *African Development*, Vol. 1, No. 1 (Dakar) October 1976.

9. See UNCTAD Secretariat, *Handbook of International Trade and Development Statistics*, Geneva, 1979, Table 2.5.

10. See UNCTAD Secretariat, *International Financial Co-operation for Development*: Current Policy Issues, (UNCTAD V—Manila, May 1979), Doc. No. TD/134.

11. UNCTAD Secretariat, *Handbook . . .*, *op cit*, Table 5.12.

12. Bela Balassa, 'The Structure of Protection in the Industrial Countries and its Effects on the Exports of Processed Goods from Developing Countries', IBRD Economics Department, Report EC-152, 28 February, 1968 (mimeo); and A. J. Yates, 'Do International Transport Costs Increase with Fabrication? Some Empirical Evidence', *Oxford Economic Papers*, Vol. 29 (November 1977).

13. See UNCTAD Secretariat, *Dominant Positions of Market Power of Transnational Corporations: Use of Transfer Pricing Mechanism*, Geneva, 1978, Doc. TD/B/C.2/167.

14. United Nations, Report of the Secretary-General, *Minerals: Salient Issues*, Geneva, 29 March 1977, Doc. E/C.7/68. (Fifth Session of the Committee on Natural Resources, 9–20 May 1977).

15. UNCTAD Secretariat, *Handbook . . .*, *op cit*, Table 1.2.

16. See UNCTAD Secretariat *Handbook on the Acquisition of Technology by Developing Countries*, New York: United Nations, 1978 and UNCTAD, *National Design and Engineering Organisations, Their Role in Strengthening the Technological Capacity of Developing Countries*, Geneva, 1978, Doc. TD/B/C.6/36.

17. The basic early works are J. Viner, *The Customs Union Issue*, Carnegie Endowment, New York 1950; J. Meade *The Theory of Customs Unions*, North Holland, Amsterdam, 1955; B. Balassa, *The Theory of Economic Integration*, Irwin, Homewood, 1961.

18. See S. B. Linder, *Trade and Trade Policy for Development*, Praeger, New York, 1967.

19. See for example, K. G. V. Krishna and R. H. Green, *Economic Co-operation in Africa: Retrospect and Prospect*, Oxford, Nairobi, 1967;

A. F. Ewing, 'Prospects for Economic Integration in Africa', *Journal of Modern African Studies*, 5 May 1967; P. Robson, *Economic Integration in Africa*, Allen and Unwin, London, 1968.

20. For a fuller description of SACU, especially as it affects Botswana, see Derek Hudson 'The Customs Union' in C. Harvey's *Essays on the Political Economy of Botswana*, Heineman, London, 1980.

21. See A. Hazlewood, *Economic Integration: The East African Experience*, Heinemann, London, 1975.

22. See R. H. Green, 'The East African Community: 1975 and After', 'The East African Community: The End of the Road', 'The East African Community: Death, Funeral, Inheritance' in *ACR*, 1975–6, 1977–7, Africana, London.

23. See J. P. Renninger, *Multinational Co-operation for Development in West Africa*, Pergamon, New York, 1979, especially Chapters 3–4.

24. See W. Demas, *The Economics of Development in Small Countries*, McGill, Montreal, 1965; R. H. Green and A. Seidman, *Unity or Poverty: the Economics of Pan Africanism*, Penguin, London/ Baltimore, 1967/8; M. Brewster and C. Y. Thomas, 'Aspects of the Theory of Economic Integration', *Journal of Common Market Studies*, VIII, December 1969.

25. Both Demas, *op cit*, and Seidman/Green, *op cit*, are examples.

26. For example Brewster/Thomas, *op cit*, C. V. Vaitsos, 'Crisis in Regional Economic Co-operation (Integration) Among Developing Countries', *World Development*, 1979.

27. See for example D. P. Ghai (ed.), *Economic Independence in Africa*, East African Literature Bureau, Nairobi, 1973, especially chapters by Ghai, Onitiri, Green, Harvey; Brewster/Thomas, *op cit*, and Seidman/Green, *op cit*, and more recently UNCTAD *Economic Co-operation Among Developing Countries* (Report of a Group of Experts), Geneva, 1976.

28. *Ibid.*

29. See C. V. Vaitsos, *The Role of Transnational Enterprises in Latin American Economic Integration Efforts*, UNCTAD, Geneva, 1978.

30. See Vaitsos, 'Crisis in Co-operation', *op cit.*

31. See L. K. Mytelka, 'The Salience of Gains in Third World Integrative Systems', *World Politics*, XXV, January 1978.

32. See W. A. Axline, *Caribbean Integration: The Politics of Regionalism*, Pinter/Nichols, London/New York, 1979, especially Chapters I, II, III, VIII.

TABLE 1
Rhodesia: Country of Origin of Adult African Employees by Sector, 1969

Country of Origin	All Sectors		Agriculture		Mining		Domestic Service	
	Total of employees	% of Total	of employees	% of Total	of employees	% of Total	of employees	% of Total
Rhodesia	415,369	65.7	107,154	47.0	23,574	49.7	69,772	73
Malawi	106,385	16.8	58,496	25.7	11,456	24.2	13,769	14
Mozambique	81,448	12.9	49,054	21.5	6,905	14.6	9,221	9
Zambia	24,622	3.9 }	13,164	5.8	5,444	11.5	2,401	2
Other	4,744	0.7 {						
Total foreign	217,199	34.3	120,714	53.0	23,805	50.2	25,391	26
Total employees	632,568	100.0	227,898	100.0	47,394	100.0	95,163	100

Source: Rhodesia, Central Statistical Office: *Census of Population 1969.*

TABLE 2
Selected Manufactured Exports of Southern Rhodesia 1965
in Thousand US$

	SITC	Angola	Bots	Les	Malaw	Mzge	Nam	Swazi	Tan	Zam	Total Region	South Africa	World
Petroleum Products	332	—	.2	n/a	2.2	—	—	—	—	167.6	170.0	—	170.0
Chemical elements, compounds	51	—	9.8	,,	140.8	14.0	—	—	—	378.0	542.6	281.4	855.4
Dyes, Tanning, Colouring	53	—	77.3	,,	332.6	2.2	—	—	—	943.9	1,356.0	.3	2,662.8
Medicinal Products	541	—	24.4	,,	345.2	9.5	—	—	25.5	533.7	938.3	282.0	1,353.8
Soaps and Cleaning	554	—	27.2	,,	220.1	—	—	—	—	2,672.3	2,919.6	7.3	2,936.4
Manufactured fertilizer	561	—	.8	,,	304.6	37.2	—	—	—	2,394.6	2,737.2	10.1	2,754.4
Explosives	571	—	—	,,	—	—	—	—	—	—	—	—	—
Plastics	581	—	—	,,	—	—	—	—	—	—	—	—	—
Pesticides, etc.	5992	—	.8	,,	77.3	9.8	—	—	4.2	478.0	570.1	4.2	621.3
Butter Manufactures	62	—	9.8	,,	1,037.7	5.0	—	—	1.1	2,047.6	3,101.2	2.0	3,269.0
Paper and Paperboard	64	—	29.7	,,	707.4	19.3	—	—	—	3,192.8	3,949.2	204.1	4,366.6
Textiles, yarn and fabric	65	—	359.0	,,	2,944.5	116.5	—	—	8.9	4,216.2	7,644.9	1,285.2	9,005.6
Cement, building products	661	—	57.1	,,	116.5	—	26.6	30.5	—	1,247.4	1,478.1	596.1	2,074.8
Iron and steel products	67	—	109.8	,,	454.4	115.1	—	—	1.1	3,821.7	4,502.1	1,882.2	18,137.6
Metal manufactures	69	210.8	357.0	,,	1,367.2	201.0	149.8	—	17.9	5,369.8	7,673.5	866.6	8,679.4
Machinery (non-electrical)	71	47.0	76.7	,,	271.6	122.4	26.9	19.6	215.6	2,458.7	3,238.5	380.8	4,020.2
Agricultural Machinery	712	42.3	15.1	,,	119.8	65.8	—	—	33.9	641.2	918.1	37.5	1,114.8
Machinery (electrical)	72	2.5	106.7	,,	748.7	17.6	63.6	—	37.8	4,242.3	5,219.2	3,716.7	9,560.3
Transport equipment	73	—	69.7	,,	1,611.1	92.1	2.5	—	18.5	8,377.0	10,170.9	136.6	10,453.8
Railway vehicles	731	—	21.6	,,	34.4	10.6	—	—	—	102.8	169.4	34.2	205.2
Road vehicles (non-motor)	733	—	8.1	,,	154.0	—	2.5	—	—	1,082.5	1,247.1	41.2	1,301.2
Furniture	821	—	198.5	,,	308.8	2.03.6	—	—	—	1,643.0	2,155.9	123.5	2,290.4
Clothing	84	—	504.3	,,	2,397.9	1.4	39.8	—	4.8	6,783.3	9,731.5	5,383.0	15,449.6

	SITC	Angola	Bots	Les	Malaw	Mzqe	Nam	Swazi	Tan	Zam	Total Region	South Africa	World
Shoes, Footwear	85	—	81.8	,,	540.1	—	15.4	—	12.0	2,545.5	3,204.8	1,613.1	4,895.8
Instruments, watches, clocks	86	—	—	,,	—	—	—	—	—	—	—	—	—
Total Exports, Domestic Merchandize		525.3	4,455.6	—	21,667.3	2,657.1	346.2	107.3	451.7	101,052.8	131,263.3	35,826.2	398,875.2

Sources: Southern Rhodesia, Central Statistical Office: Annual Statement of External Trade 1965.

TABLE 3
Trade Matrix (goods and services) Average 1974–1975
(Million US$)

Imports of → / Exports from ↓	Angola	Botswana	Lesotho	Malawi	Mozambique	Swaziland	Tanzania	Zambia	Total Regional	Others	Total	% Regional Total
Angola					6.6	0.200		0.2	7.0	1121.1	1128.1	0.62
Botswana				0.025		0.1	0.016	0.3	0.4	131.5	131.7	0.30
Lesotho								0.035	0.035	11.5	11.6	0.30
Malawi	0.017				0.1	0.003	0.003	4.4	4.5	123.5	128.0	3.53
Mozambique	13.7			2.150		1.0		0.1	17.0	280.0	297.0	5.72
Swaziland		0.030	0.6	0.007	0.6			1.5	2.8	142.0	144.8	1.92
Tanzania	0.7	0.3		1.6	0.4	0.002		3.4	5.4	378.1	383.5	1.41
Zambia	0.2	0.3		6.6	0.6	1.3	6.7		15.0	1093.9	1108.8	1.35
Total Regional	14.4	0.6	0.6	10.4	8.3	1.3	6.8	9.9	52.0			
Others	579.8	200.2		208.5	423.4	158.2	787.2	848.1				
Total	594.2	200.5		219.0	431.6	159.6	794.0	858.0				
% Regional	2.42	0.15		4.77	1.91	0.84	0.85	1.15				

TABLE 4
Trade Matrix (goods and services) Average 1976–1977
(Million US$)

Exports from \ Imports of	Angola	Botswana	Lesotho	Malawi	Mozambique	Swaziland	Tanzania	Zambia	Total Regional	Others	Total	% Regional Total
Angola					5.9	0.2		0.2	6.3	696.3	702.6	0.9
Botswana				0.03		0.1	0.02	2.8	2.95	173.25	1712	1.7
Lesotho								0.1	0.1	16.8	16.9	0.6
Malawi	0.1				3.0		0.02	3.7	6.82	178.58	185.4	3.7
Mozambique	9.3			3.2		0.7	1.9	0.2	15.30	326.9	324.2	4.7
Swaziland		0.04	0.7	0.01	0.6			2.1	3.45	190.25	193.7	1.8
Tanzania		0.3		0.2	1.7			3.6	5.5	513.0	518.5	1.1
Zambia	0.4	0.34		5.3	1.1		2.4		9.5	989.5	998.8	1.0
Total Regional	9.8	0.7	0.7	8.74	12.30	1.0	4.34	12.70	49.92			
Others	526.7		176.6	211.56	470.8		711.06	687.9				
Total	536.5		177.3	220.3	483.1		715.4	700.6				
% Regional	1.8		0.4	4.0	2.6		0.6	1.8				

TABLE 5
General Imports (CIF) by Commodities in Million US$

Commodity	SITC	1974 Angola	1974 Botswana	1976 Malawi	1974 Mozambique	1975/76 Swaziland	1975 Tanzania	1975 Zambia
Food, beverages and tobacco	0+1	84.8	29.9	19.6	36.0	20.2	128.9	57.1
Beef and meat	01	1.9	.9	—	—	1.0	—	4.2
Dairy products	02	5.0	2.0	2.8	3.2	1.4	7.8	7.4
Rice	042	2.2		—			32.5	—
Maize	044	4.3		2.4	—		38.8	—
Fruits and vegetables	05	5.2	1.3	.4	2.0	1.4	—	3.2
Sugar	06	2.7	4.4	.3	—	3.2	.1	.9
Total Imports of Goods (CIF)		624.3	176.9	205.6	463.6	171.8	718.2	928.7
Percentage of SITC 0+1 in Total Imports		13.6	17.0	9.5	7.8	11.8	17.9	6.1

Source: United Nations: *Yearbook of International Trade Statistics,* 1977; Swaziland: *Quarterly Digest of Statistics 1976;* Botswana: *Annual Statistical Abstract 1975.*

TABLE 6
Trade in Selected Manufactured Products (US$ Million)

IMPORTS (CIF)

Products	SITC	Angola 1974	Bots 1974	Les	Malaw 1976	Mzge 1974	Nam	Swazi	Tan 1975	Zam 1975	Southern Rhodesia 1965	South Africa (Cust. UN) 1976
Petroleum	332	27.3	—	—	26.2	19.4	n/a	16.6	15.1	14.9	8.9	—
Chemical elements, compounds	51	12.3	—	n/a	4.1	—	,,	3.6	11.7	30.1	4.6	227.4
Dyes, Tanning, Colouring	53	4.9	.8	,,	1.4	1.4	,,	1.4	7.2	2.2	.6	32.6
Medicinal and products	541	25.4	1.9	,,	2.3	12.7	,,	1.6	27.4	11.8	4.5	62.3
Soaps and cleaning	554	2.9	1.8	,,	1.1	—	,,	.9	1.7	2.8	.9	14.7
Manufactured fertilizer	561	7.2	.4	,,	10.5	1.9	,,	—	13.2	35.5	12.1	—
Explosives	571	1.6	.6	,,	—	—	,,	—	0.7	6.8	2.4	—
Plastics	581	23.1	1.4	,,	—	7.6	,,	.4	8.8	13.7	3.3	178.3
Pesticides, etc.	5992	4.3	—	,,	1.9	5.5	,,	1.6	7.5	3.4	4.1	31.9
Rubber Manufactures	62	4.6	3.0	,,	3.4	6.0	,,	.2	7.2	16.5	3.7	28.8
Paper and paperboard	64	12.9	3.6	,,	5.7	7.1	,,	2.5	19.3	25.1	9.7	110.6
Textiles, yarn and fabric	65	44.6	.1	,,	10.3	26.6	,,	3.1	24.8	52.6	34.8	308.8
Cement, building products	661	—	—	,,	0.6	—	,,	1.6	2.9	—	.2	—
Iron and steel products	67	45.8	12.1	,,	18.2	22.9	,,	3.3	44.7	59.0	14.4	135.6
Metal manufactures	69	23.5	—	,,	8.7	13.9	,,	5.1	33.1	41.7	11.3	126.0
Machinery (non-electrical)	71	112.1	—	,,	26.1	56.5	,,	12.7	116.1	147.5	44.6	1,628.1
Agricultural Machinery	712	9.3	—	,,	6.4	2.3	,,	4.6	10.4	14.6	6.7	171.9

IMPORTS (CIF)

Products	SITC	Angola 1974	Bots 1974	Les	Malaw 1976	Mzqe 1974	Nam	Swazi	Tan 1975	Zam 1975	Southern Rhodesia 1965	South Africa (Cust. UN) 1976
Machinery (electrical)	72	30.9	6.8	,,	13.3	25.2	,,	14.8	36.1	60.6	16.4	776.9
Transport equipment	73	70.9	—	,,	24.9	44.0	,,	17.6	83.8	120.5	45.4	1,271.2
Railway vehicles	731	2.3	—	,,	2.1	1.5	,,	.1	36.7	20.0	6.5	67.5
Road vehicles (non-motor)	733	1.7	—	,,	1.3	1.1	,,	.7	4.4	6.8	1.4	—
Furniture	831	—	—	,,	0.2	—	,,	1.6	—	—	.8	—
Clothing	84	7.1	—	,,	2.0	4.2	,,	6.3	2.8	10.1	10.6	76.2
Shoes, footwear	85	2.5	—	,,	0.7	0.8	,,	1.3	0.6	6.3	3.3	27.1
Instruments, watches, clocks	86	8.4	—	,,	1.7	—	,,	.7	5.5	9.2	4.4	189.2
Total Imports of Goods (CIF)		624.3	176.9	,,	205.5	463.6	,,	171.8	718.2	928.7		

Source: United Nations: *Yearbook of International Trade;* Swaziland: *Quarterly Digest of Statistics, 1976;* and Botswana, *Annual Statistical Abstract* 1975.

239

TABLE 7

Estimated Ad Valorem Tariffs and Freight Costs for Selected Exports to the United States, 1974 (percentages)

Imported Product by Stage of Processing	Tariffs and Freight Costs[1]	Raw Commodity	PROCESSING STAGE		
			Stage I	Stage II	Final Product
Hides and skins	T	1.1	4.7	7.7	14.0
Leather	FC	3.9	4.5	6.2	9.1
Leather goods, shoes	T+FC	5.0	9.2	13.9	23.1
Copper Ore	T	0.1	2.3		4.2
Copper Unwrought	FC	3.9	2.0		2.8
Copper Wrought	T+FC	4.0	4.3		7.0
Logs, rough wood	T	0.0	0.3	8.5	6.7
Simpled worked wood	FC	2.9	7.0	17.2	8.6
Plywood Manufactures	T+FC	2.9	7.3	25.7	15.3

Source: Commodities of export interest to the region were selected from A. J. Yates, *op. cit.*, Table 1.

[1] T = Tariff   FC = Freight Cost   T+FC = Tariff and Freight Cost

T = Tariff   FC = Freight Cost   T+FC = Tariff and Freight Cost

TABLE 8

Population, Incomes and Trade in the Region

Country	Exports of Goods (FOB) 1977	Imports of Goods (CIF) 1977	Population '000 1977	GDP US$ Million 1976	GDP US$/Capital 1976
Angola	786	720	5,470[1]	3,331	607
Botswana	200	220	710	299	433
Lesotho	28	160	1,900	190[2]	160[2]
Malawi	195	235	5,530	723	140
Mozambique	190	360	9,680	2,343	248
Namibia	753[3]	460[3]	900[1]	836	929
Swaziland	150	170	510	274	548
Tanzania	509	748	16,090	2,686	172
Zambia	897	670	5,300	2,687	533
Southern Rhodesia	490	430	6,740	3,241	496

Source: United Nations: *Monthly Bulletin of Statistics,* February, 1979; UNCTAD: *Handbook of International Trade and Development Statistics,* 1979.

[1] 1976 data

[2] GNP and GNP/capita

[3] Reginald Green, *Namibia:* Background Notes, SADCC Paper, 1979, Table 16.

241

TABLE 9
Matrix of Trade in Agricultural Commodities
(US$ Millions)

Exporters	Commodity	Angola	Botswana	Lesotho	Malawi	Mzmbque	Namibia	Swaziland	Tanzania	Zambia	Zimbabwe (S. Rhodesia)	South Africa	Region	Exported items to (160) outside	(165) Total
Angola	coffee	•								•			•	✓	250
	fish meal									•			•	✓	50
	sisal													✓	20
	cotton					✓							•	✓	12
	bananas												•	✓	8
	maize								•				•	✓	5
	pulses									•			•	✓	
	veg. oils												•	✓	1.5
Botswana	meat	•										✓	✓	✓	40
	live animals										✓		✓	✓	
	pulses												✓	✓	1
Lesotho	wool, mohair,											✓	✓	✓	5.8
	pulses							•				✓	✓	✓	0.1
	live animals							•				✓	✓	✓	2.3
	seed potato							•							
Malawi	tobacco													✓	56
	tea								•				•	✓	25
	sugar													✓	13.3
	groundnuts													✓	7.8
	maize		•			•			•	•				✓	4
	cotton												•	✓	2.2
	rice					•							•	✓	2.2
	pulses								•				•	✓	2.2
	fish								•				•	✓	1.6
Mzmbque	cashew nuts													✓	50
	prawns, lobster													✓	25
	cotton, raw												✓	✓	30
	tea								✓					✓	11
	cement								✓					✓	10
	copra													✓	21
	sugar									•			✓	✓	60
	coconut oil													✓	4
	pulses									•				✓	4
	cattle										•		•	•	
Namibia	karakul pelts											✓		✓	75
	goat products	•										✓		✓	75
	wool, mohair		•									✓		✓	4
	fish products		•					•					✓	✓	75

Importers / Exporters	Angola	Botswana	Lesotho	Malawi	Mambque	Namibia	Swaziland	Tanzania	Zambia	Zimbabwe (S. Rhodesia)	South Africa	Region	Exported items to (160) outside	(165) Total
Swaziland														
sugar	•	•	•		✓			•	•		✓	✓	✓	83
wood pulp									✓			✓	✓	21
citrus fruit	•	•	•						✓		✓	✓	✓	9
lumber									✓		✓	✓		
meat														
rice	•							•	•	•		✓	✓	2
Tanzania														
coffee		•			✓						✓	✓	✓	110
cotton				•	•				•	•	•	•	✓	60
sisal					•							•	✓	40
tobacco		•			•				•			•	✓	19
tea												•	✓	10
sugar												•	✓	7
pulses									•			•	✓	7
veg. oils									•			•	✓	2.7
Zambia														
tobacco	✓			✓	✓			✓		✓	✓	✓	✓	9
maize	•	•			•			•		•		•	•	
dairy products					•			•				•	•	
poultry	•	•			•			•				•	•	
sugar	•	•						•				•	✓	
cotton												•	✓	
S. Rhodesia														
beef, meat			✓	✓							✓	✓	✓	4
sugar			✓								✓	•	✓	
tobacco			✓									•	✓	
cotton				✓	✓			✓	•		✓	✓	✓	
maize												✓	✓	
hops, malt											✓	✓	✓	
dairy products												✓	✓	
citrus fruits												✓	✓	

Source: FAO, *Trade Yearbook, 1977* and *Production Yearbook 1977*, National Statistics: United Nations Economic Commission for Africa, FAO, IECA Joint Agricultural Division.

243

TABLE 10
Minerals in the Region

Minerals	Angola	Botswana	Lesotho	Malawi	Mozambique	Namibia	Swaziland	Tanzania	Zimbabwe	Zambia
Alabaster	*									
Asbestos		*					✓		✓	
Barutes				*						
Bauxite	*			*	✓					
Cadmium										
Chrome			*	*						
Coal		✓			✓	✓	✓	✓	✓	✓
Cobalt		✓							✓	✓
Copper	*	✓			✓				✓	✓
Crude Oil	✓		✓			✓			✓	
Diamond	✓							✓		
Gold	*					✓	✓	✓	✓	*
Gypsum	*					✓			✓	
Iron Ore	✓						✓ *			✓
Kaolin										
Lead		*	*			✓		✓		*
Letseng			*			*				
Limestone				✓	✓	✓	*	✓	✓	
Lithium									✓	
Magnetite	*									
Manganese	*	*								
Mica and Quartz	*	*	*						✓	
Natural Gas		* ✓ *						*		
Nickel		✓							✓	
Petroleum									✓	

244

Minerals	Angola	Botswana	Lesotho	Malawi	Mozambique	Namibia	Swaziland	Tanzania	Zimbabwe	Zambia
Phosphates	*							*		*
Platinum		*							*	
Rare Earth				*						
Silica	*									
Silver				*						
Strontionte						✓				
Tin						✓			✓	
Tungsten						✓			✓	
Uranium	*	*	*	*		✓				
Wolfram		*				✓				
Zinc						✓				✓

Source: American Bureau of Metal Statics: Metal Statistics Yearbook (a); World Metal Statistics.

✓ actual exploited deposits
* known to exist deposits

TABLE 11
Trade in Selected Manufactured Products ($US Million)

| Product | SITC | EXPORTS (FOB) | | | | | | | | | S. Rhod. | 1976 S. Africa |
		Angola 1974	Bots	Les	Malaw 1976	Mzqe 1974	Nam	Swazi	Tan 1976	Zam 1975	1965	(Cus. UN)
Petroleum products	332	39.6	n/a	n/a	0.003	15.55	n/a	—	20.6	—	.2	—
Chemical elements, compounds	51	—	,,	,,	0.20	—	,,	—	—	—	.9	52.2
Dyes, tanning, colouring	53	—	,,	,,	—	—	,,	—	4.1	—	2.7	21.5
Medicinal and products	541	—	,,	,,	0.66	—	,,	—	—	—	1.4	14.0
Soaps and cleaning	554	—	,,	,,	—	—	,,	—	—	—	2.9	—
Manufactured fertilizer	561	—	,,	,,	—	0.13	,,	—	—	—	2.8	10.4
Explosives	571	—	,,	,,	—	—	,,	—	—	—	—	15.0
Plastics	581	—	,,	,,	—	—	,,	—	—	—	—	12.9
Pesticides, etc.	5992	—	,,	,,	—	—	,,	—	—	—	.6	—
Rubber manufactures	62	0.74	,,	,,	—	—	,,	—	—	—	3.3	—
Paper and paperboard	64	—	,,	,,	—	—	,,	—	—	—	4.4	30.0
Textiles, yarn and fabric	65	0.81	,,	,,	0.90	4.03	,,	—	12.9	—	9.0	6.6
Cement, bldg. products	661	4.62	,,	,,	—	1.30	,,	13.8	—	—	2.1	—
Iron and steel products	67	.83	,,	,,	0.41	—	,,	—	—	—	18.1	476.5
Metal manufactures	69	—	,,	,,	0.12	—	,,	—	—	—	8.7	12.8
Machinery (non-electrical)	71	1.69	,,	,,	0.39	—	,,	—	—	—	4.0	103.8
Agricultural machinery	712	—	,,	,,	0.34	—	,,	—	—	—	1.1	20.7
Machinery (electrical)	72	—	,,	,,	0.15	—	,,	—	—	—	9.6	32.9
Transport equip.	73	5.85	,,	,,	0.007	—	,,	—	—	—	10.5	40.6

246

EXPORTS (FOB)

Product	SITC	Angola 1974	Bots	Les	Malaw 1976	Mzqe 1974	Nam	Swazi	Tan 1976	Zam 1975	S. Rhod. 1965	1976 S. Africa (Cus. UN)
Railway vehicles	731	—			—	3.93	;;	—	—	—	.2	—
Road vehicles (non-motor)	733	—	;;	;;	—	—	;;	—	—	—	1.3	—
Furniture	831	—	;;	;;	—	—	;;	—	—	—	2.3	—
Clothing	84	—	;;	;;	—	—	;;	—	—	—	15.4	—
Shoes, footwear	85	—			1.41	—	;;	—	—	—	4.9	—
Instruments, watches, clocks	86	0.08	;;	;;	—	—	;;	—	—	—	—	—

Source: United Nations *Yearbook of International Trade Statistics*; Swaziland: *Quarterly Bulletin of Statistics* and Southern Rhodesia, Central Statistical Office: *Annual Statement of External Trade 1965.*

BASIC DATA

TABLE 1
Summary Data

	Angola	Botswana	Lesotho	Malawi	Mozambique	Namibia	Swaziland	Tanzania	Zambia	Zimbabwe
Area Sq. Km.	1,247,000	582,000	30,334	118,500	783,030	824,269	17,363	364,943	743,900	389,000
Population	7,180,000	750,000	1,150	5,200,000	11,050,000	1,250,000	523,000	17,552,000	5,300,000	7,040,000
Language	Portuguese	English	English/ Sesotho	English	Portuguese	Afrikaans	English/ Siswate	Swahili	English	English
Currency	Kwanza	Pula	Loti Maloti (pl.)	Malawi Kwacha	Escudos	Rand	Lilangeni Emalengeni (pl.)	Tanzanian Shilling	Zambian Kwacha	Zimbabwe Dollar
Exchange Rate (May 1980)	1: US$.036	1: US$1.26	1: US$1.26	1: US$1.23	1: US$.032	1: US$1.26	1: US$1.26	1: US$.12	1: US$1.28	1: US$1.45
Gross Domestic Product	58.9 bn. Escudos (1973)	330 mn. US$	98 mn Rand (1977)	782 mn. US$	54.5 bn. Escudos	1,135 mn. Rand (1977)	134.9 mn. Emalengeni (1977)	25,048 mn. Tanz. Sh. (1977)	2,256.5 mn. Kwacha (1978)	2,332 mn. Z$ (1978)
Total Exports	31 bn. Escudos	169.5 mn. Pula	10.3 mn. Rand (1976)	160 mn. US$	20.955 mn. Escudos (1978)	655 mn. Rand (1977)	163.3 mn. Emalengeni (1976)	4,475 mn. Taz. Sh. (1977)	708.5 mn. Kwacha (1977)	500 mn. Z$
Total Imports	15.8 bn. Escudos	206.7 mn. Pula	173.6 mn. Rand (1976)	206 mn. US$	6,765 mn. Escudos (1978)	400 mn. Rand (1977)	168.6 mn. Emalengeni (1976)	6,160 mn. Tanz. Sh. (1977)	529.6 mn. Kwacha (1977)	322 mn. Z$
Main Exports	Oil Coffee Diamonds Sisal	Copper Nickel Diamonds Livestock	Cattle Diamonds Sheep	Tobacco Tea Sugar Groundnuts	Cashew Nuts Cotton Sugar Tea	Diamonds Base Metals Uranium Oxide Beef/Cattle	Sugar Wood pulp Iron Ore Asbestos	Coffee Cotton Cashew Nuts Sisal	Copper Zinc Lead Cobalt	Tobacco Gold Asbestos Maize

	Angola	Botswana	Lesotho	Malawi	Mozambique	Namibia	Swaziland	Tanzania	Zambia	Zimbabwe
Total Government Expenditure (Current and Capital)	26,950 mn. Escudos (1975)	74.9 mn Pula	123 mn. Rand (1978-9)	1,864 mn. US$ (1976-7)	14 bn. Escudos (1976)	140 mn. Rand (1976-7)	86.2 mn. Emalengeni (1976-7)	8,965 mn. Tanz. Sh. (1977-8)	821 mn. Kwacha (1977)	803 mn. Z$ (1978)
Most important trading partners	USA Portugal	RSA USA EEC	RSA UK	UK RSA	Portugal USA RSA W. Germany	RSA UK USA W. Germany	RSA UK Japan	UK EEC USA China	UK RSA EEC	RSA UK W. Germany Japan

(Miscellaneous Sources.)

249

BASIC DATA
TABLE 2
Demographic Data

	Area 000' km²	Population Mill.[2] as at mid 1976	Population Growth Rate 1970–75	Density People/sq.km.	Life Expectancy at birth 1970–75 (no. of years)	growth rate per cent 1960/70	growth rate per cent 1970/76	GNP per capita 1976 US$
Angola	1246.7	5.5	0.1	4.4	39	5.1	1.0	330
Botswana	570.0	0.7	3.0[3]	1.2	44	5.4	24.9	410
Lesotho	30.4	1.2	2.2	39.5	46	3.0	4.0	170
Malawi	118.5	5.2	2.3	43.9	41	5.2	8.9	140
Mozambique	783.0	9.5	2.4	12.1	44	4.8	-2.0	170
Namibia	824.3[1]	1.3	3.0	1.5	49	5.2	5.2	470[4]
Swaziland	17.4	0.5	3.2	28.7	44	8.2	9.5	470
Tanzania	945.1	15.1	2.7	15.9	45	5.4	4.2	180
Zambia	752.6	5.1	2.9	6.6	45	4.0	3.1	440
Zimbabwe	390.6	6.5	3.5	16.6	52	4.7	5.1	550
Total/Average	5678.6	50.6	2.5[5]	8.9	45[5]	4.93[6]	3.3[6]	280[5]
Republic of South Africa	1221.0	26.0	2.6	21.3	52	6.2	5.6	1340

[1] Includes the area of Walvis Bay.
[2] Migrant workers are included under their home countries.
[3] 1971–6.
[4] Only figures in this column are based on World Bank sources. For Namibia the following procedure has been used: The country profile 1977 ratio GNP/GDP has been used on the 1975 GDP figure increased by 10 per cent for inflation 1975–6. This figure has been divided with the population figure given in the table.
[5] Weighted average, using mid-76 population as weights.
[6] Weighted average, using 1975 GDP as weights.

Sources: Demographic Yearbook 1976, (UN); *World Bank Development Report 1978*; Statistical and Economic Information Bulletin for Africa No. 10 (ECA); Miscellaneous sources for certain items.

BASIC DATA

TABLE 3
Economic Structure

		Sectoral distribution of GDP per cent			Shares of merchandise imports 1975 per cent				
		Agriculture	Industry & Mining	Services	Food	Fuel	Manufactures	Machinery	Other
Angola	1960	50.0	8.0	42.0					
	—76	29.0	27.0	44.0	9.1	3.9	28.3	48.3	10.4
Botswana	—60	58.1	11.6	30.3					
	—75	37.5	28.3	34.3	14.0	6.3	35.9	29.4	14.4
Lesotho	—60	72.6	NA	NA					
	—75	37.5	7.3	54.1	30.7	6.3	48.4	9.4	5.2
Malawi	—60	58.0	11.0	31.0					
	—76	45.0	22.0	33.0	13.2	12.2	30.7	32.3	11.6
Mozambique	—60	55.0	9.0	36.0					
	—76	45.0	15.0	40.0	6.6	10.7	18.2	19.2	45.3[2]
Namibia	—60	19.1	47.4	33.5					
	—75	17.7	56.6	25.7	NA	NA	NA	NA	NA
Swaziland	—60	32.6	23.1	44.3					
	—75	30.8	35.7	33.5	13.5	13.2	27.8	25.5	20.0
Tanzania	—60	57.0	11.0	32.0					
	—76	45.0	16.0	39.0	19.8	10.8	23.4	32.9	13.1
Zambia	—60	11.0	63.0	26.0					
	—76	14.0	41.0	45.0	8.7	25.3	20.8	34.7	10.5

251

	Sectoral distribution of GDP per cent			Shares of merchandise imports 1975 per cent				
	Agriculture	Industry & Mining	Services	Food	Fuel	Manufactures	Machinery	Other
Zimbabwe −60	18.0	35.0	47.0					
−76	16.0	40.0	44.0	10.8	8.3	34.2	31.7	15.0
Total/Average −60								
−76[4]	30.4	28.8	40.8					
Republic of −60	12.0	42.0	46.0					
South Africa −76	9.0	23.0[1]	68.0	4.9	0.2[3]	26.3	53.3	15.3

Source: World Bank. Figure should probably be about twice with a concurrent decrease in the figure under services.

[2] In basic trade statistics major parts of imports are summarily classified under 'other' group 9 SITC.

[3] RSA statistics exclude oil. Based on consumption (equal to import) of about 15 m tons a year and price per ton 115 US\$ total oil imports would be 1725 mill. US\$. Total exports ex. oil was 5859.4 mill. US\$. The oil import share would then be about 20–25 per cent. Includes imports of BLS countries and Namibia.

[4] Weighted average. Weights 1975 GDP figures.

BASIC DATA

TABLE 4

Trends in Growth of Production and Allocation of GDP

| | Average Annual Growth Rates (Per cent) | | | | | | | | Distribution of Gross Domestic Product (Per cent) | | | | | |
| | GDP | | Agriculture | | Industry | | Services | | Agriculture | | Industry & Mining | | Services | |
	1960-70	1970-6	1960-70	1970-6	1960-70	1970-6	1960-70	1970-6	1960	1976	1960	1976	1960	1976
Angola	5.1	1.0	4.0	-0.7	9.8	11.6	3.9	3.0	50	29	8	27	42	44
Botswana	5.5	16.1	1.6	11.8	11.9	16.8	7.3	18.6	55	25	11	31	34	45
Lesotho	7.0	4.3	—	—	—	—	—	—	73	38	—	8	—	54
Malawi	5.2	8.9	2.9	5.5	13.9	12.4	8.9	11.4	58	45	11	22	31	33
Mozambique	4.8	-2.0	2.1	2.0	10.8	-3.8	5.8	-2.1	55	45	9	15	36	40
Namibia	—	—	—	—	—	—	—	—	11	30	40[1]	43	49[2]	27
Swaziland	8.3	5.6	7.1	5.4	12.5	3.2	6.2	7.3	30	31	22	25	48	44
Tanzania	5.4	4.2	3.7	2.5	8.0	2.9	5.3	2.8	57	45	11	16	32	39
Zambia	4.0	3.1	2.0	3.2	-0.1	3.4	8.1	4.4	11	14	63	41	26	45
Zimbabwe	—	—	—	—	—	—	—	—	18	16	35	40	47	44

Source: Drawn from IBRD, *World Development Report, 1978*—Washington, and other bank documents.

Notes:
[1] Mining
[2] Includes manufacturing

BASIC DATA

TABLE 5

Population and Rural Employment Structure: 1950–75

	(1) Population (thousands)		(2) Population Growth Rates (annual percent)			(3) Annual Pop. Growth Rate %	(4) Estimated Rural Pop. (thousands)	(5) Estate Employment (thousands)	(6) Labour Force in Agriculture (% of total)	(7) Life Expectancy at Birth	(8) Total Agricultural Population	
	1950	1975	1950–60	1960–70	1970–5	1970–7	1975		1970	1975	Per ha. Arable Land	Per 1000 ha. total land
Angola	4,258	6,394	1.6	1.3	0.1	2.3	3,886	—	64.0	38.6	3.1	32
Botswana	411	691	2.0	1.9	1.9	—	579	5	80.7	43.5	0.4	10
Lesotho	614	1,148	2.1	2.2	2.2	2.4	999	—	19.7	46.0	2.9	332
Malawi	2,787	4,909	2.2	2.6	2.6	3.1	4,253	140	88.1	41.0	1.9	461
Mozambique	5,934	9,223	1.4	1.9	2.4	2.5	6,376	150	73.5	43.5	2.3	84
Namibia	400	883	—	—	—	—	460	50	55.6	48.8	0.7	6
Swaziland	249	469	2.4	2.9	3.2	—	362	30	81.1	43.5	2.2	214
Tanzania	7,719	15,388	2.2	3.0	2.7	3.0	12,872	—	86.0	44.5	0.4	65
Zambia	2,431	5,004	2.8	2.9	2.9	3.0	3,494	—	73.0	44.5	0.7	48
Zimbabwe	2,670	6,272	3.1	3.3	3.5	3.3	3,845	360	63.9	51.5	1.6	102
Sub-total	27,473	50,381										
Republic of South Africa	12,672	24,663	2.4	2.7	2.7	2.7	7,347	1,450	30.9	51.6	0.6	61
Total	40,145	75,044										

Source: David Morawetz, Twenty-five years of Economic Development 1950–75, World Bank, 1977; IBRD, *World Development Report*, 1978, Washington; FAO, *Production Yearbook*, 1977; Miscellaneous sources for certain items.

BASIC DATA

TABLE 6

Dimensions of the Employment Problem in Southern African States, 1976/77

(Data are in '000s or percentages)

	Angola	Botswana	Lesotho	Malawi	Mozambique	Namibia	Swaziland	Tanzania	Zambia	Zimbabwe	Total all Countries
Population	7,000	700	1,200	5,200	11,000	1,250	480	17,000	5,100	6,860	55,790
Labour Force[1]	3,500	350	600	2,600	5,500	625	240	8,500	2,550	3,430	27,895
Formal Employment	300[3]	59	32	271	455	260	60	450[2]	368	1,018	3,273
% of Labour Force	(8.6)	(16.9)	(5.3)	(10.4)	(8.3)	(41.6)	(25.0)	(5.3)	(14.4)	(29.7)	(11.7)
— of which Agriculture	,,	(7.0)	(1.0)	(44.0)	(30.0)	(25.0)	(33.0)	(24.0)	(9.0)	(34.0)	
— Mining	,,	(9.0)	(2.0)	—	(10.0)	(9.0)	(5.0)	(1.0)	(16.0)	(6.0)	
— Industry	,,	(19.0)	(19.0)	(20.0)	(10.0)	(10.0)	(18.0)	(30.0)	(31.0)	(20.0)	
— Services	,,	(45.0)	(78.0)	(36.0)	(60.0)	(64.0)	(44.0)	(45.0)	(44.0)	(40.0)	
— of which non-citizens[4]	,,	4	2	5	36	36	4	5	33	110	235
% of Labour Force	,,	(7.0)	(6.0)	(2.0)	(8.0)	(14.0)	(7.0)	(1.0)	(9.0)	(11.0)	(8.0)
Migrant Workers											
— in South Africa	—	65	200	17	40	3	20	—	—	50	395
— in Southern Rhodesia	,,	5	—	100	80	—	—	—	20	N.A.	205
Migrants as % of lab. force	,,	(20.0)	(33.3)	(4.5)	(2.2)	(0.5)	(8.0)	—	(0.8)	(1.5)	
GNP (US$'000s)	710,000	370,000	252,000	430,000	1,651,000	817,000	276,000	1,500,000	1,864,000	3,200,000	8,000,000
GNP per capita (US$)	100	530	210	83	150	653	575	85	363	465	140
— % from formal sector	,,	(88.0)	(42.0)	(64.0)	,,	(97.0)	(87.0)	(73.0)	(93.0)	(94.0)	
— % from subsistence sector	,,	(7.0)	(17.0)	(36.0)	,,	(3.0)	(11.0)	(27.0)	(7.0)	(6.0)	
— % from migrants' earnings	,,	(5.0)	(41.0)	,,	,,	—	(2.0)	—	—	,,	

Notes:

[1] Definitions of labour forces vary for data available for each country. As an approximation, we have assumed labour force to equal half of the population. In most cases this is a slight underestimate of available working age people, but an overestimate of those at present economically active.

[2] Tanzanian employment data for 1974.

[3] Very rough estimates.

[4] Europeans in the cases of Namibia and Zimbabwe.

N.A. = not applicable; ,, = data not available; — = insignificant.

Sources: Data gleaned from a wide variety of sources documents, mainly Government reports.

BASIC DATA

TABLE 7

Land Use in Southern Africa: Hectares (millions)

	Angola	Botswana	Lesotho	Malawi	Mozambique	Namibia	Swaziland	Tanzania	Zambia	Zimbabwe	Total
Total Area	124.7	60.0	3.0	11.8	78.3	82.4	1.7	94.5	75.3	39.1	570.8
Land Area	124.7	58.5	3.0	9.4	76.5	82.3	1.7	88.6	74.1	38.7	557.5
Arable & Perm.	1.8*	1.4*	0.4*	2.3*	3.1*	0.7	0.2*	6.3	5.0*	2.5*	23.7
Crops¹ of which:											
Arable	1.3*	1.4	0.4	2.3*	2.9*	0.7*	0.2*	5.2	5.0*	2.5*	21.9*
Perm. Pasture	29.0*	44.0*	2.5*	1.8*	44.0*	52.9*	1.1*	44.7	30.0*	4.9*	254.9
Forest and Woodland	72.7*	1.0*	—	2.3	19.4	10.4*	0.1*	31.1	37.3*	23.8	198.1
Other Land	21.2	12.2	0.2	3.0	10.1	18.3	0.4	6.5	1.8	7.6	81.3
Irrigation (ha/(000))	n.a.	1.0	—	5.0	68.0	7.0	26.0	55.0	n.a.	55.0	n.a.

Source: FAO, Production Yearbook, 1977

Notes:
¹ * = Unofficial or estimate.
² — = Less than 0.05.
³ Arable Land refers to land under temporary crops, temporary meadows, market gardens and grass and temporary fallow. Permanent Crop refers to crops which occupy the land for long periods and need not be replanted after each harvest such as coffee, fruit trees, nut trees and vines. It excludes land under trees for wood or timber. Permanent Pasture refers to land used for five years or more for herbaceous forage crop either cultivated or wild. Forest and Woodland refers to land under natural or planted stands of trees, whether or not productive, and forests which have been cleared but which will be replanted in the foreseeable future. Other Land refers to potentially productive land, built on areas, parks, roads, etc.

BASIC DATA

TABLE 8

Agricultural Production and Food Supply Trends 1966–77

Country	Food Production Indices (1969–71 = 100)				Agricultural Output Per Capita Production Indices (1969–71 = 100)				Food Per Capita Production Indices (1969–71 = 100)				Supply of Calories per Capita per day (Number)		Supply of Protein per Capita per day (Grammes)	
	1966	1970	1974	1977	1966	1970	1974	1977	1966	1970	1974	1977	1961–3	1972–4	1961–3	1972–4
Botswana	86	92	121	130	95	92	110	110	94	93	110	110	2,055	2,062	72.7	69.5
Lesotho	92	97	105	111	100	98	93	95	99	97	98	97	2,091	2,204	63.7	67.5
Malawi	82	90	117	121	90	92	108	112	89	90	106	103	1,942	2,413	52.4	67.9
Mozambique	85	100	106	100	93	101	96	82	92	100	97	85	2,006	1,988	39.3	37.3
Namibia	79	100	127	132	92	100	113	108	91	100	113	108	2,187	2,162	70.1	71.1
Swaziland	77	102	121	129	86	102	112	110	85	102	109	106	1,957	2,118	55.4	57.0
Zimbabwe	88	93	129	125	112	94	109	97	103	93	113	99	2,480	2,476	73.3	72.1
Republic of South Africa	82	94	121	118	94	95	106	96	93	94	109	97	2,783	2,858	76.3	77.8

Source: FAO, Production Yearbook, 1977.

Note: For Angola, Tanzania and Zambia, the Food Production Indices and the Food Per Capita Production Indices (1969–71 = 100) were as follows:

	Food Production Indices			Food Per Capita Production Indices		
	1967	1972	1977	1967	1972	1977
Angola	93	97	105	99	93	88
Tanzania	90	103	116	98	97	94
Zambia	94	108	132	102	102	107

257

BASIC DATA
TABLE 9
Balance of Trade, Major Exports

	Total Imports (CIF) mill US$		Total Exports (FOB) mill US$		Trade Balance mill US$		Major Export Commodities 1975		
	1975	1976	1975	1976	1975	1976		mill US$	% of exports
Angola	614.3[1]	316.8	1,202.4[1]	535.1	587.9[1]	218.3[1]	crude oil	595.2	48.5
			0 3 0 6				coffee	247.1	22.3
							diamonds	96.9	7.9
							sisal	51.7	4.2
Botswana	183.2	208.4	120.9	176.2	-62.3	-32.2	beef	34.7	41.9
							diamonds	36.9	20.6
							copper/nickel	25.3	20.9
Lesotho	135.5	206.5	10.6	16.9	-124.9	-189.6	mohair	2.5	23.9
							wool	1.7	12.0
							foodstuffs	1.3	12.0
							diamonds	0.6	5.4
							cattle	0.3	3.3
Malawi	252.0	206.1	139.9	160.0	-112.1	-46.1	tobacco	57.6	41.2
							tea	23.8	17.0
							sugar	10.1	7.2
							groundnuts	7.4	5.3
Mozambique	409.8[1]	300.0	298.1[1]	149.8	-111.7	-150.2[1,4]	sugar	64.7	21.7
							cotton	33.3	11.2
							cashew nuts	24.3	8.1
							fresh fruit	21.4	7.2
							vegetable oils	12.3	4.1
							shell fish	11.3	3.9

258

	Total Imports (CIF) mill US$		Total Exports (FOB) mill US$		Trade Balance mill US$		Major Export Commodities 1975		
	1975	1976	1975	1976	1975	1976		mill US$	% of exports
Namibia	N.A.	460.0[2]	N.A.	753.3[2]	N.A.	293.3[2]	diamonds	271.2	36.0
							uranium	105.5	14.0
							fishing produce	75.3	10.0
							meat produce	75.3	10.0
							karakul pelts	75.3	10.0
							copper	67.8	9.0
Swaziland	110.7	146.0	166.8	193.7	56.1	47.7	sugar	58.2	33.0
							timber	31.1	19.0
							iron ore[5]	28.8	16.0
Tanzania	722.3	638.8	370.0	490.1	-352.3	-148.7	coffee	65.3	17.6
							spices	46.5	12.6
							sisal	40.8	11.0
							cotton	40.0	10.8
							fruit	29.8	8.1
							diamonds	24.3	6.6
Zambia	928.8[3]	714.1[3]	809.8	910.8	-119.0	196.7	copper	721.3	89.1
Zimbabwe	N.A.	460.0[2]	N.A.	685.0[2]	N.A.	225.0[2]	tobacco, maize, beef, cotton and sugar	308.3	45.0
							gold, asbestos, nickel, copper and chrome	274.0	40.0
							manufactured goods	102.8	15.0

	Total Imports (CIF) mill US$		Total Exports (FOB) mill US$		Trade Balance mill US$		Major Export Commodities 1975		
	1975	1976	1975	1976	1975	1976		mill US$	% of exports
Republic of South Africa	7,594.9[6]	6,742.0[6]	8,850.8[6]	7,939.0[6]	1,256.8	1,197.0[6]	gold	2,921.3	33.0
							diamonds	457.8	5.2
							maize	407.6	4.6
							sugar	390.9	4.4

Notes:
[1] 1974 figures.
[2] 1977 figures.
[3] F.O.B.
[4] In 1977 cashew nuts became the major export commodity (23 per cent), cotton and sugar second (12 per cent each), shell fish fourth (8 per cent), and copra and tea fifth (4 per cent each).
[5] Almost depleted now.
[6] Includes Botswana, Swaziland and Lesotho. Import figures exclude oil.

Sources: International Financial Statistics 1978; Direction of Trade 1970–6 (IMF); Yearbook of International Trade Statistics 1976 Vol. I and II; South African Statistics 1978 (Department of Statistics, Pretoria); Miscellaneous sources for certain items.

BASIC DATA

TABLE 10
Direction of Trade 1976

	Exports			Imports		
	1976 Total mill. US$	Major Countries of destination	% share of total	1976 Total mill. US$	Major sources of imports	% share of total imports
Angola[1]	1,202.4	USA	38.3	614.3	Portugal	22.0
		Portugal	26.9		Germany	12.9
		Canada	7.7		USA	10.2
		Japan	5.7		Rep. of South Africa	9.9
		Germany	4.1		UK	6.8
					Italy	4.9
					Japan	4.8
Botswana	176.2	UK	41.3	208.4	Rep. of South Africa	81.4
		America (N + S)	34.1		Zimbabwe	12.2
		Rep. of South Africa	15.1			
		Zimbabwe	7.5			
Lesotho	16.9	Rep. of South Africa	90.0	206.5	Rep. of South Africa	94.0
Malawi	160.0	UK	45.7	206.0	Rep. of South Africa	29.0
		USA	12.2		UK	22.0
		Netherlands	6.7		Japan	7.7
		Rep. of South Africa	5.5		Zimbabwe	4.9
					Canada	4.6

	Exports			Imports		
	1976 Total mill. US$	Major Countries of destination	% share of total	1976 Total mill. US$	Major sources of imports	% share of total imports
Mozambique	149.8	Portugal	25.0	300.0	Rep. of South Africa	15.0
		USA	23.7		West Germany	12.7
		Rep. of South Africa	7.7		Portugal	9.4
		Japan	5.5		Japan	6.2
		Europe—Portugal	20.0		Iraq	5.9
					Portugal/Europe	21.7
Namibia[2]	753.3	UK	36.2	460.0	Rep. of South Africa	60.0
		Rep. of South Africa	10.2			
Swaziland	193.7	UK	33.0	146.0	Rep. of South Africa	87.0
		Rep. of South Africa	20.0			
		Japan, Europe				
		USA + Canada				
Tanzania	490.1	West Germany	14.8	638.8	UK	14.4
		UK	13.5		Iran	12.1
		USA	10.1		Germany	9.9
		Singapore	7.2		Japan	8.9
		Italy	6.6		China	7.2
		Hong Kong	5.6		USA	6.9
		India	5.5		Saudi Arabia	5.2
		China	3.0			

	Exports			Imports		
	1976 Total mill. US$	Major Countries of destination	% share of total	1976 Total mill. US$	Major sources of imports	% share of total imports
Zambia	910.8	UK	22.5	714.1[3]	UK	19.8
		Japan	17.6		USA	12.5
		West Germany	14.2		Saudi Arabia	11.7
		Italy	12.9		Japan	9.0
		France	8.4		West Germany	7.3
		Yugoslavia	4.2		Italy	4.0
		China	2.5		China	2.9
Zimbabwe[2]	685.0	Rep. of South Africa	16.0	460.0	Rep. of South Africa	38.0
		Japan, France	N.A.		Japan, France	N.A.
		West Germany			West Germany	
		Spain, USA			Spain, USA	

Major Source: Yearbook of International Trade Statistics.

Notes:
[1] Figures refer to 1974.
[2] Figures refer to 1977.
[3] F.O.B.

BASIC DATA

TABLE 11

Central Government Finance 1974 US$ Mill[1]

	Total Receipt	Total Current Expenditure	Total Capital Expenditure	Total Expenditure % of GDP	Total Expenditure ODA 1974[2]	Revenue from SACU
Angola	665.6[3]	534.2[3]	107.1[3]	21.9[3]	0.37	—
Botswana	103.9	45.4	45.3	24.4	36.6	30.8 30% of total
Lesotho	32.7	21.5	11.0	28.9	20.9	13.3 41% of total
Malawi	108.9	59.8	39.6	16.6	41.7	—
Mozambique	580.3[3]	467.3[3]	111.6[3]	18.8[3]	0.69	—
Namibia	N.A.	N.A.	N.A.	N.A.	—	—
Swaziland	52.8	32.8	19.4	19.0	15.9	19.6 37% of total
Tanzania	618.8	387.0	228.9	28.2	162.5	—
Zambia	1,244.3	678.4	246.3	33.0	58.3	—
Zimbabwe	663.9	484.1	209.6	25.5	—	—

Notes:
[1] *Main Source:* Statistical Information Bulletin No. 11. See Page 103 for definition of concepts.
[2] DAC Statistics.
[3] 1973.

Abbreviations

ACP	African, Caribbean and Pacific countries
ADB	African Development Bank
ADF	African Development Fund
ADMARK	Agricultural Development & Marketing Corporation (Malawi)
AFRAA	African Airlines Association
ANDEAN	Northern South American Nations
ASEAN	Association of South East Asian Nations
CAF	Central African Federation (former N. & S. Rhodesia and Nyasaland)
CAFRAD	Centre Africain de Formation et de Recherche Administratives pour le Développement (African Centre for Administrative Training and Research for Development)
CIF	Cost, Insurance, Freight
CIPEC	Conseil Intergovernmental de Pays Exportateurs de Cuivre (Inter-Government Council for Copper-Exporting Countries)
CSO	Central Selling Organization (Diamonds)
EAC	East African Community
EADB	East African Development Bank
EAP	Economically Active Population
ECA	Economic Commission for Africa (of UN)
ECOWAS	Economic Community of West African States
EEC	European Economic Community
FAO	Food & Agricultural Organization (of UN)
FOB	Free on Board
FRELIMO	Frente para Libertaçao de Moçambique (Mozambique Liberation Front)
GDP	Gross Domestic Product
GNP	Gross National Product
GSP	Generalized System of Preferences (of USA)
GWH	Generated Watts per Hour
IBRD	International Bank for Rural Development
ICAO	International Civil Aviation Organization
ICRISAT	International Centre for Research in Semi-Arid Tropics

ILO	International Labour Organization (of UN)
IMF	International Monetary Fund
KWH	Kilowatts per Hour
MNC	Multi-National Corporation
MPLA	Movimento Popular para Libertaçao de Angola (Peoples Movement for the Liberation of Angola)
MSA	'Most Seriously Affected' nations
MULPOC	Multi-Lateral Planning & Operational Centre
MW	Megawatts
NDP	National Domestic Product
OAU	Organization for African Unity
OECD	Organization for Economic Co-operation & Development
OPEC	Oil & Petroleum Exporting Countries
PANFTEL	Pan-African Telecommunications Union
PTA	Preferential Trade Area
RMA	Rand Monetary Area
RSA	Republic of South Africa
SACU	Southern African Customs Union
SADCC	Southern Africa Development Co-ordination Conference
SDR	Special Drawing Rights (of IMF)
SECID	South East Consortium for International Development
SOEKER	Southern Oil Exploration Corporation (of RSA)
SWAPO	South West Africa Peoples Organization
TAZAMA	Tanzania-Zambia Mining Association
TAZARA	Tanzania-Zambia Railway Association
TEBA	The Employment Bureau of Africa (of RSA)
TNC	Trans-National Corporation
TTL	Tribal Trust Land
UDEAC	Union Douanière et Economique de l'Afrique Centrale (Customs & Economic Union of Central Africa)
UDI	Unilateral Declaration of Independence
UN	United Nations
UNCTAD	UN Conference on Trade & Development
UNDP	UN Development Programme
UNESCO	UN Educational, Scientific & Cultural Organization
UNIDO	UN Industrial Development Organization
UNITA	União Nacional para a Independencia Total de Angola (National Union for Total Independence of Angola
USAID	United States Agency for International Development
WENELA	Witwatersrand Native Labour Association (now TEBA)
WHO	World Health Organization (of UN)

Record of those Present
at the Meetings
(1) *Arusha*

ANGOLA

Hon. Mr Ismael Gaspar MARTINS	*Minister of Finance*
Ms Deolrida Bebiano D'ALMEIDA	*Director for Co-operation (Secretariat of State for Co-operation)*
Mr Fernando TEIXEIRA	*Director, National Bank of Angola*
Mr Joao Baptista DA COSTA	*Ministry of Planning*
Mr Vergilio FARIA	*Ministry of Foreign Affairs (Planning)*
Mr M. DIEGO	*Ministry of Finance*

BOTSWANA

H. E. Sir Seretse KHAMA	*President*
Hon Dr Quett MASIRE	*Vice-President, Minister of Finance*
Hon Archibald M. MOGWE	*Minister of External Affairs*
Mr Kenneth MATAMBO	*Director of Economic Affairs*
Mr L. T. LEGWAILA	*Senior Private Secretary to H.E.*
Mr Ben MOTLHALAMME	*External Affairs*

MOZAMBIQUE

Hon Mr Rui Baltazar SANTOS	*Minister of Finance*
Mrs Janet MONDLANE	*National Director of International Co-operation*
Mr Abdul MAGID	*National Director of Finance*
Mr Subhasandra BHATT	*Deputy National Director of Transport*
Mr Rui FONSECA	*Ministry of Transport and Communication*
Mr Hernando PEREIRO	*Interpreter*

267

TANZANIA

Hon Mr Edwin MTEI	*Minister of Finance & Development Planning*
Mr Ndewirwa KITOMARI	*Commissioner for Sectoral Planning*
Mr Marcel NAMFUA	*Ministry of Foreign Affairs*
Mr Richard MARIKI	*Director of External Finance*

ZAMBIA

Hon Gen. Kingsley CHINKULI	*Minister of Transport, Power and Communication*
Hon Ben KAKOMA	*Minister of State for Finance*
H.E. G. R. ZIMBA	*Under Secretary for Foreign Affairs*
Mr Nedson NYONI	*Director, Contingency Planning*
Mr C. L. M. CHIRWA	*Ministry of Finance*

AFRICAN DEVELOPMENT BANK

Mr Iddi SIMBA
Mr Gabriel KARIISA

ARAB BANK FOR ECONOMIC DEVELOPMENT OF AFRICA

Mr Salah KHEIR	*Development Officer*

BELGIUM

H.E. Mr E. KOBIE	*Ambassador to Tanzania*
Mr F. ROELANTS	*Deputy Chef de Cabinet to Foreign Minister*
Mr R. Van OVERBERGHE	*Counsellor, Ministry of Foreign Affairs*

CANADA

Mr Noble POWER	*Vice-President CIDA*
Mr Andrew McALISTER	*High Commission, Dar es Salaam*

COMMONWEALTH SECRETARIAT

H.E. Mr S. R. RAMPHAL	*Secretary-General*

DENMARK

H.E. Mr Bjorn OLSEN	*Ambassador to Tanzania*

Mr Niels LASSEN	*Head, African Division, Ministry of Foreign Affairs*
Mr J. A. NIELSEN	*Director, DANIDA*

ECONOMIC COMMISSION FOR AFRICA

Mr Bax NOMVETE	*Head, Office of Economic Co-operation*
Mr Peter MATOKA	*Senior Regional Adviser, Economic Co-operation*

EUROPEAN ECONOMIC COMMUNITY

Mr Maurice FOLEY	*Deputy Director General DG VIII*
Mr John SCOTT	*DG VIII*
Mr Bertil ENGVAL	*DG VIII*

FOOD & AGRICULTURAL ORGANIZATION

Mr Salah ABD	*Resident Representative*
Mr William JAMES	*Programme Officer*

FEDERAL REPUBLIC OF GERMANY

Mr H. UHRIG	*Embassy, Dar es Salaam*
Mr K. KIRCHHOF	*Head, Southern African Department, Ministry of Economic Co-operation*

NETHERLANDS

H.E. Mr Van Der WILLEGEN	*Ambassador to Tanzania*
Mr R. HARKEMA	*Development Co-operation, Ministry of Foreign Affairs*
Mr Fred ROOS	*Embassy, Lusaka*

NORWAY

Mr Arne ARNESEN	*Director General, NORAD*
Mr Rolf HANSEN	*Embassy, Dar es Salaam*

SWEDEN

Mr Anders P. FORSSE	*Director General, SIDA*
Mr Hendrik SALANDER	*Office for International Development Co-operation, Foreign Office*

UNITED KINGDOM

Mr Martin LYNCH — *Under Secretary for Africa, Overseas Development Administration*

Dr Robert STONE — *High Commission, Dar es Salaam*

UNITED NATIONS

Mr Gordon GOUNDREY — *Assistant Secretary General*

Mr Michel DOO-KINGUE — *Assistant Administrator of UNDP and Regional Director for Africa*

Mr A. T. KABBAH — *Resident Representative, UNDP*

UNITED STATES

Mr William C. HARROP — *Deputy Assistant Secretary of State for African Affairs, State Department*

Mr W. Haven NORTH — *Deputy Assistant Administrator for Africa, USAID*

WORLD BANK

Mr Ravi GULHATI — *Chief Economist for Africa*

NON-GOVERNMENTAL ORGANIZATIONS

Mr Marc LENDERS — *Director of Ecumenical Centre, Brussels*

Mr Thom KERSTIENS — *President, Liaison Committee European Development NGOs with the European Communities*

STEERING COMMITTEE

H. E. Mr Amon NSEKELA — *Chairman*

Mr. David ANDERSON

Prof. Reginald H. GREEN

Mr Tim SHEEHY

Ms Margaret M. FEENY — *Co-ordinator*

(2) *Lusaka*

ANGOLA

H.E. Mr Edwardo dos SANTOS — *President*

Mr Alexandre Rodrigues KITO — *Deputy Minister of Internal Affairs*

270

Mr Afonso VAN-DUMEM (M'Binda)	*Secretary, Department of External Affairs*
Mr Venancio de MOURA	*Deputy Minister of External Affairs*
Mr Pinto JOAO	*Director Minister of Commerce*
Mr Assuncio do ANJOS	*Director of the Cabinet of the President*
Major Jose MARIA	*Secretary to the President of the Republic for Defence and Security*
Mr Rui XAVIER	*Member of the Department of External Affairs*
Ms Luisa FILIPE	*Translator*

BOTSWANA

H.E. Sir Seretse KHAMA	*President (Conference Chairman)*
Hon Dr Q. K. J. MASIRE	*Hon Vice-President*
Hon Mr A. M. MOGWE	*Minister of External Affairs*
Mr L. M. MPOTOKWANE	*Secretary of External Affairs*
Mr O. K. MATAMBO	*Director of Economic Affairs*
Mr M. J. MELAMU	*High Commissioner to Zambia*

LESOTHO

Hon M. V. MOLAPO	*Minister of Commerce, Industry and Tourism*
Mr T. J. M. MASHOLOGA	*Permanent Secretary for Transport & Communications*
Mr A. M. MONYAKE	*Permanent Secretary for Finance*
Mr T. MAKHAKE	*Deputy Permanent Secretary for Commerce, Industry and Tourism*
Mr T. MOTSOPA	*Deputy Permanent Secretary for Water, Energy & Mines*

MALAWI

Hon D. T. MATENJE	*Minister of Education*
Hon L. J. CHIMANGO	*Minister of Finance*
H.E. Mr J. B. ITIMU	*High Commissioner to Zambia*
Mr G. J. CHIUNDIRA	*Principal Secretary, Ministry of Transport & Air Communications*
Mr M. V. L. PHIRI	*Under Secretary, Minister of External Affairs*

271

MOZAMBIQUE

H.E. Samora Moises MACHEL — *President*

Mr Joaquim A. CHISSANO — *Minister of Foreign Affairs*

Mr Jose Luis CABACO — *Minister of Transport and Communications*

Mr Rui Baltazar SANTOS — *Minister of Finance*

Mr Abdul Magid OSMAN — *Secretary of State for Coal and Hydrocarbonates*

Mr Fernando HONWANA — *Personal Assistant to His Excellency the President*

Mr Aquind de BRAGANCA — *Director of Centre of African Studies*

SWAZILAND

H.E. the Hon Prince MABANDLA — *Prime Minister of the Kingdom of Swaziland*

Hon Prince NQABA — *Minister for Commerce, Industry, Mines and Tourism*

Hon Dr V. G. LEIBRANDT — *Minister for Works, Power and Communications*

Hon L. M. MNCINA — *Minister of State for Foreign Affairs*

Mr T. M. J. ZWANE — *Permanent Secretary, Department of Planning & Statistics*

Mr V. E. SIHONDZE — *Permanent Secretary, Ministry of Finance*

Mr G. MOTSA — *ADC to the Prime Minister*

TANZANIA

H.E. Mwalimu Julius K. NYERERE — *President*

Hon B. W. MKAPA — *Minister for Foreign Affairs*

Hon Dr K. MALIMA — *Minister for Planning and Economic Affairs*

Hon A. MWINGIRA — *Minister for Communication and Transport*

Hon C. D. MSUYA — *Minister for Industries*

Mr C. KILEO — *Tanzanian Ambassador to Mozambique*

272

| Prof S. M. MBILINYI | Personal Assistant to the President (Economic Affairs) |
| Mr H. HALAHALA | Assistant Press Secretary to the President |

ZAMBIA

H.E. Dr. K. D. KAUNDA	President
Hon D. M. LISULO	Prime Minister
Hon W. P. NYIRENDA	Member of the Central Committee and Chairman of the Economic and Finance Committee
Hon W. M. CHAKULYA	Minister for Foreign Affairs
Hon K. S. K. MUSOKOTWANE	Minister of Finance
Hon Gen G. K. CHINKULI	Minister of Power, Transport and Communications
Hon H. Y. MWALE	Minister of Works and Supply
Hon A. B. CHIKWANDA	Minister of Agriculture and Water Development
Mr S. J. KAZUNGA	Special Assistant to the President (Administration)
Mr S. G. MWALE	Special Assistant to the President (Economic Co-operation)
Mr E. I. L. WILLIAM	Secretary to the Cabinet
Mr P. L. KASANDA	Permanent Secretary, Ministry of Foreign Affairs
Dr L. S. CHIVUNO	Acting Permanent Secretary and Director General, National Commission for Development Planning
Ambassador K. KANGWA	Under Secretary, (Inter-Co-op) Ministry of Foreign Affairs
Mr J. M. S. LICHILANA	Senior Economist of Foreign Affairs

ZIMBABWE

The Hon Robert Gabriel MUGABE	Prime Minister
Mr Enos NKALA	Minister of Finance
Mr Emmerson MUNANGANGWA	Minister of State in the Prime Minister's Office
Mr Witnesse MANGWENDE	Deputy Minister of Foreign Affairs

273

IN ATTENDANCE:

SWAPO/NAMIBIA

Mr Sam NUJOMA — *President of SWAPO*

Mr Kapuka NAUYALA — *Member of SWAPC Central Committee, Secretary to the President*

ORGANIZATION FOR AFRICAN UNITY

H.E. Mr Edem KODJO — *Secretary-General*

ECONOMIC COMMISSION FOR AFRICA

Prof Adebayo ADEDEJI — *Executive Secretary*

Mr B. D. NOMVETE — *Chief Economic Co-operation Co-ordinator*

Mr O. MATOKA — *Regional Advisor*

Mr S. S. SANGWENI — *Acting Director, Lusaka MULPOC*

Mr P. M. MANGOAELA — *Co-ordinator Transport*

Mr P. N. MWOK-HANDA — *Trade Economist*

Mr D. J. NJAU — *Agricultural Economist*

Conference Secretariat

H.E. Mr Amon J. NSEKELA — *Conference Secretary-General*

Mr David ANDERSON

Mr Iddi SIMBA

Mr Tim SHEEHY